Take Me Under the Sea

THE DREAM MERCHANTS OF THE DEEP

by Thomas N. Burgess

1994

THE OCEAN ARCHIVES

Salem

Library of Congress Catalog Card Number 93-87618

ISBN 0-9639840-0-4

Cover design by Thomas Burgess, illustration by Will Nelson, and undersea photography by Cathy Church
Text design by Balfour Smith
Set in 11 point Monotype Calisto

First OCEAN ARCHIVES edition published 1994.

This book is dedicated to

DR. ROSALYN EDELSON

Educator extraordinaire.
Seaperson of boundless enthusiasms.

and to

The late GEORGE WILLIAMSON JUNIOR

A dutiful son and an unpretentious man.

Acknowledgments

⬦

The Men Who Wrote an Undersea Novel

For research assistance in Europe, I wish to thank Ms. Elaine Friedman of the University of Michigan, and the staff of the Bibliothèque Nationale. In the United States, research liaison was initiated by Drs. Paul and Edith Nickel of Michigan State University and the University of Michigan. Also invaluable were research efforts by the staffs of the New York Public Library, the Library of Congress, the Chicago Public Library, and the San Francisco Public Library. For their translations from the French, I would like to thank Franchesca Taylor and Brigitte Guttridge of San Francisco, Gisèle Cervisi of Alliance Française de San Francisco, and Dr. Rosalyn Edelson of the Department of Education at Willamette University.

The Man Who Painted Under the Sea

In Tahiti, I wish to thank historian Bengt Danielsson, and Al Prince of the Tahiti Bulletin. In New York, I am especially grateful to Mrs. Francesca Yates for her research efforts. I also thank Ms. Mildred Bobrovitch of the Research Library and Mr. Joel Sweimler of the Special Collections Department at the American Museum of Natural History, as well as the staff of the Metropolitan Museum of Art. In California, invaluable assistance was provided by Ms. Mayers of the Archives of California Art at the Oakland Museum. The staff of the Shields Library, Department of Special Collections, University of California at Davis was additionally helpful. I wish also to express my gratitude to the staff of the Los Angeles County Museum of Art Library as well as the staffs of the Los Angeles,

Pasadena, and San Francisco Public Libraries, and to the officials of the United States Immigration and Naturalization Service. The staff of the Ryerson and Burnham Libraries of the Art Institute of Chicago also has my gratitude, as does Carole Camillo and her associates at the Cleveland Museum of Natural History.

The Brothers Who Launched Undersea Movies

Most importantly, I am grateful to the late George Williamson Junior and his wife, Shirley, for their time, attention, and generous correspondence, and also for Mrs. Williamson's donation of photographs to the author. In New York, I wish to thank Mr. Richard Koszarski, Curator of the American Museum of the Moving Image; also the staffs of the Film Study Center of the Museum of Modern Art, the Lincoln Center Library for the Performing Arts, and the Explorer's Club, particularly Marie E. Roy. At the Library of Congress in Washington, D.C., my thanks go to Paul Spear, David Francis, and Charlyn Pullmann of the Motion Picture, Broadcasting, and Recorded Sound Division. In Norfolk, Virginia, I am grateful to Lucile Portlock and the staff of the Sargeant Memorial Room of the Norfolk Public Library. At the Academy of Motion Picture Arts and Sciences in Los Angeles, I thank the staff of the Margaret Herrick Library; and also M. Lou Ellen Kramer, at the U.C.L.A. Film and Television Archives. In addition to these scholars, I would thank Mr. William Martin Hill and Mr. Harry Motte Joyner, historians of motion picture technology, as well as Dave Sheppard of Film Preservation Associates.

•

In manuscript preparation and editorial assistance, I am grateful to Deanna Ruth Spake, formerly of the Hopkins Marine Station Library and the Monterey, California Public Library; as well as Nancy Winbigler Hindershot, formerly of the University of Oregon; and Dorothy Whitnah and Balfour Smith in San Francisco.

TAKE ME UNDER THE SEA

Foreword

ON FEBRUARY 28, 1954, CBS WAS AIRING ONE OF TELEVISION'S earliest and most noble efforts to elevate the broadcast culture. The show was called *Omnibus*, then in its second season, and for the benefit of both urban and heartland Americans, its host, Alistair Cooke, vivified all manner of cultural, scientific, and geographic pursuits.

That particular Sunday afternoon, there appeared for certain regions the first true undersea films ever broadcast. They were the work of a team led by Capitaine Jacques Yves Cousteau, a French naval officer and co-creator of the Scaphandre Autonome – the Aqua Lung. His inaugural book, *The Silent World*, had been published in English the year before, and, much as his writing had done, Cousteau's films now propelled the audience under the Red Sea and through its submarine kingdoms; a geography never before seen by the home-viewing public in this country.

I was sitting there. At an impressionable seventeen years of age, in a tiresome, landlocked town in the South, I was sitting there awestruck. The engravings and photographs I had studied as a child were coming alive on the screen and the image wasn't an animation or a Hollywood tank but actual moving pictures from beneath the sea. In the most outrageous interpretations of the experience, I, suddenly, could see myself gliding over the lost continents of Plato's *Timæus*, or through the ribs of the *Mary Celeste*, or simply viewing firsthand any of a million supernatural, submarine vistas that had, heretofore, been denied me and all the others participating in Cousteau's vision. At the time, I was unaware that such films predated not only *Omnibus*, but both World Wars. For me, it was television that first transported the undersea, and, over the months, "aquanauts" continued to swim the broadcast band into our home.

As a consequence, I saw one day the same otherworldly apparatus I had seen in Cousteau's films. It sat in the window of a downtown store looking every bit like a time machine; like a giant passkey to the vaults of phantasma revealed on *Omnibus*. In France, the device had been marketed for seven or eight years, and in the United States for five. What I saw at that moment, however, was the first factory model to arrive in my town. Predictably, but briefly, a companion and I owned the thing. With no permission, no ocean access, and no training, we nevertheless owned it, and, furtively, it took us into a rooftop reservoir, into a muddy river, and into a near-opaque quarry.

To these pitiful forays the Navy then added scope. The following summer, they packed me off to school and then to the western Pacific, where I spent the rest of my boyhood doing adult – but pleasurable – chores. I worked around and explored within the gin waters of Oceania, most literally living the undersea experiences I had seen on television only a year before. And, for the most part, I was alone. Experientially, I owned almost every place I went. The involvement was indeed that new and the territory virgin.

It was the translucence that held me. Having this quality, the sea could offer up all its dimensions, and looking from above, I could see them. Clear water had made an inverted geography – a viscous interior that often had floors or horizons, and, just as often, did not. It was a solid space yet penetrable, and, at will, I could enter and view the crystal element from within.

Physically, it was life in immersion and psychically, it was man's love of the inner sanctum. Slipping under the surface, the ceiling would close over me and I would sink into a chamber of the strangest optical peace – down into living submarine cathedrals of organic ribs and vaultings; life forms that were fantasy because they followed few dictates from the world above. They were both dreamlike in shape and dreamlike in their illumination. The light either diffused an object or chattered around it but rarely brought clarity.

This was God's stagecraft and I soon realized that, in the visible undersea, mystery is wedded to æsthetics. For a young, ocean-struck artist, it was the ultimate freedom and the ultimate visual conquest combined.

Accordingly, from that time on, as I dived various waters, I remembered the *Omnibus* films. Never had media so affected me and I often wondered about earlier people whose introduction to the deep was less comfortable – but whose amazement could have equalled or surpassed my own. Penetrating the ocean, someone long ago sought to retell the experience; imaging within the framework of their own particular talents at a time when both undersea access and communication were limited.

Who first novelized this place, the undersea? Who, from personal experience, first crafted a sketch or a painting of it? Who first photographed it or made a movie of it?

This is the product of my curiosity. It is not always about results. It is not a critique. By means of artistic valuation, the works of these people could well be judged deficient, and indeed many of their creations have long since been lost or destroyed – the people forgotten. Their esteem, however, is less important to me than their lives, their efforts, and especially, their enthusiasms – the same impractical, inapplicable enthusiasms that led me to write this book.

TNB

Introduction

(1994)

THE UNDERSEA. THE BOTTOM OF THE SEA. FARAWAY ZONES STILL exist on this planet, but few have names that sound so forbidding. Early in the last century, visionary children sat in large, overstuffed chairs and uttered those words with a reverence – the same reverence today's child might feel when saying "black holes in space." For that earlier generation, it was the most mysterious place on earth because it was the most inaccessible. The naturalist poets thought so, too, and most of them attempted at least once to paint a word picture of the deep.

Then scientists developed dredges and sounding devices to probe this hidden realm from above. Industrial Age tinkerers worked with ballast and force pumps, building diving suits and submersibles so that man could enter this realm physically. From these developments came new questions as to what man might next contrive and how far he could penetrate. Most of all, men wanted to know what they would encounter in their descent.

Already, the vast interior of the ocean was the stuff of dreams and nightmares. Her life forms were so illusive and so different from those of the surface world that the deep had long been the birthplace of even stranger biotic concepts. But now, scientific publishers had expedient ways to air these concepts. Journalists had fanciful – and profitable – new stories. Close behind them, the serialists and engravers adopted the subject, and the results were tabloid adventures from the penny press.

"Media explosion" may be a new term, but the subject is not particular to our century. Neither is "ocean awareness." In a less credible form, the nineteenth century saw an era similar to that of Cousteau in the twentieth. Fueled by the breakthroughs in science, the rotary press, and a literate population, magazines of the mid-1800s reaped the benefits of bringing ocean phenomena to their readers. As a result, the public was starting to learn what the undersea looked like, and, as they had suspected, it was consummately strange. Their visions were enhanced by writers and illustrators who relished stretching the imagery to its most haunting and grotesque extremes. At that point, the mystery of the undersea was no longer just its inaccessibility. The undersea now had both psychic and æsthetic properties that were nurtured by the press and purveyed to the general populace. "The world beneath the brine" had become a marketable literary theme.

Inevitably, the undersea novel was written, and its scope was vast and romantic. It played to man's love of secret places. It told of the horrors and the enchantments of a submarine world. It paid homage to both the industrial and the scientific revolutions which had made undersea exploration possible. Finally, it was a testament to the imagination and the artistry of its creators who, in their lifetimes, would never see the undersea firsthand.

When the twentieth century arrived, there were new artists – graphic artists – who were fascinated enough by the sub-ocean to explore it themselves, instead of just rendering from a vision. In those early decades, however, diving was the occupation of a few, and was far more laborious than it is today. There wasn't the freedom of the aqualungers. There weren't the camera refinements, the lavish photoengravings, or the mass air travel to turn pretty pictures into a personal experience. Those who descended even a modest distance did so with a full complement of Victorian hardware. Two or three trifling fathoms meant crawling into some metal monstrosity and peeking out through a tiny port.

Despite its inaccessibility – or perhaps because of it – there were men who decided that the undersea was a theme worth romancing. They, in fact, spent a good part of their lives expressing their enthusiasms – or simply exploiting an untapped artistic resource. This, then, is the story of a few such men: writers, painters, and movie makers who, regardless of their motives, were fascinated by the undersea. Each used his talents to bring that mystical geography to armchair travelers of the world – this despite the unorthodox and difficult methods of their era. Moreover, in evoking this place, they took an immense æsthetic gamble. Although the public had acquired a fascination for it, they had yet to acquire an affinity.

Today, it is commonly acknowledged that the undersea is beautiful. This awareness, however, was hard won by some interesting yet forgotten people. The physically dangerous undersea can also be historically lethal. She has obliterated the names of many who pursued her. Through earlier times, some of the explorers did indeed make lasting names for themselves. A handful of image makers also briefly prospered, but given the trouble they went to, their path to obscurity was terribly straight and quick. Only in literature were there exceptions.

Artistic attachment is not always a practical matter. But then, neither is adventure.

The Men Who Wrote
an Undersea Novel

(1817–1869)

AS LATE AS THE 1940s, THE SEA FLOOR WAS STILL THE STRANGEST place imaginable. It was especially so when one spent large portions of a childhood looking through encyclopedias in order to feed sea dreams. Yet, for some youngsters the mystery was more aggravating than for others. On library shelves, we the addicted ones had found lustier reading for our dream mill, and it wedded us inexorably to the idea of visiting Neptune's domain. The authors of these texts were very special men who *did*, in fact, go under the sea, and then wrote of it in a wildly romantic fashion. There were William Beebe who had biological adventures and Edward Ellsberg who had salvage adventures. David Masters sent diving stories from England – and we children sat reading away, imprisoned by domestic life. In those earlier decades, it would have taken the powers of either a great navy or a great museum to have rescued us from our surface captivity.

In the years since that time, of course, technology has made the interiors of the ocean far more accessible and the media has put at least a small dent in its mystery. Mankind now has new transport, new ways of seeing, and can better communicate images to the less mobile; however, until the day people can just walk into it, breathe its liquid atmosphere, and tour its wonders on a monorail, the undersea will always be what it is today – still the most isolated and otherworldly environment on this planet.

If armchair explorers of the twentieth century could be so intrigued, imagine the wondering of their counterparts in the nineteenth. In the early years of that century, Western man's inventions didn't take him down very far and he certainly didn't try that often. Accordingly, his few modest penetrations left an even greater mystery. When parlor urbanites read of the undersea, they might as well have pondered heaven, hell, or a far-off planet, and, indeed, the water world would remain an enigma. It would, however, soon improve its obscure literary standing.

When Victoria began the third decade of her reign, there emerged an author whose name came to embody the very concept of the undersea. Even to this day, people only aware of his works might refer to some ghostly subaqueous vision as "Just like Jules Verne!" Others might peruse an antiquated piece of diving gear and say, "Now there's a real Jules Verne for you!" The most common image is that of a brooding genius – one who sparked an age of technology and whose novel was the first to envision man's undersea travels.

Well, Verne was indeed imaginative. As a lay scientist and geographer, he was scrupulous about details. He was also a hard worker and consequently one of the most prolific writers of his time. But unlike his character Nemo, the visionary author didn't stalk dark regions or retreat from society. He didn't brood and he didn't swear vengeance. Jules Verne was an artistic dandy in the prosperous empire of Louis Napoleon. He had an abundance of rollicking friends; he dressed up for costume parties; he harmonized at the piano and he teased women about their corsets. In his early years he even wrote librettos for comic opera, and like many good Frenchmen, he drank plenty of wine and passed from this world with an abused pancreas.

More important, Verne's celebrated undersea story, *Vingt Mille Lieues sous les Mers* (*Twenty Thousand Leagues Under the Seas*) was not so much a portent of things to come as it was a chronicle of existing technology. It also wasn't the archetype of science fiction, and it wasn't the first novel to have people cruising the ocean's floor. Quite a few eventful decades preceded Verne's novel and contributed to its gestation. Like most literature, the book was part of an evolution and very much the product of its time.

The story of *Twenty Thousand Leagues* is the story of the nineteenth century. That century formed for man the world's first science–machine symbiosis – where artists spoke through the rotary press, commerce spoke through a telegraph cable, and young readers could see undersea geographies through the viewports of a literary submarine.

By the time Verne was ready to create his undersea epic, the nineteenth century would place the theme into his hands. Industrial developments would provide the hardware for his vessel, and ocean commerce would spawn the sciences which served as his muse. Before any of this was to happen, however, the century saw another sort of ocean awareness. It wasn't as well publicized because it was largely unrelated to physical progress. Verne's literary predecessors ushered it in, and their chosen device was what used to be called "the language of the gods." Of course, a good text on conchology was always available and naval ministries could be counted on to report some new salvage device at least twice a year, but when people wanted a more romantic treatment of the world below the waves, they had a complement of poetry to choose from.

Today, the word "poetry" is more likely to be used in describing an Olympic skater or a movie about horses. In its literary form, the world seems to have tagged poetry as a dated commodity and even good material resides today in basements. In the period of Verne's childhood, however, people sat down and read poetry and they did it quite often. They copied it, memorized it, translated it, and swapped it. The practice was as popular as Sunday promenades. In England alone, there were nearly seventy magazines that reviewed poetry – a scale movies today enjoy.

In all that poetry, the undersea theme appeared a surprising number of times and mostly because a surprising number of authors had to try it at least once. Naturally, if those sub-sea verses were tallied against the rest of the world's sea poems, they would be very few in comparison. Some might think it pretentious to carve even a small niche in literary history for such esoteric stuff. But in the years between 1817 and 1833, there was such a pronounced concentration of fantasies about the ocean's floor that the period bears singling out. None of the poets had ever descended in a bell and they were usually operating from healthy imaginations. Nevertheless, their imagery was surprisingly accurate when they visualized density, colors, motion, and the overall dream quality that pervades the sea's interiors.

The subject was a literary challenge. It was too inaccessible not to be. Other than what was seen in tidal pools or shallow water, the visions were hardly a result of first-hand experience. Yet when early poets wrote of the undersea, they compounded their boldness. They didn't just stand back from it or look down into it. They went ahead and placed themselves squarely within the element – as if submerged and traveling about like a twentieth century aquanaut. In a literal sense, that fantasy couldn't be corroborated, and, in a literary sense, it was difficult to share – a least in the early 1800s.

When the poets took this imaginary viewpoint, they gave the undersea a new and special geography – and with it, an obscure set of references. To be sure, it was daring æsthetics. It dared to exist without the familiar. But for many readers, such a world, although intriguing, was difficult to fit into the framework of their other experiences. For most writers, it soon became an unwieldy vehicle, especially if trying to extract metaphors or relate to the human condition. Many notable poets experimented with the undersea, but most did so once or twice and then dropped the theme. They felt it was too quickly exhausted and they promptly returned to more fertile – and recognizable – terrain. On top of all this, any poet had a big job convincing the public of beauty in such an alien place. It is only from today's more comfortable vantage point that people can appreciate just how accurate some of those poetic visions were.

Despite these inherent problems, nineteenth-century literature began its undersea excursions with a man who managed to conquer almost every obstacle. Unlike the writers who would follow him, he repeatedly used the undersea motif and yet found fresh material for his philosophies each time he did so.

In the afternoon of July 8, 1822, the winds and waves of a sudden storm capsized a sailboat off the coast of Viareggio in northwest Italy. One crewman who sank to the ocean's floor had long before written these lines:

He plunged through the green silence of the main,
Through many a cavern which the eternal flood
Had scooped as dark lairs for its monster brood;
And among mighty shapes which fled in wonder,
And among mightier shadows which pursued.[1]

It was prophetic that Percy Shelley should have died this way. Of all lyric verses in the English or any other language, his were unparalleled in the abundance of their undersea imagery.

English scholars know Shelley as the unrivaled poet of his age and philosophers regard him as a humanist and social reformer. Water wasn't the predominant concern in Shelley's life: He was consumed by the question of man's place in the universe and society. But he loved the idea of an undersea world. When his pen touched paper, he quite often used the ocean or the sub-ocean as a thread on which to string his ideas.

Shelley's persuasions were all part of a literary era that he helped to launch called the Romantic Era. It was populated by a group of quiet and solitary folk whose writing was characterized by, among other things, a strong interest in nature. For these people, however, the natural world wasn't just a place in which to wander. It was an extension of man's psyche as well. When their writing dipped below the ocean, for instance, they were really answering to their own sensitivities. They found philosophic counterparts in the undersea as they did in all of nature.

Because these poets attempted to paint word pictures of the undersea world, we know that their references were obscure. They were envisioning something others hadn't seen. However, by their immersion, they had also created another problem: justifying their presence in the undersea. In those days, it was all very correct and logical to romance the earth's terrain. One did it from a terrestrial vantage point because that was where human beings belonged. But man's presence beneath the ocean didn't make a lot of sense – at least not for the purpose of just being an observer. Judging from the works produced, we can assume that most poets of the time felt a need to adopt some device – something to transport them or else a familiar object to relate to or to work through. They also needed

11

a justification for displacing themselves and their readers from the beauty and safety of terra firma and into an environment that was so unknown and unfriendly.

It was also often assumed that, by themselves, submarine landscapes were not sufficient themes. That assumption had some validity, but there were those who did, in fact, brave raw environmental descriptions. They simply loaded their poems with many metaphors from the surface world. And so, all things considered, if a Romantic Age poet decided to indulge in undersea themes, he had at least three obstacles to deal with: an unknown terrain, his unexplained presence there, and a limited interest if other thematic elements were not introduced.

As it happened, Percy Shelley settled into the Romantic Age with at least one large solution to all the problems. In addition to his love of mankind and the ocean, he brought with him a life-long infatuation for ancient Greece. He translated its mythologies, and he adopted its fables as a format for his epic poetry. It was a liberating move because mythology brazenly took its readers anywhere it chose and it was especially notorious for occupying all sorts of celestial, subterranean, and submarine places. As a civilization, Greece had lived in more intimate contact with the sea than most others. Consequently, the Greeks used the sea's hidden regions as a habitat for many of their mythological creations. Obviously, undersea awareness didn't originate in the nineteenth century, it was simply rescued from a two-thousand-year suspension by Shelley.[2] Once he adopted their epic styles and themes, he could take his pen and travel from air to water and back just as freely as had the Greeks. Mythology didn't have to be the subject, although quite often it was. The classical style and the fable were, in themselves, a passkey to the sea floor – without either excuses or devices necessary.

Shelley's greatest involvement with the ocean was in the four years between 1817 and his death, roughly the period of his residence in Italy. Though he couldn't even swim, he never lost contact with the sea for all of that time. Once a friend watched him kick off his clothes, jump into the deep water, and then stretch out on the bottom. Shelley expected to be rescued, and he was, but the lack of any forewarning caused his friend some anguish. Between such hair-raising excursions, Shelley produced more than 150 separate lines, quatrains, and stanzas that embellished the concept of the undersea.[3]

The young poet also infused his friends, Lord Byron and John Keats. In contrast to Shelley, Byron was a robust swimmer who once confirmed the plausibility of a legend by swimming the 37-mile Dardanelles. It was only natural that he wed his undersea contributions to his swimming themes in *The Two Foscari* ("Roll on, thou deep and dark blue Ocean – roll!"). Keats, on the other hand, stuck to mythology with a vision of an aging Neptune[4] and another work, *Endymion*:

> Fish semblances, of green and azure hue,
> Ready to snort their streams. In this cool wonder
> Endymion sat down and 'gan to ponder . . .
>
> The visions of the earth were gone and fled –
> He saw the giant sea above his head.

Once fables and legends made it permissible to go under the sea, Shelley's contemporaries dispersed. Nearly a dozen poets went in search of other transporting themes, and without much effort they soon discovered the categories of mermaid, monster, and mortality.

Of course, the mermaid was just another child of mythology, but she had far more universal appeal than other creatures. Mermaids also had one characteristic that especially served a poet's interest. Though their amours were suspect, it was always taken for granted that the love of a sea-maiden automatically gave her man the power to live under water as she did. She could then take her fully human guest down into the depths without any danger, and in this way, the mermaid was the tour guide, and the poem could speak in the person of the newcomer. With that kind of mythos provided to them, one wonders how many ancient sailors claimed to have seen the ocean's floor.

Mermaid stories number in the hundreds, they appear in

many languages, and they probably predate historic records. The theme wasn't original with the Romantics, just the treatment. A year before Shelley's death, Walter Scott devoted a Canto of his *Verses From The Pirate* to the undersea people. It was an interchange or poetic song between *Mermaids* and *Mermen*, but it was really quite limited compared to a work by his old friend, John Leyden. When the two writers were gathering historic ballads for Scott's book, *Minstrelsy of the Scottish Border*, Leyden had composed *The Mermaid* which had its origins in one of those ballads.[5] It was an ambitious poem and contained some reasonably vivid images of a sea-lady's surroundings:

> With tranquil step to trace the deep,
> Where pearly-drops of frozen dew
> In concave shells unconscious sleep,
> Or shine with lustre, silver-blue.

Leyden's contribution was the first mermaid theme of the period and actually preceded Shelley's work by 15 years. After Leyden and Scott, the subject lay at rest until Tennyson got hold of it in 1830. Regarding sub-ocean romance, Tennyson was a lustier thinker. His companion poems, *The Merman* and *The Mermaid* were a little thin on the environment, but they certainly were bountiful on the side of sensuality – as when a mermaid speaks:

> In the purple twilights under the sea;
> But the king of them all would carry me,
> Woo me, and win me, and marry me,
> In the branching jaspers under the sea.
> Then all the dry pied things that be
> In the hueless mosses under the sea
> Would curl round my silver feet silently
> All looking up for the love of me.

Much later, in 1849, Matthew Arnold would compose *The Forsaken Merman* which was the most metaphoric treatment of all.

Mermaids aside, there were still other ways to justify a presence under the ocean. A second was as witness to man's mortality. That included the temporal nature of everything he ever crafted or conquest he ever sought. In those days, man's appetite for commerce and immigration often ran ahead of his marine engineering, and as late as the 1850s, passage across the Atlantic was held as quite a serious undertaking. Most people drafted a will before they sailed. That was the stark reality of an age we today romanticize. There were, in fact, so many losses that, in mid-century, a book on shipwrecks was a best seller. Even when ships regularly made the crossing, they were frequently overdue for days and sometimes weeks. Consequently, the newspapers would cater to the public's morbid inclinations and alternate between doom mongering and hope mongering.

Such calamities were very much in people's minds and, philosophically, no death seemed as ominous as a death at sea. Of course, many poets wrote about life's mutable properties. But for some, the image of poor mortals and their enterprises, strewn across the ocean's floor and mingling with the inevitable sea life, seemed to drive home the point more effectively. Also, like the mermaid vision, many of these poetic inspirations came from earlier ballads, and when it came to lost souls at sea, there were plenty of elegiac ballads around.

Around 1820 Longfellow wrote *The Sea-Diver*, which followed the path of sea tragedies from the surface to the seafloor – all as seen through the eyes of a waterfowl. Also in the early twenties, there appeared *The Treasures of the Deep*, in which Felicia Hemans tells the undersea to keep its lost fortunes (in favor of returning only the dead):

> Yet more, thy depths have more! What wealth untold
>   Far down, and shining through their stillness, lies!
> Thou hast the starry gems, the burning gold,
>   Won from ten thousand argosies!
>   Sweep o'er thy spoils, thou wild and wrathful Main!
>   Earth claims not these again.

Yet more, thy depths have more! Thy waves have rolled
   Above the cities of a world gone by;
Sand hath filled up the palaces of old.
   Seaweed o'er grown the halls of revelry.
     Dash o'er them, Ocean, in thy scornful play!
     Man yields them to decay.

Within Europe's middle-class reading public, Hemans was mostly appreciated because she espoused the current morality. Aside from this, however, her feeling for the undersea was as substantial as any who ever wrote of it. She spent most of her life in a solitary mansion on the coast of North Wales – raising her sons, playing the harp, and generally communicating with the ocean like some Druid priestess. Prolific in her own works, Mrs. Hemans also translated poetry from the German, French, and Spanish as a service to magazines, and she corresponded with both Shelley and Scott. Her involvement with the ocean's depths came from a lifetime of surveying the tragic flotsam that the tides would deposit on her doorstep, and, even as a child, she had developed a melancholy obsession with sea burials. Among her other works was *The Diver*, a tribute to that daunting profession of wresting pearls with a lungful of air.

After mermaids and mortality,[6] there remained the poetic recognition of beasts – either real or imagined, but mostly the latter. John G.C. Brainard's *Sonnet to the Sea Serpent* came out in 1825 and it reflected the current serpent publicity. Another example was Alfred Tennyson's *The Kraken* which appeared in 1830. His particular devil was believed to be a giant cephalopod which haunted Scandinavia, and in its own quiet way, Tennyson's poem struck a terrifying picture of unseen life in the ocean (although his vegetation was somewhat misplaced):

Below the thunders of the upper deep,
Far, far beneath in the abysmal sea,
His ancient, dreamless, uninvaded sleep
The Kraken sleepeth: faintest sunlights flee
About his shadowy sides; above him swell
Huge sponges of millennial growth and height;

And far away into the sickly light,
From many a wondrous grot and secret cell
Unnumbere'd and enormous polypi
Winnow with giant arms the slumbering green.

After the more popular themes were explored, there still
remained a few who would write of unadorned scenics and the
purely physical. They wanted no help from other agents of
the sea. Brainard made a contribution with *The Deep*, although
the poem was more an abstraction of responses as opposed
to physical description. Another Yankee, John Greenleaf Whittier, composed *Ocean* in 1827, but it was so frightening an image
that it made Tennyson's environment look like a land of sugar
castles. The second stanza is a particularly foreboding example:

O'er what recesses, depths unknown,
    Dost thou thy waves impel,
Where never yet a sunbeam shone,
    Or gleam of moonlight fell?
For never yet did mortal eyes
    Thy gloom-wrapt deeps behold,
And naught of thy dread mysteries
    The tongue of man hath told.

Whittier was one of many who made generous use of sea
imagery in a way that revealed an underlying fear and distaste.
Equally gruesome were Thomas Miller's *The Sea-Deeps* and, of
course, Edgar Allan Poe's *The City in the Sea*.

Of the nineteenth-century men who wrote sub-aqueous
descriptions, no one surpassed the accuracy of a very peculiar
American named James Gates Percival. Percival was an eccentric, intellectual hobo who, at different times in his life, was a
doctor, a journalist, a linguist, a state geologist for Connecticut,
a chemistry teacher at West Point, and periodically, a patient in
mental wards. During all this shuttling, he must, at one time,
have acquired some means to view the undersea because the
vision he penned was rather incredible. It was entitled *The Coral
Grove* and even a few lines indicate some personal experience

beyond pure imagination – except for his incorrect belief that red is intensified:

> (Far down in the green and glassy brine)
> The floor is of sand like the mountain drift
> And the pearl shells spangle the flinty snow;
> From coral rocks the sea plants lift
> Their boughs, where the tides and billows flow;
> The water is calm and still below,
> For the winds and waves are absent there,
> And the sands are bright as the stars that glow
> In the motionless fields of upper air:
> There with its waving blade of green,
> The sea-flag streams through the silent water,
> And the crimson leaf of the dulse is seen
> To blush, like a banner bathed in slaughter:

Lastly, William Wordsworth made a contribution. Wordsworth was an example of great poetic output that utilized the sea solely to allude to man's destinies. Rarely did he dwell on the physical properties of the sea. Of the few times he did so, it was, interestingly enough, when his writing dipped *below* the sea's surface. The result was a profound statement about our relationship to the sub-ocean. *By the Seashore, Isle of Man* was published in 1833; as Percival was accurate in visual details, so Wordsworth was accurate as to why human beings respond to the water element and to life in immersion:[7]

> Why stand we gazing on the sparkling Brine,
> With wonder smit by its transparency,
> And all-enraptured with its purity? –
> Because the unstained, the clear, the crystalline,
> Have ever in them something of benign;
> Whether in gem, in water, or in sky,
> A sleeping infant's brow, or a wakeful eye
> Of a young maiden, only not divine.
> Scarcely the hand forbears to dip its palm
> For beverage drawn as from a mountain well;
> Temptation centres in the liquid Calm;

Our daily raiment seems no obstacle
To instantaneous plunging in, deep Sea!
And revelling in long embrace with thee.

Such was the state of undersea poetry in the early nineteenth century. It wouldn't be the main catalyst for undersea
awareness, but for the first time in history there were enough
compositions to constitute a "body" of literature. Largely an
English-language phenomenon,[8] in a small way the subject had
attained the status of a repetitive theme. In verse, however, the
undersea would not make another published appearance until
mid-century; and, by then, writers in other literary forms would
have picked it up as well.

In the tenure of Wordsworth, Percival, and Tennyson, the gifted
Jules Verne was born, and from his first breath, he was in unavoidable contact with the ocean. His father was a maritime
lawyer and his home was on a small island near the mouth of
the Loire called Ile Feydeau. Its parent city, Nantes, was a
bustling Atlantic Ocean port built on the fortunes of the old
West Indies Company. But seasonal floods, sinking foundations, and the demise of their Caribbean empire had caused the
resident Santo Domingo traders to abandon their estates and
the island transformed from an opulent polity to a middle-class
preserve. Ground floors were converted into shops, and perpetuating the wares of a century before, they sold everything from
coral trinkets to bananas to tropical birds. The entire quarter
was like a boat. At its bow was a green esplanade looking seaward and its stern, the Place Neptune, had become a great mal-
odorous market for cod, tunny and other delights from the Bay
of Biscay. By modern standards, Ile Feydeau was a veritable
maritime movie set.

For young Jules Verne, a certain die was cast in this magic
place. He fished for bleaks on the sea wall, he played in a floating bath house, he sailed, and he rummaged in his father's old
documents for descriptions of cargo, insurance, and shipboard
squabbles. At eleven, he even swapped places with a cabin boy

one day and headed out aboard a three-master for the Caribbean. But, his father was tipped off by a ferry worker, and, on horseback, he intercepted the ship at an outgoing port before it got off to open sea.

Jules' appetites weren't created just from the insular world of Ile Feydeau. The larger world outside was starting to produce and promulgate a wave of dream material for the reading public. Its points of origin were of no matter. By the educational standards of the day, children like Jules were often polylingual, and even had they not been, the international translation and distribution of literary material was big business. In addition to the *poetry* of English-language authors, a new phenomenon had recently arrived. The adventure tales of James Fenimore Cooper were being released in dozens of European locations as soon as they were published in America.

In 1824, Cooper had made the sea and life at sea the predominant elements of a story, and in doing so, he created the first true sea novel. The immediate popularity of his book, *The Pilot*, was so great that he spawned ten other such sea novels over the next two decades. They became staples of escape the world over and especially in France, where Cooper was often in residence and was once U.S. Consul at Lyons.

As Cooper's fame was spreading, a much-decorated British naval officer named Frederick Marryat also stepped into the picture. Marryat determined that it would be quite shameful if the greatest maritime power on earth wasn't represented in this new literary market. Consequently, in 1831 he left the navy to start his own string of more than a dozen British-flavored sea adventures and soon they, too, were lining bookshelves all over Europe.

But the phenomenon didn't end there. In Verne's native language, Cooper and Marryat had an equal in Marie Joseph Sue, a former ship's surgeon. Sue actually antedated Marryat by several years, and like the Englishman, he retired from the navy to begin writing wildly romantic sea novels. The ocean *poets* of England and America had French counterparts as well: Victor Hugo was writing extensively about the sea, as was Alphonse De Lamartine, who, with his lyric treatment of all of nature, was called the "French Byron."

Regarding these and many other of man's pursuits, Jules Verne grew up on the threshold of a renaissance. The sense of adventure that novels and poems created was further enhanced by tremors from a real and practical world. It was the beginning of a new era in civilization's curiosity about this planet. Between 1830 and 1832, when Sue's and Marryat's first novels appeared, America was commencing substantial programs in maritime science. The U.S. Coast Survey embarked on its first sustained period of mapping, and the U.S. Depot of Charts and Instruments was established to begin astronomical observations to aid navigation. In exploration, both French and English investigators were sending back reports from Africa's interior. Elsewhere, the Mississippi River was finally traced to its source; John Ross solved the riddle of positioning the north magnetic pole; and Fitzroy, with Darwin, embarked on his five-year scientific cruise.

In this climate, the undersea also would soon yield to man's persistence; however, literature at the time – at least the novel and the short story – was inclined not to pace itself ahead of scientific progress. In the earlier days of the industrial and scientific revolutions, only the English language poets exhibited an undersea awareness. Here and there, the French poets touched on a sub-oceanic phrase, but it wasn't until much later in the century that one of them would extend the idea. Of the novelists – French, British, or American – none was prepared to risk much time on the undersea either. Rarely was its presence acknowledged. When it did occur, it was a brief observation in the course of voyaging through southern waters. In *The Cruise of the Midge*, Michael Scott, a contemporary of Cooper, gave the undersea more text than any other novelist of the era was inclined to do:

> The reef, like a bow, hemmed in a most beautiful
> semicircular pool of green sea water, clear as crystal,
> its surface darkened and crisped by tiny blue sparkling
> wavelets, which formed a glorious and pellucid covering
> to the forest, if I may so speak, of coral branches and sea-
> ferns that covered the bottom, and which, even where
> deepest, were seen distinctly in every fibre. When you

held your face close to the water, and looked steadily into
its pure depths, you saw the bottom at three fathoms perfectly alive and sparkling with shoals of fishes of the most
glowing colours, gambolling in the sun, bird-like amongst
the boughs, as if conscious of their safety from their rav-
enous comrades outside, while nothing could be more
beautiful than the smooth sparkling silver sand as the
water shoaled towards the beach.

This sort of passage was unusual in sea prose. But then,
Scott was more sensitive to the physical properties of the sea in
general. Where others often concentrated on the relationship
between sailors, their ships, and each other, Scott portrayed as
many seascapes as character studies. In that, he was the finest
of the genre and his awareness was heightened by years spent
in the Caribbean. Yet, even Scott knew that the sea beneath the
surface had a limited value in the literary genres of his day.
Jules Verne would be 17 years old before the first *fantasy* of sub-
ocean travel would appear in the bookstalls of Europe.

In all the diving schemes of previous centuries, inventors had
descended – often theoretically – in an assortment of kegs,
drums, bags, bladders, and armor plating. They all wrote questionable reports and they always complemented their tales with
a beautifully grotesque little drawing. Well into the nineteenth
century – poetic viewpoints aside – when some backyard engineer envisioned himself on the sea-floor, his account usually
described the activity as simply "walking." He didn't "glide" or
"soar" or "hang suspended." His vision was, understandably, a
prisoner of his mechanics, and it was also a popular image.
"My divers were able to walk around," reported Maillet in
1748[9] as he tried to trace undersea tides. Recounting a demonstration for the King of Sweden, the *Gazette de France* in 1774
said, "Mr. Jonas Dahlberg descended to the bottom of the lake
where he walked around over a space 120 feet in area in a way
that permitted the King and the princess to see him walking."[10]
Dahlberg was also, by some means, able to render a song for

the King that was quite audible. It's certain, however, these men weren't able to step around as effortlessly as reported – if they did at all. Walking was just an easy frame of reference. Readers identified with the action, and they could imagine strolling about as easily as if passing Sunday in a public square.

After centuries of such tales, a trio in England did, nonetheless, figure a practical method for walking underwater. Back when Tennyson wrote of the sea bed, three Saxon engineers fashioned a compressed air helmet that allowed the kind of mobility and duration men had sought. The 1830 helmet of Charles Deane, John Deane, and Augustus Siebe was open at the bottom or could be affixed to a jacket which was open at the bottom. Either way, the diver was required to remain upright at all times; yet, in contrast to everything that had preceded it, the device actually worked. Oddly, the simple concept of an inverted bucket required a gestation of centuries, but much of its success had to do with the recent advent of the reciprocating and portable compressor. In some ways, Siebe and the Deanes were simply in the right place at the right time.

Extended walks under the water were certainly an exciting prospect. But, while the Siebe-Deane helmet gave practicality to a dream, stories about it didn't spread far beyond the newspapers and the naval office. By themselves, neither the diving rig nor the act of using it were enough to inspire the literary mills. Another diving device called the submarine would have more potential. With "A. Siebe's" first production models, the diving dress was somewhat resolved, but submarines appeared in ever more fantastic forms and would for decades. Also, the sub had enticing properties that a solitary diver lacked.

First, when readers of the day fantasized an unusual journey, they much preferred a vehicle to pedestrian means. Aside from scaling mountains, hacking through jungles, or descending caverns, there was far less geographic conquest associated with travel on foot. Society had fast carriages and fast ships. Steam locomotion had become a reality and balloon flight was spreading. With the arrival of the submarine, there would be no reason for people to settle for an imaginary undersea journey on foot.

Secondly, the diving helmet and its rig weren't intended for adventurers seeking terrain. Siebe's rig found its way into the commercial harbors of England to aid in salvage, dredging, and the construction of sea walls, bridge foundations, and lighthouses. In contrast to all those unromantic applications, warfare had been the predominant force behind the submarine. At least to the reading public, warfare was and always has been romantic – more romantic than a hard day's work, unfortunately.

Once he started writing his "Voyages Extraordinaires," Jules Verne would spend a good part of his literary life in paying tribute to Yankee genius. As the sea novel had come from America in James Fenimore Cooper, so did the submarine arrive from America with Robert Fulton.[11]

Most people remember Fulton as a Pennsylvania engineer who created the steamboat. But, in fact, his mechanical genius first took root under the water and not on top of it – in Jules Verne's country and not in his own. Although the pioneering David Bushnell had tried to sell France one of his "Turtle" designs from the American Revolution, it was the younger Fulton who received France's first contract for a submarine in 1801. To challenge England's sea power, his sales pitch actually called for an entire fleet of submarines. The result, however, was two boats – one wooden and one copper-hulled. They didn't constitute a fleet, but they were fully operating submarines. Each had ballast tanks, force pumps to blow them out, viewports, manual propeller drive, anchor and windlass, and a detachable explosive charge. In the harbor of Brest, Fulton's copper-hulled boat gave the French quite a show. Fulton, with three companions, remained submerged for over an hour, navigated using a compass, and ultimately succeeded in damaging an old schooner – either by diving below it and attaching his charge or by trailing one on a line so that it smacked into the target ship.

Interestingly, though the accomplishments were duly reported, the "romance" of the submarine enticed singular inventors and entrepreneurs more than it did the navy. The naval establishment had experienced a change of heart. Under pressure from the admirals, Napoleon fired Fulton as soon as the general declared himself emperor in 1804. Much to their credit, many in the seagoing hierarchy couldn't stomach the idea of risking or taking lives in such a secretive and ungallant fashion. Also, Fulton had scrapped the second boat before Napoleon could see it, so the Emperor assumed he was a fraud. Fulton, however, was no more political than he was moralistic. He simply crossed over to England and served for two years in an effort to blow up the French fleet.

All this was history more than twenty-five years before Verne was born, and, of course, Bushnell's adventures predated him by a half-century. In pointing out this probable influence on Verne's work, it should be noted that Fulton's ingenious undersea boats were both named "Nautilus."

Moral dilemmas aside, as an engineering stimulus the submarine found an early home in France. For roughly thirty years after Fulton's departure, there were documented some 14 to 16 submarine efforts. With the exception of two English proposals, one American,[12] and one Spanish, the projects were all born in the minds of Frenchmen. The majority of these submersibles got no further than the design stage, however. Of those few that were built, most had a quick mechanical death and at least two took their creators with them. One effort had rather ironic circumstances, considering that it was Bonaparte who gave both a birth and a death certificate to his country's first working submarine. After his second exile, a group of Frenchmen had commissioned an English engineer to help them in rescuing Napoleon from Saint Helena. Money was put forth for the construction of a submarine to spirit him away, but the banished emperor died in 1821, just before the launching, and the boat was abandoned.

In this period, although most of Fulton's successors predated Verne, others overlapped his childhood. In 1834, when Jules was six years old, he heard of a tragedy at Saint-Valery-sur-Somme. There, at the river's mouth, a physician named Jean Baptiste Petit had been maneuvering his submarine around and on descent had become stuck in the river's mud bed. When the tide ebbed, Doctor Petit's creation was hauled out and he was found asphyxiated. Three years before, the

25

Spaniard Cervo, under similar circumstances, had totally disappeared. After Petit, however, there were no more recorded efforts for more than a dozen years. The inventive minds of Europe and America were merely taking a rest. The period was the calm before an immense 20-year-long storm of submarine interest – one which would have a starting point in France, and also in Germany.

Although there was no actual construction of submarine boats between 1834 and 1846, undersea travel and undersea habitation were nevertheless starting to seep into the public consciousness. Once the seed was planted, the proposals, jokes, and crackpot stories never really waned; the newspapers knew good filler when they saw it. From London's *Comic Almanack* of 1843 is this excerpt from a "Letter from a Passenger on Board the Submarine Steamer" which indicates not only a widespread frame of reference, but also that "corn" wasn't confined to the music hall:

> Well, here we are, safe and sound at the bottom of the
> Bay of Biscay, where we intend to sleep one night, for
> the purpose of testing the qualities of the bed of the
> ocean, which consists, as you will suppose, of several
> sheets of water, and plenty of wet blankets, with billows
> instead of pillows on the top of it.
>
> Not being able to keep my head above water I determined on making a bold plunge, and therefore took
> my passage in the submarine steamer, where several
> others, who, like myself, over head and ears, were
> anxious to keep out of the way, and having sunk all
> my available capital, I thought it better to sink myself
> by way of looking after it.
>
> We have had a very delightful voyage, but we met on
> our way with some very odd fish, who stared rather
> rudely in at our cabin windows, and a party of lobsters

looked exceedingly black as we passed very near to them. The mermaids were much alarmed at first, but soon became reconciled to our appearance, and, when we talked of weighting our anchor, they, with much simplicity, offered us the use of their scales.

You are aware that a company is forming for the purpose of turning the tide of emigration towards the bottom of the sea; and if people can live under water, they ought not, from mere motives of pride, to be above it . . .

. . . and so forth and so on. Adhering to the flavor of the publication, this literary masterpiece was signed "David Drink-water" and was postscripted with a quip concerning Davy Jones.

For the verbose Mister Drinkwater and others, submarines presented an undersea situation that was logically inclusive of the reader – the reader as passenger or the reader as identifying with passengers. But during this 12-year hiatus in construction, the public didn't need either submarines or the articles or jokes that surrounded them to sustain their curiosity. Other things were happening and one of these gave the solitary diver's trade new emphasis.

In 1837, Victoria began her incredible 64-year reign, and, no doubt, the grand lady saw little more water than was in her bath or around the fleets she reviewed. But Victoria's rule was concurrent with the Industrial Revolution and is a convenient reference point for so many historical purposes – undersea technology is no exception. In fact, 1837 found A. Siebe the world's first firm involved in the factory production of helmets for diving. Then, in the second year of the monarch's reign, a harbor engineer, George Edwards, approached Siebe with plans to affix the open helmet to an enclosed suit – thus, except for exposed hands, fully surrounding the diver's body with pressurized air. With weighted shoes for stability and an exhaust valve to bleed the excesses in air pressure, a diver could then assume any working position necessary without "flooding." These innovations were more significant to the history of diving than the establishment of A. Siebe in 1819 – the year of Victoria's birth.

Shortly afterward, the new Siebe diving rig was put to work in what was to become Britain's most publicized salvage job of the day, the wreck of the *Royal George*. Since the construction of submarines was then inactive, the *Royal George* significantly compromised the submarine's supremacy for public attention. The immense ship had gone down right at the fleet anchorage, taking a thousand souls to the bottom and every attempt to raise her had failed for the last 57 years. Once Siebe's suit was introduced to the military engineers,[13] more meaningful work commenced; yet the project still required another five years.

During that time, the *Royal George* became an incubator for diving techniques, salvage methods, and the kind of stories that enjoyed years of barroom retelling. Underwater demolition with explosives was refined and divers brought up articles of great size and smaller ones of great value. The first actual school was established to teach diving – the army engineers teaching the navy. A much publicized fight occurred between two divers on the bottom and the salvage project gave birth to the first "diver's hangout" at the oystering point of Whitstable. All this provided the newspapers with a never-ending flow of material. Press correspondents were attached to the salvage ships and the workers received more individual attention than perhaps anyone in the military had ever received while engaged in their duties. Charles Dickens was then writing for the papers and he romanced the new diving branch of the military:

> . . . As they go up into the air, so they go down into the
> sea. They were Sappers and Miners who were busy in
> removing the submerged wreck of the "Royal George,"
> about whose timbers and guns at the bottom of the sea
> they worked, under a pressure that cracked the strongest
> cask, sent down empty, as if it were an egg-shell. There,
> Corporal Jones of the Sappers and Miners, while at the
> bottom of the sea in his Siebe's dress, happened to come
> close upon his friend, Private Skelton, and could hear
> him singing at his work –
>
> Bright, bright are the beams of the morning sky,
> And sweet are the dews the red blossoms sip;

which was the first intimation of the fact that the voice of
a diver could be heard under the waves.

The colonel in charge found ways to encourage competition and rewards were given for the biggest slingload of material
brought up. Interesting articles were sketched by a sergeant using
a camera lucida. Finally, Siebe himself used the project to promote his equipment and he commissioned a color lithograph of
the operation with his company's name prominently displayed.

The *Royal George* project took place between 1840 and
1845, and during those years, with a push from Siebe's equipment, an industry suddenly burgeoned all over the world –
especially in America. For Americans, at the outset, diving and
salvage was unequalled for its quick and plunderous profits. By
1843, the Coast Wrecking Company, which would evolve into
the largest of such companies, was based in Staten Island and
worked the sea lanes into New York. Its competitor, Wells and
Gowen of Boston, was already taking diving contracts as far
away as Gibraltar. Down south, on the edge of its coral trap,
Key West sat like a predator. It was on its way to becoming the
richest community per capita in the United States – and all
from diving shipwrecks.

America started nurturing still another sub-ocean industry
on its shores – the undersea or submarine telegraph cable.
Samuel Morse himself began by laying an insulated copper
wire across New York Harbor in 1842,[14] and three years later,
Ezra Cornell, founder of the university, laid one across the
Hudson. Then interest shifted to England and efforts to put
one under the English Channel. They were all modest but necessary preludes to an adventure of such incredible scope that,
before the first Atlantic cable was finally completed, more than
20 years of catastrophes would ensue. Over that one big wire,
millions of dollars would be lost, corporations busted, politi-
cians enraged, sabotage committed, and poetry written. As it
paid-out against a profile of the ocean's floor, the cable would
also give added significance to the new science of oceanography. Questions would be raised about life in the abyss as broken sections were retrieved from that mysterious realm.

Fortunately, not all sub-ocean activity lay in the nuts and

bolts of the Industrial Revolution – or in man's greed. There was a scientific revolution beginning as well and the biotic and physical undersea received its modest share of funding. As the salvors and the cable men began their enterprises, Captain Charles Wilkes was bringing his wayworn United States Exploring Expedition home after four years of trying to emulate the Europeans in specimen collecting and classification. Also, Americans Matthew Maury and Alexander Bache were installed in their respective offices to begin some twenty years of bureaucratic rivalry. Between them, it ultimately resulted in the first sustained study of the Gulf Stream, the first current charts for the Western Hemisphere, classification of sea-floor sediment, comprehensive whaling charts, and the first contour map of an ocean basin. In Great Britain, Edward Forbes was generating interest in deep sea regions and had convinced the scientific community to sponsor his dredging research, first off his own coast and later in the Aegean. A year later, in 1842, Charles Darwin published *The Structure and Distribution of Coral Reefs* which sent both biologists and geologists scampering to disprove him.

However, with soundings, dredgings, and marine rivalries, no one in those early years came into more physical and intimate contact with undersea life than Belgian-born Henri Milne-Edwards. He was a zoologist at the Paris Museum of Natural History and a remarkable individual: not only did he pursue the study of marine invertebrates when hardly anyone else cared to, but he was determined to break his science out of the pickle jar and bring it to the ocean. Examining his creatures in their habitats, he established their localizing according to tides, and he authored the first rigorous reports on their patterns of feeding and reproduction.

In the spring of 1844, on an extended field trip to Sicily, Milne-Edwards also became history's first recorded diving scientist. The Minister of Public Instruction supplied the funds, and, for his baptism under the sea, the Academy of Sciences supplied Henri with a French version of Siebe's helmet. The rig was originally an apparatus to help firemen penetrate thick smoke. Its creator, the Commandant of the Paris Fire Brigade, had then converted it for use in flooded cellars. In that state, it was presented to Milne-Edwards, "to pursue marine animals into their most hidden retreats" and to do so "in the enjoyment of perfect liberty of action." And, indeed, the intrepid professor descended into the transparent Straits of Taormina and poked, prodded, observed, and collected to his heart's content.

News of the historic undersea field trips got around. The intrepid scholar assembled a report to his sponsors, and it was published by the following year. The truly vivid accounting of his adventures, however, was not by his own hand but through his naturalist companion on the trip, Armand de Quatrefages. Ten years later, in his two-volume *Souvenirs d'un naturaliste*, Quatrefages gave near lyric descriptions of their experiences:

> Leaning forward in front of the boat, we stared down
> at the hills, valleys and plains passing before our eyes.
> Sometimes the sides of the hills were bare, sometimes
> they were covered with growth of a brownish tinge.
> It was all very much as it was above water. We
> examined the slightest ruggedness in the rocky
> precipices that plunged down for perhaps a hundred
> feet into the depths, and everywhere the undulations
> of the sandy bed, the sharp crests of rocks and the
> tufts of seaweed and rock-weed stood out with such
> astonishing clarity that we began to lose a sense of
> reality. Between us and that smiling picturesque land
> we no longer observed the water which served it as
> atmosphere and which bore us along on its surface.
> We seemed to be suspended in mid-air, or rather
> to be in the middle of one of those dreams all men
> have from time to time, that feeling of gliding through
> the air like a bird and looking down at the thousand
> and one features of the landscape beneath.

Poetic accounts like this helped commit Milne-Edwards to history but, oddly enough, did not inspire his contemporaries to copy him. Many decades passed before the concept of natu-ralist/diver would take hold and those who wore diving dress continued to be the rough and tumble men of salvage and con-struction. Only one man of science immediately followed the professor. He wasn't a zoologist, however, but a physician, and his descent was not physical but literary.

Not much is known about Clement Jules Briois, except that he was a man of medicine with a strong leaning to biochemistry. In 1841, after years of interviewing the afflicted, he produced an extensive catalog of maladies according to personal complaint. But medicine aside, Briois also had a few thoughts on the reign of Louis Philippe and society in general, and wanted evidently to impart them to the children of France. So, as a metaphor, he created the idyllic kingdom of "Piscipolie" and placed it on the ocean's floor to remove it as far from corrupting European monarchies as possible. *Voyage au Fond de la Mer* (*Journey to the Bottom of the Sea*) was published the year after Milne-Edward's Sicilian expedition,[15] and in the story, the author descends into the Indian Ocean to visit his submarine utopia. Writing under the pen name of "Capitaine Merobert," Briois describes Piscipolie's social fabric in terms half moralizing and half personal fantasy.

To begin, Capitaine Merobert arrives at the bottom of the sea to find nothing but men around. The ladies, it appears, all bear their young at the same time every year and Merobert just happened to drop in on delivery day. Later, he finds that the newborn are really still in an egg stage. Males are in blue shells, girls in pink, and similarities to fish are maintained throughout the book. Briois also develops his fish folk into practitioners of everything virtuous: simple dress, contented labor, respect for the elderly, and humility toward God. The inbuilt order of ocean life is seen as a complement to the inbuilt order of a religious community. Evidently, too many women were saying "yes" in Doctor Briois' time because he also throws in an endorsement for Piscipolien women – who are quite adept at saying "no." The whole empire combines the influence of Neptune with that of Puritanism.

Being a conservative sort, the Piscipoliens also have saved everything that ever fell down into their habitat from above. They don't quite understand the articles, so Merobert has a field day explaining the surface world to them. Using firearms, instruments, and other scuttled junk, he draws a picture of terrestrial society and its problems. He also tells them that if they're smart, they'll stay right where they are – especially after he explains war. Merobert even spots Grecian statuary and proceeds to give a lecture on Xerxes. For a physics course, the captain tells them about air and life in a different ambient pressure.

Regarding air and pressure, Briois did some very independent thinking – especially regarding Merobert's mobility from surface to sub-sea world. There was no chamber, no diving suit, and no submarine. Despite the technical advances on the horizon, Briois didn't use them to assist his traveler. Instead, Merobert – already graced with an unusual stamina for being underwater – gets into the prospect of solidifying gases. After much experimentation, he solidifies breathing air, divides it up into manageable tablets, and descends with one always tucked in his mouth. Indeed, the pills were visionary, but still Briois refused to employ any transporting hardware. His hero simply swam down to Piscipolie as if in a Greek legend.

And the Industrial Revolution wasn't the only source that Briois passed up. Although descriptions were now coming in from near and far, he also ignored any opportunity to romance the true physical and sensory aspects of the undersea experience. Granted, in his story, homes and utensils are made of sea material, skin is really scales, and people ride fish in order to hunt other fish. They even have fish pets. But these are just fanciful borrowings. Not even in establishing scenery did Briois indulge himself in thoughts about the visual quietude or the ethereal qualities of his new environment. Since the book was for children, such descriptions might have given it a special magic. Tidepools provided Briois with life sciences, but he evidently extracted no imagery from them. Only in his initial transitionary plunge did he mention a visual association with the water:

As I was sliding down along the cable of the boat,
I went through three zones which were a different color
due to the refraction of the light. The first zone was
azure, then changing to the color of aquamarine which

was the second and middle zone. The third one displayed tones of tender green progressively changing to a deeper one, the color of emerald.[16]

That passage was both the beginning and the end of Briois' underwater sensations. After his descent, all ambience and quite a few objects are borrowed from above. Indeed, many embellishments take the form of jewels, as if the sea-floor is abundant in them. When they're played upon, musical instruments emit smells and they're all earthly flower smells. In the final analysis, Briois' book was really a "Land of Pan" concept and the location was just a vehicle for his moralizing. Despite its neglect of a true ocean environment, *Voyage au Fond de la Mer* was, in fact, the first undersea novel and no doubt had some small influence on a certain boy of Nantes named Jules Verne.

When Briois' novel came out Jules Verne was seventeen. He might have been a little old for the book's fantasy, but he was a prime age for its sciences, however flawed. Briois had annotated his text throughout with explanatory notes on minerals, ancient history, and marine biology: a very marketable format for the times. Milne-Edward's report also was published then, and the following year came Fitzroy's narrative on the voyages of the *H.M.S. Beagle*. Sir John Clark Ross was soon going to press with his *Voyage of Discovery and Research in the Southern and Antarctic Regions*. It, in turn, was joined by a host of other geography books – staples in any educated household.

As the Ross adventure came out in 1847, Verne graduated the lycee. His commencement took place as Livingston explored South Africa and the missionaries Krapf and Rebmann discovered Mount Kilimanjaro. In this climate of global news and literature, young Jules was chafing for contact with the outside world – but to no immediate end. Despite the siren call of sailors and explorers, he wasn't really in a position to respond. In fact, Jules Verne was in a domestic stranglehold. As the older of two sons, it was his obligation to prepare himself for the family business – in this case, his father's law practice.

Ironically, it was his younger brother Paul who was allowed to pursue a maritime career in the merchant marine.

Verne had spent his entire childhood witnessing other people's departures and now his own brother was setting out as well. In late December, Jules watched Paul sail from Nantes as a novice pilot aboard the three-masted *Regulus*. It was bound for Africa and not due back for eight months. After his departure, the tedium of the family circle was much too burdensome for Verne, who took the only avenue of escape that was open to him. His liberation was law school, for it necessitated a journey of its own – a move to the dazzling boulevards of Paris in 1848. Paris didn't have the geographic scope of an ocean voyage, but Verne sorely needed the social and literary involvement his father had suppressed.

In fact, for the next ten years, Verne had as much contact with the ocean as would a parlor raconteur. His hunger for the Romantic coteries of the Left Bank easily predominated his law studies, and, through family contacts, Verne parlayed his salon etiquette and repartee into hundreds of invitations. It was all to penetrate the literary set and it worked. For his efforts, the plum was a close and lasting relationship with Alexandre Dumas, the elder. Dumas not only enticed Verne into bohemia, he produced Verne's first opera. More important, he gave the young Breton courage to finally buck his father and give up law for writing. Verne took the trouble to pass his exams, but, after that, he started pouring his quick wit onto paper. The result was pretty frivolous stuff at first: vaudeville sketches, libretti for mime-plays, and a number of trifling comedies for operetta and theater – the kind where flirtatious wives and outwitted husbands are standard elements. Despite the encouragement of friends – and fortunately for the world – his theatrical efforts led nowhere.

However, life changed when Verne began freelancing stories for an illustrated monthly magazine, the *Musee des Familles*. There he discovered his talent for narrative fiction; the magazine's editor, P. M. F. Chevalier, was as much a mentor along those lines as Dumas had been for his dramatic work. Interestingly enough, Verne's first effort for the periodical – and his first known prose to be published – was a sea tale in the manner of

James Fenimore Cooper called *The Mutineers*. The first of his balloon stories followed – a horrific thing influenced by his love of Poe – then another nautical yarn entitled *The First Ships of the Mexican Navy*. Verne was suddenly finding direction because, in addition to literature, the serialized stories allowed him to indulge another long-suppressed love, geography. The geography aspect intensified when Chevalier sparked a friendship between Verne and a garrulous, half-blind world traveler named Jacques Arago. When they met, Arago had worked the California gold fields and sailed from Northern China to Antarctica; his *Voyage autour du Monde* was a publisher's dream come true.

As Dumas' chateau had been a gathering place for playwrights, so did Arago's home attract travelers. There, the soirées gave Verne a vision – a clue to the potential of exploration as a literary framework – not just for chronicles but for novels as well. Moreover, since Arago's brother Francois was a famous astronomer, their house also attracted physicists, naturalists, and mathematicians, and, from all those disciplined minds, Verne formed ideas for still a third literary element – that of science. While these thoughts crystallized in his mind, more travel stories followed, as well as more insipid comedies from which he couldn't seem to wean himself. A lot of the misdirected energy was due to his collaborations with a hometown friend named Aristide Hignard who, in turn, collaborated with names like Delibes and Offenbach.

Between these various projects, however, Verne relinquished some of his socializing to become a somewhat bookish lay scientist. He spent time studying with his cousin, Henri Garcet, a professor of mathematics at the Ecole Polytechnique, and he crammed himself with Garcet's brand of cosmography and mechanics. While the precise realities of law may have bored him, the seductions of the physical universe entranced him.

The first result of the novel-travel-science amalgam was a tale entitled *Master Zacharius* which started appearing in the *Musee* in 1854. It also contained a bit of moralizing with the bizarre, and if it wasn't the first actual science fiction, it was at least Verne's first science fiction. In the story, Zacharius is a Swiss clockmaker who invents the escapement principle. He gets into terrible psycho-kinetic trouble when he starts regarding this mechanism as the secret of life. As a consequence, his body and mind start functioning well only when the clocks around him function well. The story was a portent to hundreds of fantastic scenarios to come; however, in *Zacharius* and all the efforts preceding it, Verne didn't consider himself a writer because the work alone wasn't keeping him alive.

For those early years in Paris, Verne was engaged as a tutor, a bank clerk, and the director of a small theatre. His writing came either in periods or by lamplight and he labored in furnished apartments, to the annoyance of bohemian roommates. Naturally, when love came calling, it was untimely. Verne exacerbated his problem in 1856 by marrying a lady whose matrimonial status included two daughters. Although his bride had a stipend of her own, domestic pride drove Verne to the financial district to get a steady job. At the end of the '50s, a decade after his arrival, the future creator of Captain Nemo's epic undersea journey was fatigued from his literary aspirations, playing with two adopted daughters, and working as a stockbroker in the "Bourse" of Paris.

In reality, Verne never wanted to be an explorer or a scientist. He wanted, instead, to be a literary creature and write about exploration and science. He was domiciled in a perfect place. The libraries and universities of Paris afforded him as much printed and personal contact with his subjects as he could ever use. Missing was the physical presence of the sea, but Verne chose to renew his relationship to the sea by degrees. Only later would his pursuit of it be intense; ultimately, the sea became a subject in more than two dozen of his works as it was in his first published story. Therefore, it's still ironic that, through most of the 1850s, Verne should have been so removed. It was in that very decade that the ocean became a vast proving ground for both the industrial and scientific revolutions – especially as a proving ground for more undersea enterprises. Likewise, the ocean came into the public consciousness as it had never done before.

To begin with, ocean traffic was increasing rapidly and no

country was more responsible for this than Great Britain. Her metals and coal now made her the workshop of the world, and to get the manufactured goods to market, she needed a vast maritime fleet. Guarding that merchant fleet meant building a vast navy, and her navy, in turn, formed one big patrol around the globe. While this was happening, ordinary citizens became ocean-bound. The great age of passenger travel had begun. The Nova Scotian, Sam Cunard, was already in his seventh year of plowing the North Atlantic and now, as the decade started, the fleet of Samuel Knight Collins emerged for a contest. Then, William Inman appeared, but, ignoring the elite altogether, he built his empire running emigrants from the Irish famine to jobs in the United States.

Through steam power, ships had already attained greater speed, regularity, and carrying capacity. Now, in the fifties, there were commercial carriers trading sidewheel paddles for screws and simple engines for compound ones. The image of ocean travel was further enhanced when the moneyed gentry took iron and engines to sea on their own. Cornelius Vanderbilt, for instance, built the grandest private yacht in history in 1853. He steamed across the Atlantic in it and spent a summer dropping in on royalty, impressing journalists, and generally acting like a potentate from Neptune's realm.

Soon commerce was funding the sciences: the crossover from one to the other came with men like Matthew Maury whose contour maps and depth charts were published, as was his opus magnum, *The Physical Geography of the Sea*, in 1855. Maury was also instrumental in launching the huge Brussels Maritime Conference where international cooperation for collecting and compiling data was established. He had wrested two research vessels out of the U.S. government and was recording depths, sub-surface temperatures, and taking sub-surface water samples. With a newly patented device, he was also taking bottom samples from progressively deeper regions.

While Maury collected sand, clay, and sediment with a line, others collected animals with trawls and dredges. At 300 fathoms, the pioneer Edward Forbes had mistakenly established limits to the azoic or life-supporting zones. But now, a Norwegian father-son team, Michael and G.O. Sars, were not only

38

bringing up life from 450 fathoms, but much of it was so primitive that it had previously been regarded as extinct. Another Norwegian, named Absjornsen, also helped to extend the zone downward by capturing sea lilies and luminous starfish from incredible depths. No one believed just how deep life existed, however, until the undersea telegraph cable was laid. The biologists advanced into the so-called "lifeless zones" little by little, but the cable surveyors dragged their sounding lines right down to the abyssal regions and the lines were being retrieved with extraordinary animals attached. As Jules Verne was groping for direction, selling stocks on the exchange, and writing comic operas, the words "trawling" and "sounding" became part of the public parlance as people read about the strange creatures and sediments being lifted from the mysterious deep.

Meanwhile, though sounding zones were physically inaccessible, lesser depths were not, and underwater industry progressed above the 130-foot level. Joseph Cabirol responded to Siebe and the Deanes and created a French version of the compressed air diving suit. His rig made its appearance at the International Exposition in 1855. The following year, near Washington, D.C., a gas device called Gould and Lamb's Patent Sub-Marine Lantern was tested. It was carried to a depth of 100 feet and lit a 12-foot radius in murky water. But solitary divers weren't the only means of getting a job done. The working potential of many men was consolidated when inventors started perfecting the diving bell. Intended mainly for construction, bells had cables and chain slings, were sunk by water ballast or weights, and got pressurized air through a hose. Then a Frenchman named Payerne advanced the technology. In a 10-year period, he built three construction submersibles which were untethered, could be directed by a steam system, and had air locks where divers could exit and re-enter.

Quite possibly those features were all common knowledge. In 1854, even something as utilitarian as Payerne's iron monsters could command generous space in the *Illustrated London News*. People read about it for the same reason they read of Brooke's sounding device or Cabirol's diving suit. For the weekly and monthly magazines, the great ocean quest was romantic news and the great sub-ocean quest made even better news. In the life forms of the deep or in the hardware for descending, mysterious business took place under the sea – and that made for good circulation. For the mid-nineteenth century reader, sub-ocean conquest was an incredible prospect and journals saw to it that the prospect became even more incredible. Embellished articles were hawked by the *Illustrated News*, the *Gentleman's Magazine*, and *Le Monde illustre*. At those and dozens of lesser European and American "rags," no enterprising editor would decline magnifying a biological discovery or a device for diving and probing.

However, as to the machine age, readers were snared by something more intriguing than just bells and helmets because when the '50s arrived, the submarine returned. As for *living* things, the public definitely had a new and spectacular topic. In zoology (and journalism), the '50s and '60s were the apogee of a speculative craze that swept across the world. Its subject was an elusive creature called the sea serpent.

In Verne's early manhood, news publications and sea serpents were almost correlative; they emerged together, proliferated together, and generally kept company for years. Although dated serpent reports had actually begun in 1650, they started multiplying in the early 1800s, and by then, newspapers were numerous as well. However, it wasn't until mid-century that a substantial change took place for both. First, the printing capacity of newspapers and magazines was markedly increased. Secondly – and at the same time – the concept of the sea serpent ascended from dubious reports to scientific recognition and it came to include a lot of animals we now know to exist.

The printing explosion on both sides of the Atlantic was caused by the rotary press. Despite the fact that the British were master machinists, many printing innovations took place in America as well: R. Hoe &Company first developed a rotary press for the *Philadelphia Ledger* in 1847. Soon they were making larger presses which could run off 5,000 to 12,000 impressions an hour. Another press by Thomas Nelson could print both sides simultaneously from a continuous roll of paper and it was demonstrated at the 1850 World's Fair. Nelson's machine was experimental, but refinements and adaptations came rapidly, bringing about an awesome increase in newspaper and periodical production.

Of course, all these new papers had to be sold, and a little sensationalism could often help the process. Occasionally, an outright sea monster hoax was perpetrated. As the rotary press had come from America, so did a lot of tall tales – with the remainder coming from Ireland. But, in defense of reporters, few actually fabricated a serpent story. They were just extravagant in their retelling. Even that technique was not always effective, because, if excessive, it ended reader speculation rather quickly. And while sightings were frequent, about three a year, they had no lasting editorial value. There was rarely a good way to extend the stories through corroborative evidence or opinion – that is, not until the "Daedalus incident."

The year Verne first arrived in Paris, the 19-gun *H.M.S. Daedalus* was coming home to Plymouth from the East Indies. Near St. Helena, she encountered what by all descriptions was a serpent, and when her commanding officer filed a report to the Admiralty, it was published in *The Times*.[17] Evidently, this was the first time a member of Her Majesty's Navy had dared to submit such a paper. It sparked a series of both supportive and critical letters and also subsequent reports from other captains in the area. Coming from the navy, the report was also an honorable precedent and it served to legitimize future sightings. Once involvement became respectable, two-thirds of the reporting shifted from America and Norway to the more populous England and France.

Together with navies and merchantmen, the scientific community also had been afraid to become involved for fear of ridicule. After the *Daedalus* sighting, however, some well-established naturalists vigorously pursued the issue and those who would have feared making a report were now doing it. Sightings and strandings of oarfish, basking sharks, and nemertean worms became more detailed and circumstantial. Official catalogings of giant squid already had begun and Edward Newman, editor of *The Zoologist*, now bravely opened his journal to sea monster articles. Institutions that were cradles of zoology adopted the sea serpent for lecture and debate. In that regard, probably no one did more for the cause than the Swiss-American naturalist, Louis Agassiz. In a lecture at Philadelphia, he supported a sea serpent theory that even today is plausible – one which claims that prehistoric Plesiosaurs and Elasmosaurs could still be roaming the depths. Newspapers and magazines loved this new consciousness and so did the readers. By the time Captain Nemo would fight his own particular monsters on the printed page, the world would be primed and ready for the contest.

It would be primed for his submarine as well. After some 14 years of disinterest, suddenly the undersea boat was a subject of news again, and this time there would be a greater number of boats and a greater amount of news. As it had with sea serpents, the '50s would witness the submarine's evolution from a fanciful absurdity into an accepted idea. In that decade alone, ten inventors from five countries constructed approximately 13 different boats. And to the degree that Robert Fulton had dominated the first decade, so did one man prevail in the fifth. His name was William Bauer.

Bauer was a doggedly persistent personality. Although he was a Bavarian artilleryman at the outset, like Fulton he quickly developed a capricious nationalism when it came to submarines. He peddled his ideas to any government that had the funds. While Jules Verne was experimenting with omelettes and sauces in Alexandre Dumas' kitchen, Corporal Bauer was experimenting with his first submarine. He christened it the *Brandtaucher* or *Sea-Diver* and intended to use it breaking the Danish blockade of Germany's coast. It was 25-feet long, made of sheet iron, and shaped like a porpoise. In 1850, the year Agassiz endorsed the sea serpent, Bauer launched his stubby vessel. Although he never got to blow anybody out of the water, he managed to scare the Danish fleet, which broke its line trying to get away from him. The following year, he got stuck at 60 feet, but, by gradually flooding his interior, he and two other crewmen made it to the surface. It was history's first submarine escape, but the accident cost him the confidence of the military.

After his dunking in home waters, Bauer went to Austria and wooed the Archduke Maximilian. He got as far as a ship-

42

yard contract, but a conservative finance minister cut off his funds. Undaunted, he then went to England in 1853 where concern over the Crimea was growing. There was no having audience with Victoria, but her beloved Prince Albert was an enthusiast for gadgetry and he surrounded himself with inventors. Through Albert, Bauer met John Scott Russell and Isambard Kingdom Brunel, who were the reigning monarchs of engineering. The outcome was ultimately two boats. The first one even had a sort of gas-driven engine, which failed. Unfortunately, early in the planning, Russell and Brunel adopted Bauer's ideas, but rejected both Bauer and his drawings. The resulting boats both sank with the loss of their crews and Bauer took off for Russia – by way of an unrewarding sales trip to the United States.

For some reason, Bauer's undersea ideas were always a good passkey to royal audience. In Russia, he persuaded still another nobleman, the Grand Duke Constantine. The collaboration resulted in a 57-foot submersible named the *Sea-Devil* and it turned out to be the most ambitious project of the decade. It was still a manually driven affair, but it dived to an incredible 150 feet. It also had oxygen regeneration, an airlock, an observation dome, and carried 13 crewmen. In 1856, Bauer made 134 dives in it and then topped off his success by staging an underwater concert for the new Czar. At the coronation of Alexander II, he carried four brass players down with him and rendered martial music for hours. It could be heard by people in boats above for 600 feet in any direction.

As with the *Brandtaucher*, Bauer had a submerged accident in the *Sea-Devil*. He narrowly escaped from it after letting all the other crewmen out first. Nevertheless, the sub's worth was established and Bauer was instated in the Russian Navy as official submarine engineer – the world's first such title. In 1858, he began an even grander boat, but his never-ending feud with jealous admirals caused him to quit Russia as well. France was the last country he tried, but this came to nothing, so Bauer went home to Germany. He later died in his bed – a pretty comfortable way for a man to go when he had flirted so often with the prospect of drowning.

In addition to some lesser talent in Europe, Bauer had a

counterpart in America. He wasn't as traveled, prolific, or self-promoting, but he possessed just as much ingenuity. His name was Lodner D. Phillips and he was a shoemaker in Chicago. Over the years of helping pedestrian transport, Phillips also managed to build two 40-to-50-foot vessels for underwater travel. He once took his wife and children down for a whole day in Lake Michigan while they gazed out of the ports onto a terrain somewhat more visible than that of today. One of his subs was a real workhorse, for it even had a mechanism for sawing timbers that was operated from inside. However, Lodner's other boat was designed for warfare, and, in that regard, he joined the ranks of all the other submarine tinkerers of the '50s. Through periodicals, news of his work, Bauer's work, and everyone else's work, brought the sub out of fantasy and made it a popular idea. The boats still didn't have motors and not one had yet made a successful wartime attack, but it was no matter. Those points would be resolved in the coming decade, and, besides, people loved the submarine, albeit unperfected. The newspapers certainly loved it – it sold as many editions as the sea serpent. Whether it was a strange creature who came from the undersea or a strange vessel going down into it, both made otherworldly reading for hard-working people in need of escape.

Submarines and sea serpents could only add to the mystique that the cables, bells, research ships and divers had been promulgating. For the news periodicals – and the public – the undersea was now no longer just an industry or a science, but an awareness. Briois' *Journey to the Bottom of the Sea* had been a somewhat related portent. Yet, from the time of the *Daedalus* reports and Bauer's first vessel, it would be 20 more years before a true sub-ocean theme was carried from newspapers to novels – 10 years after Bauer's success in Russia. Indeed, though enough inspiration existed for most writers, still more events would have to transpire before someone saw the literary potential. The coming decade of the '60s was to be, in some ways, more ripe with invention than even Bauer's.

Along with locomotives and bacteriology, the undersea

had an incremented popularity. Despite its newsworthiness, it had to wait – alongside steam pistons and microbes – for the eminent storytellers to adopt it. With the poets, of course, there was less hesitation. Poets – both naturalist and humanist – were intoxicated by the Industrial Revolution and its scientific counterpart. The novelists, however, were not yet ready to sing songs of progress – or incorporate science into an adventure story. As for the undersea aspect, there was yet another consideration. The undersea couldn't very well emerge in novels when the sea in general wasn't holding its own as a literary muse. In contrast to the '30s and '40s – and in spite of everything that was happening – the decade of William Bauer saw a scarcity of sea fiction. The year before Jules Verne moved to Paris, Frederick Marryat published his last work. Three years before, James Fenimore Cooper had done likewise and Joseph Sue also terminated his sea writing in that period. Suddenly England, France, and America had all lost their pre-eminent sea novelists. As for newer writers, steam power had completely disoriented them. Once the romance of sails started waning, it created a limbo where potential sea authors didn't quite know what to do with the subject. The end result was that, during the decade of the '50s, hardly anyone shaped literary adventures from either science or the sea. This was in spite of great technical, scientific, and commercial dramas that were occurring on the ocean every day. A new and special romance was emerging out of sea explorations, yet little of it was treated artistically.

This neglect, however, did not prevent the occasional æsthetic statement. There was one very important exception in the lean period of ocean novels – Herman Melville. His books had actually emerged in the '40s, but, in 1851, he delivered a consummate masterpiece into the world. It was a sea novel of such broad human scope that many today think it the most metaphysical writing since the *Holy Bible*. The book was *Moby Dick*. Few people at the time understood what Melville was saying, and his popularity diminished soon after its publication. In this epic work, however, Melville crafted profound statements about mankind. He also devoted text to the sea's visual mystique, and he included some acknowledgment of the undersea as well – such as when Ishmael reflects on equatorial water – and the beauty of its largest creatures in their element:

> But far beneath this wondrous world upon the surface, another and still stranger world met our eyes as we gazed over the side. For, suspended in these watery vaults, floated the forms of nursing mothers of the whales, and those that by their enormous girth seemed shortly to become mothers. The lake, as I have hinted, was to a considerable depth exceedingly transparent; and as human infants while suckling will calmly and fixedly gaze away from the breast, as if leading two different lives at the same time; and yet while drawing mortal nourishment, be still spiritually feasting upon some unearthly reminiscence; even so did the young of these whales seem looking up toward us, but not at us, as if we were a bit of gulf-weed in their new-born sight. Floating on their sides, the mothers also seemed quietly eyeing us.[18]

. . . or a passage where Starbuck indulges in the same pleasure:

> Loveliness unfathomable as ever lover saw in his young bride's eye! Tell me not thou of thy teeth-tiered sharks, and thy kidnapping ways. Let faith oust fact; let fancy oust memory; I look deep down and do believe.[19]

Later, Melville wrote *The Encantadas or Enchanted Isles*. It was 10 sketches of the Galapagos which first appeared in *Putnam's Magazine*[20] and was later reprinted in *The Piazza Tales* in 1856. In it were less poetic but still vivid descriptions such as this one:

> The winged life crowding Rodondo had its full counterpart in the finny hosts which peopled the waters at its base. Below the waterline the rock seemed one honeycomb of grottoes, affording labyrinthine lurking places for swarms of fairy fish . . . Here hues were seen as yet unpainted and figures which are unengraved.

In addition to prose writers like Melville, there were still poets who carried on in the Romantic tradition of the '20s and '30s. The Englishman Matthew Arnold, for instance, conceived an unusual turnabout of mythology in *The Forsaken Merman* – wherein an undersea family laments for its mother, who has left them for the allurements of a land-bound life. At any rate, Arnold's construction of the family's home gives good insight into a Victorian's concept of the sea floor:

> . . . Sand-strewn caverns, cool and deep,
> Where the winds are all asleep;
> Where the spent lights quiver and gleam,
> Where the salt weed sways in the stream,
> Where the sea-beasts, ranged all round,
> Feed in the ooze of their pasture-ground;
> Where the sea-snakes coil and twine,
> Dry their mail and bask in the brine;
> Where great whales come sailing by,
> Sail and sail, with unshut eye . . .

With considerations for the period, there was an artistry in Arnold's work, but there were also some sentimentalists at large. Bayard Taylor, for one, was more known for his travel books and German translations, but he also composed poetry like *Sunken Treasures* in 1852. In that piece, the undersea was used as a metaphor for human maturing and recall:

> When the uneasy waves of life subside,
>   And the soothed ocean sleeps in glassy rest,
> I see, submerged beyond storm or tide
>   The treasures gathered in its greedy breast.
>
> There still they shine, through the translucent Past,
>   Far down on that forever quiet floor;
> No fierce upheaval of the deep shall cast
>   Them back, – no wave shall wash them to the shore . . .

Of course, no discussion of the era could exclude Walt Whitman. Especially during the 1850s, he haunted Long Island shores from Brooklyn to Montauk and he composed to a host of ocean themes. Whitman had a robust and mystic identification with the universe. Verne's countrymen thought he was indelicate, but Whitman couldn't have cared as he raggedly spread himself out over all sorts of earthly experience. It's little wonder then, that in the course of all his sea visions, he even went under the surface as in *World Below the Brine* from his *Leaves of Grass*:

> The world below the brine,
> Forests at the bottom of the sea, the branches and leaves,
> Sea-lettuce, vast lichens, strange flowers and seeds, the thick
>   tangle, openings, and pink turf,
> Different colors, pale gray and green, purple, white, and
>   gold, the play of light through the water,
> Dumb swimmers there among the rocks, coral, gluten, grass,
>   rushes, and the aliment of the swimmers,
> Sluggish existences grazing there suspended, or slowly crawling
>   close to the bottom
> The sperm whale at the surface blowing air and spray, or
>   disporting with his flukes
> The leaden-eyed shark, the walrus, the turtle, the hair sea-
>   leopard, and the sting ray,
> Passions there, wars, pursuits, tribes, sight in those ocean-depths,
>   breathing that thick-breathing air, as so many do.
> The change thence to the sight here, and to the subtle air
>   breathed by beings like us who walk this sphere,
> The change onward from ours to that of beings who walk
>   other spheres.

And so, these visions were largely what the '50s gave to the undersea's obscure literary stockpile. Remaining were a few to the deep-sea diver. In one case, Nathaniel Hawthorne wrote a short story entitled "A Prize From the Sea" about the recovery of sunken treasure. The rest occurred when documentation crossed into the literary realm. For example, in 1859, 20 years after he wrote about the *Royal George*, Charles Dickens was still interested in divers. In his *Uncommercial Traveler*, he described a tour around the site of another wreck, the *Royal Charter*, which sank in a storm: "Even as I stood on the beach with the words 'Here she went down' in my ears, a diver in his grotesque dress dipped heavily over the side ... and dropped to the bottom ...." Dickens then went on about recovering both bodies and gold from the ill-fated ship.

Another example was a tiny book printed in Buffalo, New York, in the same year that the *Royal Charter* went down. It was verbosely titled *Diving With and Without Armor, Containing the Submarine Exploits of J.B. Green, The Celebrated Submarine Diver* and it was probably the first diver's autobiography. Crippled by the bends, Green had it printed up and he peddled it on street corners for a quarter. Basically, he had been a tradesman of northern waters and never indulged in descriptions of his working environment – that is, not until he was sent to the vicinity of Grand Turk Island on a salvage assignment:

These [cannon] we could see from the surface of the
water, sixty feet beneath, lying among the pillars of
coral. Here is presented to the diver one of the most
beautiful and sublime scenes the eye every beheld.
The water varies from ten to one hundred feet in
depth, and is so clear that the diver can see from
two to three hundred feet.

The bottom of the ocean in many places on these banks,
is as smooth as a marble floor; in others it is studded with
coral columns, from ten to one hundred feet in height,
and from one to eight feet in diameter. The tops of those
more lofty, supporting a myriad of pyramidal pendants,
each forming a myriad more; giving the reality to the
imaginary abode of some water nymph. In other places,
the pendants form arch after arch, and as the diver stands
on the bottom of the ocean, and gazes through those
lofty winding avenues, he feels that they fill him with
as sacred an awe, as if he were in some old cathedral,
which had long been buried beneath "old ocean's wave."
Here and there, the coral extends even to the surface
of the water, as if those loftier columns were towers
belonging to those stately temples now in ruins.

There were countless varieties of diminutive trees, shrubs, and plants in every crevice of the coral. They were all of a faint hue, owing to the pale light they received, although of every shade and entirely different from plants I am familiar with, that vegetate upon dry land. One in particular, attracted my attention; a sea-fan of immense size, of variegated colors, and of the most brilliant hue.

To enumerate all the kinds of fish that I beheld while diving on these Banks, would were I enough of a naturalist so to do, requires more than my limits will allow.

As J. B. Green sold his book in the streets of Buffalo, the decade of Jules Verne's deliverance was close at hand. In fact, it was just before the '60s that Verne initiated his first escape from the stock market and embarked on a voyage that wasn't imaginary. He and his musician-friend Hignard got a free trip to Scotland through Hignard's brother who was a shipping line agent. At age 31, not only was it Jules' first journey outside of France, but his first experience in the open sea. Starting at Bordeaux, the two comrades sailed for Liverpool, trained to Edinburgh and on to Glasgow. A number of ferry trips across Lochs Lomond and Katrine were included and the water adventure was further enhanced by a storm which forced their rescue in rowboats.

But of all the experiences on his journey, for Verne the most vivid occurred after they had traveled by sea to the Hebrides. As if a portent to his future craft, Verne kept a detailed narrative of the trip – travel notes that were literally novelized.[21] At Fingal's Cave, where a natural canopy creates a temple for the sea-floor, Verne committed to paper for the first time his intimate contact with the world below the surface. His words reveal an early love of all such secret places and this theme of inner space would recur again and again in the years to come:

From this point in the cave, there is an admirable vista broadening out to the open sky, and the water, filled with clear light, allows one to see every detail of the sea bed.

On the side walls, one sees an astonishing play of light
and shadows. When a cloud covers the entrance to the
cave, everything grows dark, as when a gauze curtain is
dropped over the theatre proscenium. But everything
sparkles and glints gaily with the seven colours of the
rainbow whenever the sun breaks through again,
reflected off the crystal of the cave bottom and glancing
upwards in long luminous streaks to the threshold of the
central nave. Beyond that, the waves break at the foot of
the gigantic arch which forms the opening to the cave:
and this frame, black as ebony, throws all the foreground
features into full relief. Further out still, the horizon
between sea and sky stretches out in all its splendour,
with the dim heights of Iona two miles out in the open
sea, and the pale silhouette of its ruined monastery.

What an enchanted palace this Fingal's Cave is! Who
could be so dull of soul as not to believe that it was
created by a god for sylphs and water-nymphs!

From the floor of the sea, Verne soon returned to the floor
of the Bourse and economic realities. In the summer of 1861,
however, he and Hignard once again secured passage on a
freighter. This time, it was to Norway with a load of coal and
they spent six weeks ingesting the atmosphere of the "midnight
sun" and those bleak northern waters. At the end of this second escape, Verne then returned to an even greater economic
reality – his newly arrived and only child.

Between voyages one and two, the soon-to-be-famous
author had continued trading stocks. He also wrote again for
the frivolous end of theatre. One work was a musical comedy
he produced with Offenbach about a well-attired monkey who,
with his exceptional manners, penetrates the human social register. It was all the very worst kind of Second Empire silliness.
However, once Verne returned from his second voyage, this
kind of nonsense ended. His scientific and geographic interests
had been incubating too long to lay dormant any longer – new
child notwithstanding.

It had been fully seven years since he had written *Master*

51

Zacharius and a literary career seemed to be passing him by. What with family and the stock market, Verne had neglected cultivating new friends. After all, it was Alexandre Dumas who had spurred him to writing. P.M.F. Chevalier had channeled him into narrative fiction, and Jacques Arago had exposed him to the society of scientists. And so it happened that in 1862, with his new resolve, Verne met two fresh personalities who finally drove him straight to his predestined mark.

The first was an ebullient character named Felix Tourna-chon who used the pseudonym of Nadar and who pursued every novelty that presented itself. Verne found him at a club for science writers. Nadar was a political cartoonist and a society photographer; and most importantly for Verne, he was a master publicist and an aerial enthusiast. In that regard, it would be misleading to say that Verne was totally consumed by the sea, either above or below the surface. His love of geography led him in many directions and especially into schemes involving aircraft. To further align the facts, the prospect of air travel had a lot more romance for the public than its sub-ocean counterpart. Even to this day, the undersea, for many, cannot compete with the spatial qualities attached to flying.

Though Verne's first published prose had been a sea tale, his first balloon story had immediately followed and he now wanted to expand the concept. As he set himself to the task, Nadar became a godsend. In addition to supplying enthusiasm for Verne's work, Nadar decided to make the story manifest. He organized the Society for Aerial Locomotion, and, to attract subscriptions, he began construction of a real balloon – a huge multi-passenger affair. As tall as Notre Dame, it was to be launched with maximum publicity and roughly timed to coincide with Verne's book. Verne was secretary of the organization and heartily approved of the schedule. When news of the forthcoming aero-monster had spread, he pushed himself to complete his manuscript. Through a friend of Dumas, he then presented himself to that second personality – the single most influential figure in his life, Pierre Jules Hetzel.

As colorful as any of Verne's other associates, Hetzel was a political activist who had just returned from seven years of exile. He was an author in his own right, and, as a publisher, his personal stable of writers had come to include Honore Balzac, Alfred Musset, and George Sand. From the day Verne first walked into his office, Hetzel became Verne's principal representative. He was the man who "discovered" and helped nurture Verne – tutoring the young writer and encouraging him to mold himself into his specialized calling. The result was a literary composite of science, geography, futurism, and fiction – a maverick, new blend that would make rich men of them both.

When Verne met Hetzel, a particularly timely atmosphere prevailed. Hetzel had recently begun cultivating a share of the youth market. As well as books for children, he was laying down plans for a children's magazine – the format to be both educational and entertaining. Verne easily married science fact with fictional narrative and the combination was perfect for the tone of the *Magasin d'Education et de Recreation*. After a slight reworking, Hetzel bought the balloon story. With the future in mind, he also signed Verne to a contract for three stories a year which could be serialized for the *Magasin* before they took book form.

In more ways than one, Verne and Hetzel were men of the hour. In literature, they stood ready as the pioneering opportunists of the scientific revolution. But, in addition to their science-fiction posture, they were participants in a more general literary change. As sea serpents, diving exploits, and other phenomena – like balloons – had benefited the newspaper market, so a new device called the *feuilleton* caused that market to literally explode. The *feuilleton* was simply a story section – the purveying of a tale in installments – either as the sole means of publication or as a prelude to some forthcoming book. Once the penny press discovered its value, many novelists started tailoring their romances to a structure for easy serialization. In this sense, the *feuilleton* became the basis for a whole new art form.

Contributing writers had once created for a small elite, but now they were in no position to reject the change. Private patronage had begun to disappear and they needed the new mass market to keep working. Moreover, France had remained at the tail end of paper manufacturing and bindery progress. Book production in Verne's country was an expensive proposition and the new reading masses could more easily afford a tabloid newspaper. Verne's friend, Dumas, was one of the first to conform to this new medium and the results were outstanding. In a three-week period, one of his novels, *Le Capitaine Paul*, attracted 100,000 new subscribers for a paper called *Siecle*. As rotary presses paved the way for this mass literature, Pierre Hetzel intended to supply the children's share of that prose. The popularizing of science and geography would be his merchandise. Jules Verne would be the romantic pitchman to sell it.

While Hetzel's paper was still in the planning stage, Verne's first efforts went straight to book form. The long and prosperous relationship was officially launched early in 1863 when *Cinq Semaines en Ballon* (*Five Weeks in a Balloon*) was released and immediately became a best-seller – both for its intrinsic value and the not-so-coincidental assembly of Nadar's dream-ship. With the publication of his first true novel, Verne set out on the 40-year's labor of his "Voyages Extraordinaires" – a collection of more than 100 books. In them, he would take his readers up into the heavens, down into subterranean grottoes, and across every earthly zone from tropic to polar. Of course, in the greatest of his works, he would take them under the sea as well.

In the real world, that quest had continued its momentum. When Verne had returned from Scotland, Charles Darwin's controversial *Origin of Species* had been published, and, in England, the treatise helped to spark a rash of biology books – for the general public as well as academia. Many of them were on sea life, and nearly all of those were magnificently bound volumes sporting lavish illustrations. They had romantic titles like *The Sea and Its Wonders* and "nature-printed" plates where engravings had been made using actual sea plant and coral dissections.[22] Off Sardinia, the shallow water azoic theory was shattered when a submarine telegraph cable was hauled up for repair. After three years at a depth of 6,000 feet, it not only had animals attached to it, but encrusted upon it as well. It was sent to Paris, and Milne-Edwards, still very much active, filed a landmark paper with the French Academy of Sciences concerning the cable's biological importance.

Later, when Verne had returned from Norway, his countrymen were presented with their own version of the *Dædalus* sea-serpent affair. In November of 1861, a French gunboat, the *Alecton*, had encountered a giant squid some 40 leagues off its home port. The captain returned with a piece of the monster, and, by way of his remnant and the testimony of his crew, a length of 24 feet was established. It wouldn't stand as a record, but, at the time, it was quite enough to start a renewed interest in sea serpents, particularly giant squid.

In that same period, in France, new developments occurred in diving. Some 20 years after the English had established a school for military divers, the French followed the example. Their own diving rig design, the Cabirol, was now five years in use and Louis Napoleon's navy started training divers as well. In addition, the French re-entered the submarine business – in a very important way. Two gentlemen, Simeon Bourgois and Charles-Marie Brun, started to work on the first submersible to *successfully* use something besides manpower for propulsion. Three years from blueprints to reality, the result was a 435-ton, 140-foot boat. By the time Jules Verne saw his first printed copy of *Five Weeks in a Balloon*, Bourgois and Brun were piloting *Le Plongeur* under the surface using a compressed air engine that was rated at 80 horsepower.

Despite the inspirations around him, it was a while before Verne gave any serious thought to the undersea. The gestation of a story would take more time still, and once begun, his first commitments to paper would be sporadic. In all, it was six years after he met Hetzel before the world saw *Twenty Thousand Leagues Under the Seas* in the bookstores. After the success of his balloon tale, Verne took up his pen, created an English character named Captain Hatteras, and, via Hetzel's *Magasin*, commenced a journey to the North Pole. Following that, he formulated a German expedition and led them down through the crater of an ancient Icelandic volcano in *Journey to the Center of the Earth*.

With these early stories, Verne and Hetzel formed a close and permanent collaboration in sensing the public's appetites. Undersea exploration was deferred for a while in favor of other conquests and it well could have been a joint decision.[23] Once their travel machine was in motion, Verne discussed all his concepts with his publisher and he easily tolerated Hetzel's injunctions to revise the manuscripts. As the newspaper's format developed, an ever-increasing amount of science was skillfully incorporated into each text. To facilitate the gathering of facts, Hetzel influenced Verne to meet specialists who could contribute to their stockpile. Verne would then steer his nineteenth century Ulysses through a framework of this accumulated knowledge. In later years, the science/geography themes would be complemented with wry humor and political allusions. Most of this probably escaped the children, but Verne's audience ultimately would extend beyond its youth-oriented beginnings and the barbs would not be wasted.

From the first novel, his following mushroomed. Not only were the stars of literature, science, and printing all in position, but so was society. In a way, Verne's success was assured because he entered an immense and hungry market. In the 1860s, social equality was still more an ideal than a fact, but compared with earlier times, incomes grew and literacy expanded at a rapid clip – both hitching a ride on the other revolutions. Victoria wanted an educated populace, and so did Verne's sovereign, Louis Napoleon. Although he had a penchant for military ventures – all badly conceived – the French emperor championed a progressive society. During his reign, the muddy walks of Paris became spacious boulevards, France became the center of art and culture, and, despite the fact that Louis was a scheming mountebank, many people were more decently housed and paid that they ever had been. It was no small feat in a country that was still principally agrarian and still mechanically far behind England and the United States. France was deficient in metals and metallurgy, and the farming interests worked to keep a lid on what mining there was.

Despite these lesser resources, Louis Napoleon literally worshipped the era of inventions, and he conceived a temple to it called the international exposition – forerunner of the modern-day trade fair. There, through the years, an enlightened audience would see the industrial and scientific manifestations of Verne's thinking – either in current use or in magnificent models and projections. Verne, himself, picked up ideas in the exhibits. Many of his concepts were aligned with reality and certainly all of them were aligned with Louis' relentless belief in progress. If an invention increased man's control over nature in any way, then it was considered fruitful. With this attitude, the monarch saw gadgetry as a key to international markets and great prosperity for France. Accordingly, even though Verne despised both Louis Napoleon's sleazy politics and his military aspirations, he still became a literary extension of Louis' enticing mechanical dreams.

His inspirations, however, fell short of chauvinism, because Verne frequently acknowledged the greater progress happening in other countries. He simply would not create many French heroes. Knowing where greater sales might occur, Hetzel probably helped the decision, but it was still an honest preference. France was doing well in the natural sciences, had a fine navy, and, indeed, became a showplace for technology. But, in other important arenas of commerce, France was so technically deficient that her manufacturers had to develop a system of industrial smuggling in order to get English machinery and blueprints across the English Channel. Consequently, Jules Verne's heroes were more often English and American. In fact, a great stimulus, at least for his mechanical creations, was the American Civil War. It was in its third year when Verne's first novel was published, and France was keenly interested in those faraway battlefields.

France was especially interested in the Confederacy and had lent the South large sums of money against cotton bonds. Although Louis Napoleon would later spurn the Confederacy, it was Southern cotton that kept French textile mills humming, and the mills were France's largest mechanized industry. Verne, however, was neither an industrialist nor a warmonger; his fascination was with the futuristic aspects of the conflict. The "War Between the States" was the first modern war; one where technology and industrial capacity would be a deciding factor. From the front came reports on the first time-fuse projectiles, the first military telegraph, and the first balloon reconnaissance. There were also the first machine guns, electrical mines, armored trains, and ironclad warships.

In fact, after his third novel, Verne's next project was *The*

Blockade Runners – a tribute to the sleek, shallow-draft steamers that sped in and out of Southern ports and defied Union warships. As he was completing the manuscript, however, an incident occurred that, more than any preceding one, caused Verne and Hetzel to theorize that the time for a tale of undersea conquest was close at hand.

It was on the night of February 17, 1864, in Charleston, South Carolina. Standing out in open water and blockading the port was an armed Union screw-steamer, the *Housatonic*. Inside the harbor, eight seamen and two engineers from the 21st Alabama Regiment left the docks at sunset. They were manning a 35-foot submarine named the *H.L. Hunley* and mounted on the bow was a spar torpedo that was marked for the *Housatonic*. The Confederate boat went out on an ebb tide, with a nearly full moon, and by 8:45 she was lined up for the kill. When the explosion went off, its 200-foot target heeled over to port, sank stern first, and became the first warship in history to fall victim to a submarine. Unfortunately for the Confederate seamen, the blast was multidirectional, and the *Hunley* was lost as well. Nevertheless, after almost a century of serious submersible experiments, the first successful wartime attack had happened.

Early in the conflict, the Confederacy had begun testing subs. They were built on the Gulf Coast, and particularly at Mobile, Alabama, because iron and ingenuity were plentiful there. Although the *Hunley* was manually propelled, her creators had experimented with steam and other power sources. When the war started, Paccinnoti and Gramme had just perfected the dynamo and Rebel engineers even tried installing electricity in their undersea boats. In the North, a French engineer named Villeroi was commissioned to build submersibles for the U.S. Navy. His work occurred late in the fighting, and, though it never saw action, at least one functional Yankee sub was launched.

For Verne and Hetzel, the American Civil War, and especially the *Hunley* incident, drove home the ominous importance of submarines. Through the sensationalist treatment of

Le Monde Illustré, news of Civil War technology reached Verne in abundance, and though Bourgois and Brun were now navigating *Le Plongeur* under *French* waters, it didn't dilute the effect of *Le Monde*'s fanciful reporting from *American* waters. The paper had fleets of oversized submarine behemoths pitted against one another and the French public devoured it. Louis Napoleon loved it, too. It was one of the reasons that submarines were starting to reappear in France. The other reason was that Louis was as fanatic about ships as he was about boulevards and libraries. Despite his country's limited iron resources, he became an innovator in armored vessels and was determined to have a fine navy at all costs – and that included having submarines.

As the American conflict ended, other countries emerged with new and better subs. A Barcelona man built one that sported both a cannon and a steam auger. Then *Le Monde*'s oversized fantasies came true when a 265-foot boat – almost twice the length of *Le Plongeur* – was launched in England. By 1865, large submarines were suddenly as much a reality as undersea warfare. They were limited to their home waters because crew life was grueling and power systems couldn't take them very far. In adapting the sub to literature, those details would be left for Verne to solve. Warfare wasn't his interest, but living in strange environments and conquering geography was. For a journey around the world, he had only to conceive better propulsion and to make his machine habitable. There were few restraints on Verne's thinking and he ultimately created a power system that was perfect for the task and an interior that was not just habitable, but undeniably opulent. All he needed now was mobility for his men – or rather, a real-life inspiration that would place his men in closer touch with their new world.

As far as subaqueous experience, the submarine itself was only an iron-clad vehicle and a confining habitat at that. It didn't place its crew in contact with the elements, and, on the whole, it offered little awareness of the undersea environment. Men needed to leave the mother ship and walk about before Verne's sense of freedom would be satisfied. Air-locks had already been built, and from them, tethered divers had made exits and reentries. But still greater freedom was at hand. As the *Hunley* and *Le Plongeur* had caused Verne to speculate on an undersea novel, so a second invention committed him. This time, like *Le Plongeur*, it was spawned in the waters of France.

Midway into the American Civil War, two of Verne's countrymen had revealed a new concept in diving. One man was a naval officer, the other a mining engineer, and they called their new device the *aérophore*. It shared a common incumbrance with both the Siebe and Cabirol units in that the diver was still tethered to a hose and surface pump – at least most of the time. However, instead of the pump-forced air going directly to a helmet, it passed first into a metal canister that he wore on his back. There it was pressurized a little more and became a surplus above his immediate needs. After that, the revolutionary part of the rig went to work. Sitting atop the canister, a valve and membrane device released air at ambient pressure – rising and falling in concert with the diver's lungs as they drew from it by way of a tube. Benôit Rouquayrol and Lieutenant August Denayrouze had created nothing less than the basic concept of our modern demand regulator – 70 years before the first experiments in modern scuba.

Requiring neither a helmet nor a suit, the diver wore a nose-clip and goggles – later, a full-face mask. The real attraction for Verne was that the diver could detach the air hose from his canister and briefly exist with no connection to the surface – an independent agent walking around on the sea floor. The limiting factor was that no one had yet figured how to store large amounts of air at very high pressures. Consequently, the *aérophore*'s storage canister – and the diver's freedom – was only good for a few minutes and in shallow water at that.[24] The fact that men could have this freedom, even briefly, fired Verne's imagination. He envisioned entire submarine crews stalking the deep ocean's floor without effort. As an honest chronicler, he would ultimately give Rouquayrol and Denayrouze their credit, but, as an incurable visionary, he would sketch their invention in outrageous extremes. One of Nemo's treks would require the 14-inch canister to provide air for nearly 10 hours at 450 feet. Together with suits sealed at surface pressure and no decompression on re-entering the unpressurized sub, Verne's crewmen would need extra lives just to survive his armchair concepts.

Armed with a large submarine and portable life-support, Verne prepared to descend into the oceans of the world. As well as marine steam engines, there now existed compressed-gas engines, electric motors, and dynamos. Air could be pressurized then stored and oxygen-regeneration systems were decades old. So were air-locks, diving bells, and underwater compasses, lanterns, and tools. Scholarly friends were very willing to contribute data and Verne's brother Paul, now a merchant marine officer, would aid him in physics and navigation. Verne sought-out Jacques Conseil who, six years earlier, had launched a manually-driven submersible and, later, one powered by turbine.

In his mind, abstractions about the undersea were now omnipresent. So were they in the mind of his publisher. But in crediting all this male-dominated technology, the first real encouragement for writing *Twenty Thousand Leagues* could well have come from a woman. At the very least, hers may have been the first suggestion from a fellow author. Through Hetzel, Verne had developed a friendship with George Sand and, two years before, had made her a gift of his first two novels. In reply, she said, "I have only one regret – that I have finished them and have not another ten volumes to read. I hope you will take us soon into the depths of the sea and that you will make your characters travel in one of those submersible boats which your imagination and knowledge will be able to make perfect." Whether Verne had given it any serious consideration before 1864 is not known, but a synopsis was drafted and sent to Hetzel around January of 1866.[25]

For today's undersea enthusiast, it might be romantic to imagine Verne then obsessively throwing himself into the book, but that wasn't the case — at least not at first. After the synopsis, nothing else was written for 15 months, though not from apathy. Throughout that year, many letters were exchanged between himself and Hetzel regarding the concept and ways to extend it. Verne was impatient and wrote, "If I were to botch this book, I would never get over it. I've never had my hands on a finer subject." But already, there were other projects in gestation. In discovering his talents, he had accepted too much work and was contracted to see it through. Before any more sub-ocean efforts were expanded, Verne had to first complete a novel entitled *The Children of Captain Grant* – a South Pacific journey by two people in search of their seamaster father. On top of this, one of Hetzel's other writers became terminally ill in the middle of an *Illustrated Geography of France* and Verne agreed to take that job over as well. It was a monumental piece of work, but, for Verne, it was merely a potboiler to straighten out his finances. Once these two commitments were honored, he would later allow *From the Earth to the Moon*[26] to also encroach on his undersea time. During the course of his life, it was perfectly natural for him to temporarily break off from one novel if inspiration for another presented itself.

Creative energies notwithstanding, Verne's involvements became burdensome. He finally moved himself and his family out of Paris and up to the shrimp fishing village of Le Crotoy. There, near Saint Valery, he found provincial inspirations for his unprovincial visions. A rented cottage looked out over the mouth of the Somme, and a stretch of sand dunes and beech trees buffered the family from the English Channel. Verne loved the place and what was intended as a short escape from urbana became a two- to three-year residence.

In Le Crotoy, he kept his first sailboat since childhood – a converted fishing smack he named the *Saint Michel*. Despite its original commercial design, it was quite habitable and became his deliverance from the hack labor of the *Illustrated Geography*. Sailing acumen returned, and casting off his natty attire, he would tack for days along the Picardie coast, clad in a seaman's jersey. When it was time to trade halyards for a pen, two permanent crewmen took over and shipmaster Verne would sprawl on the deck with his writing.

The boulevardier of Paris was rediscovering the magic and simplicity of a port town – and the extent to which he had deferred his sensitivity for the ocean. In this environment, Professor Aronnax, Captain Nemo, and the *Nautilus* would have their incredible undersea journey committed to paper – the mouth of the Somme the spawning ground for their adventures.

By March of 1867, Verne had retired his other commitments, and he now prepared to prowl the ocean. The *aérophore* of Rouquayrol and Denayrouze had, weeks before, been utilized in a spectacular recovery of gold in Marseilles harbor. As a result, the term "sunken treasure" was now frequent in the popular parlance and Verne was inclined to give it scope. His less relevant priorities may disenchant the modern aquaphile, but at least one romantic notion is valid: *Twenty Thousand Leagues* was both researched and written not just by the sea, but, literally, on the sea. The regimen on the *Saint Michel* was decidedly productive, but her captain was to temporarily transfer his work to yet another vessel; one that would prove to be additionally inspiring.

That same month, Verne and his brother Paul decided to fulfill two sea-faring ambitions at one time. The first, to cross the Atlantic together; and, the second, to travel on the largest ship then built – the *Great Eastern*. A 693-foot iron behemoth, the ship was leaving Liverpool in late March for New York, with a return that would land them in Brest. The French port was part of a cooperative venture between the ship's English directors and Louis Napoleon to carry hundreds of wealthy New Yorkers to the emperor's latest and biggest exhibition, *Le Grand Oriental*. For Verne, the advantages were visiting America, sailing the open ocean, exploring the *Great Eastern*, and, in the midst of it all, taking his work with him – the embryonic draft of his undersea novel. In his usual fashion, he also took notes for another story – one inspired by the vessel which transported him, *Une Ville Flottante* (*A Floating City.*)

On March 27, a ship, four times larger than anything afloat, left the River Mersey and started knifing its way west. She had a 22,000-ton displacement and 11,000-horsepower that could drive either paddlewheels or a 24-foot screw. But size wasn't her only attribute, for the *Great Eastern* was also a technological marvel and the ultimate in sea-going modernity. With new concepts in instrumentation, propulsion, and steering, she was the magnum opus of Isambard Kingdom Brunel, the brilliant and daring engineer. Her hull and paddle engines were built by the equally venerated John Scott Russell. The work started only a year after Russell and Brunel had collaborated with William Bauer in submarine construction.

For Captain Paul Verne, the *Great Eastern* was a high caliber busman's holiday. For his brother Jules, it was a classroom; *Twenty Thousand Leagues* was the first novel to bring the whole industrial and scientific revolution to sea literature. Brunel's great ship became a surface-bound cradle for Verne's subsurface ideas – an air-breathing mother to his undersea equivalent, the *Nautilus*. Like the *Great Eastern*, the *Nautilus* would incorporate every scientific advantage conceivable as well as every accommodation possible; this in order that Nemo could reveal with exactitude, and in comfort, the wonders of an undersea world he called home. Verne took notes on every accessible place aboard, but technology wasn't his only quest. There was the ocean itself. The voyage was undertaken to absorb the open sea and not just a group of inventions. Verne hoped to find the spirit and omnipotence of the Atlantic, and, as it turned out, he got a very good concentration of it.

First, despite "progress," the gravity of a seaman's lot was evident before they even left port. Four crewmen were killed by flying capstan bars when a pin broke and the anchor ran away. Later, a fifth man lost his life when a block fell, and, as a result, Verne witnessed a burial at sea. The nautical pathos accumulated as a few days out the great ship came upon a drifting wreck with no survivors. A week later, the situation was further intensified as they passed slowly through a field of ice – a frequent, unpredictable menace in the North Atlantic. Verne, of course, was keeping his customary log of images all the while.

His ultimate lesson came as they neared Newfoundland. The *Great Eastern* drove straight into a violent storm, and, for a time, her captain refused to yield. When the towering seas struck, Verne made sure that he spent his time on the bridge cataloguing events. He watched in disbelief as the tempest smashed nine-foot bulwarks and ripped away enormous sheets of cast iron covering the forecastle's hatchway.

"I had forgotten," he wrote, "that the power of the sea is infinite and nothing made by [the] hand of man can resist it." He went down in the "tween-decks" to see the crew fight with 2,000 tons of water that had flooded the holds. There, thanks to a Frenchman who was exporting 30,000 mâché infants, Verne recorded a surreal image: "New spars covered the sea, and amongst them were thousands of dolls, which my countryman had thought to acclimatize in America. The little bodies, torn from their cases by the sea, danced on the summits of the waves."

When quite enough dolls, spars, and men had been either swept up or crumpled, the captain relented, turned head to the wind, and outran his adversary. Verne watched and wrote of the resulting calm: ". . . the ocean . . . took on the fresh green of a meadow in the rays of the rising sun. The waves rolled voluptuously by, and a few porpoises leapt and tumbled like clowns in the ship's milky wake. Upon this whiteness moved other more clearly defined patterns, so that one had the impression of an immense veil of lace laid upon a blue background."

Amid these technical and elemental confrontations, Verne mingled with engineers, boatswains, and the black gang. In contrast to that, was salon life, but even there he never stopped working. As with his engine room treks, the champagne and cigar socials were often for research. It was a chance to talk at length about the Atlantic submarine cable – with men who planned it, wrestled it, and generally paid in blood to see telegraphy take place between the United States and Europe. As a passenger ship, the *Great Eastern* was actually a disappointing investment for her builders, so, in 1865, she had been temporarily converted for cable-laying operations. As part of a decade-long saga of persistence and repeated failure, it was this ship that had completed the temperamental project eight months before. Many of the workers who had grappled with the wire day and night, across the ocean, still served on board. Also aboard was the man who had promoted and built the Atlantic Telegraph Company, Cyrus W. Field – a magnetic Yankee who had gambled his entire fortune on the cable.

Before Field's farsighted enterprise, the whole of international trade and culture had operated on month-old inquiries and two-month replies. Louis Napoleon communicated with America no faster than had Louis XIV. Messages were only as fast as the ship which carried them. Once the cable was down, however, trans-Atlantic contact instantly changed from months to eight seconds. For that reason, the Western world had placed a lot of hopes in the wire and they were not all related to trade. Commercial value was obvious; but the Victorian era was one of those naïve periods when people thought a single invention would end conflict. Prose writers and poets everywhere celebrated the cable and affixed to it all manner of benevolent properties. Thackeray and Lady Byron were stockholders. Bayard Taylor wrote a hymn to the cable and John Greenleaf Whittier went on to give it providential blessing:

> O lovely bay of Trinity,
>   O dreary shores, give ear!
> Lean down unto the white-lipped sea,
>   The voice of God to hear.
>
> . . . And one in heart, as one in blood,
>   Shall all her peoples be;
> The hands of human brotherhood
>   Are clasped beneath the sea.

In literature, the cable possessed a humanistic correlation that lasted for generations. But also present was a mysterious vision – the image of man's thoughts traveling across the very bottom of the ocean – man's thoughts in a place man had never seen. Rudyard Kipling's *The Deep-Sea Cables* was composed a few decades after Verne's voyage, but, more than any other writing, it imparts the awesome feelings that prevailed when Kipling was a boy – and the cable, too, was young.

> The wrecks dissolve above us; their dust drops down from afar –
> Down to the dark, to the utter dark, where the blind sea
>   snakes are.
> There is no sound, no echo of sound, in the deserts of the deep,
> Or the great grey level plains of ooze where the shell-burred
>   cables creep.
>
> Here in the womb of the world – here on the tie-ribs of earth
> Words, and the words of men, flicker and flutter and beat –

Warning, sorrow, and gain, salutation and mirth –
For a Power troubles the Still that has neither voice nor feet.

Of course, that "Power" couldn't physically transport man beneath the ocean. However, many cultural hopes were riding on it and the signals took a wondrous and otherworldly route. The cable might just as well have been a submarine or a diving suit, for it certainly generated as much undersea awareness. For ten years, people had read of the testing, the sounding, and the tribulations. The electric serpent was almost 2,000 miles long, and it submerged to an average depth of three miles. Would the insulation hold up? One puncture could – and did – ruin their schedule. How much slack could it take? Would its own weight break it as it hung across undersea chasms? Special grapnels were built to retrieve the cable, and, ultimately, they had to be used. Would subsurface currents damage it? Would pressure squeeze it too much? Would large sea animals attack it?

As he listened to the men who had lived with these questions, Verne learned much about the undersea. Its physics were awesome and he was made to realize that only sound technical knowledge would allow man to penetrate the deep. While on board the *Great Eastern*, he recorded images of a world unforgiving of ignorance and that fact soon became a primary theme in his novel. By the time he arrived in America, voluminous notes lay waiting for their delivery into prose, but Verne was now attuned to New York. He wanted to attend the theatre, to cruise up the Hudson, and to see what he regarded as the greatest natural wonder outside of the ocean itself – Niagara Falls.

It was April 9 when the great iron ship tied up to its West Street pier on what was then called the North River. As Jules Verne disembarked, one of history's fortuitous crossing of paths may have then occurred. There was no real communication involved – only the simple occupation of space – an unresolved moment where sheer proximity creates a potential for encounter and then quickly snuffs it out. Among the customs inspectors who lined up for duty that morning was one No. 75 – a weary, reclusive man on the lee shore of his life. His remaining joy was a steady living; his job much in keeping with an obscurity he had finally accepted. In 1867, neither the passengers nor his co-workers could attach any significance to Herman Melville. Passenger Verne was writing an epic novel where the undersea was a backdrop for philosophy. He was little known to Americans. Inspector Melville, unbeknownst to his comrades, had already written the most philosophical, and indeed the most cosmic, of all sea literature. America had already forgotten him. There, on the docks of Manhattan, it is more than possible that these two men traded glances and civilities. It is quite definite that they then went their separate ways, each never knowing the other.[27]

Jules Verne had doubtless read Melville's works, as *Moby Dick* is mentioned in *Twenty Thousand Leagues*. However, like many Frenchmen, he idolized James Fenimore Cooper – not only for his sea novels, but for his pioneer and Indian tales as well. For that reason, Jules and Paul took a train through the Mohawk Valley, returning to Manhattan just in time to catch the *Great Eastern* back to France. At that point, if Verne thought that socializing would interfere with writing, his concern was soon put to rest. The ship was prepared to take 4,000 eager Americans to the Paris Exhibition. When they left the docks, however, exactly 191 passengers were onboard. Verne would get a lot of work done, but the ship's financial loss was crippling and America would never see the the *Great Eastern* again.

Despite this disappointing manifest, Louis Napoleon's *Le Grand Oriental* was a successful exhibition. Fifty-seven monarchs were entertained and European attendance was phenomenal. When the Verne brothers landed at Brest, they joined the handful of Yankee passengers and swung by Paris for an immersion in science and festivities. Louis was showing off his new boulevards. Verne's old collaborator, Offenbach, was premiering new operettas and Johann Strauss was introducing the *Blue Danube Waltz*. Krupp paraded new cannons and something strange called aluminum was presented. Among the exhibits of art, bacteriology, and propulsion was an incredibly large item – something that most people had read of but few had ever seen – a submarine. It was a model of Bourgois and Brun's *Le Plongeur*, and 10 million attendees of the exhibition would peruse her. The visitors, of course, included Jules Verne.

Mentally, he dropped into her deep interiors and studied her systems. Surrounding him were 21 copper cylinders, each containing air compressed to 200 pounds per square inch. Verne soon discovered that air operated everything. Not only were the ballast tanks voided by air, but her two "inclined" engines were air driven as well. All her pumps were air driven. Indeed, *Le Plongeur* represented the latest in pneumatic science, yet Verne also knew that the magic word "electricity" was on the lips of anyone of futurist persuasions. The exhibit was, nevertheless, a marvelous way to cap his ocean-bound research. It was also an indication that, with all of those witnesses to undersea progress, Verne ought to work faster. *Le Grand Oriental* had just given him an eager audience for his novel.

Back in Le Crotoy, he was reunited with the *Saint Michel* and his writing-sailing regimen continued. It was now springtime and Verne engaged his two-man crew, stocked the cabin with his copious notes, and set out for Le Havre, Dieppe, and a dozen other ports. The sea was to be the heroine of his story and Verne wanted the closest possible proximity to her. Collectively, almost two years would pass on the water while his epic literary voyage took shape. Rusticating back on land was his family. The relationship with his wife, Honorine, his stepdaughters, and his own son, Michel, was stable yet largely utilitarian. In almost all of his stories, science and heroics would eclipse romance, and one can assume that in the domestic, as well as the literary, applications of relationships, Verne was little more than indifferent.

Needing the elements more than the family, Verne convinced himself that his boat was the only place where subaqueous ideas could flower. The *Saint Michel* became a dream factory for the journeys of the *Nautilus* and Verne would draw vast, intrepid visions from the simple and modest events of a day's sailing. As the *Saint Michel* slipped along the surface, the *Nautilus* glided through undersea forests. As the sea's respirations were heard from above, Verne constructed the endless geographies that lay beneath him. Carefully, he walked his

Captain Nemo through blue-canopied worlds, and, like passage in the submarine, he used those walks to deliver all his carefully accumulated lectures. Jules Verne loved being instructive. He *was* the precise and pedantic Captain Nemo.

For his reference, there were now four rich decades of undersea quests, and their origins were scientific, commercial, and even literary. Facts and imagery ranged from the brusque testimonies of a working diver to the poetic musings of a Tennyson or a Hemans; from the sensationalism of tabloid reporting to the academic texts of Quatrefages or Milne-Edwards. In the overall scheme of things, the eloquent orations of Cyrus Field would be just as useful to Verne as the sober reports of Alexander Bache. This tale of adventure would become a veritable textbook for ocean enthusiasts and its contributors would be hand-picked from all over the Western world.

Even as Verne wrote, new material was being generated. Reports came in from both sides of the Atlantic where marine naturalists were wielding their dredges with a flourish. Edward Forbes even wrote a poem to his dredge. Michael Sars was finding new animals in Norway and Louis Pourtales and Louis Agassiz were leading scientific cruises in America. Submitting their first proposals for oceanographic exploration to the British Admiralty were botanist Charles Wyville Thompson and physician William B. Carpenter. Before Verne's manuscript was completed they would set out on the first of their voyages, leading ultimately to the famous *Challenger* expedition. Meanwhile, on the floor of the Dover straits, geological surveys were being conducted for a proposed tunnel from Dover to Calais.

Also in England, Thomas Henry Huxley had decided to re-examine the primordial ooze he had stockpiled in his laboratory. Discovering a mucous-like jelly under the microscope, Huxley concluded that it was protoplasm and his announcement suddenly enlarged the potential biology of the abyss. Journalists couldn't resist declaring that "living slime" carpeted the ocean's floor. Both within and without the scientific world, findings such as Huxley's were homogenized with a lot of conjecture. As a result, the deeper sea floor changed its image from that of a lifeless void to, as Kipling would say, "the womb of the world." As scientists promoted this image – and their involvements with it – they, in turn, popularized the sub-ocean for nonscientists. Then, as now, more public curiosity was the result, and Jules Verne was inheriting an ever larger audience.

Some of that curiosity was evident at Belle Isle, near Verne's Brittany birthplace. There, the world's first undersea observatory for the general public was now in operation. Two years before, in 1865, an Angers man named Ernest Bazin had constructed this steel turret and crane affair and equipped it with a 900-pound electric searchlight. The chamber had accommodating viewports and a renewable air system. For the benefit of seaside visitors, it descended as much as a hundred feet and soon Bazin was towing his device up and down the French Coast to preach the beauty of the undersea – and, of course, to make more money.

Ultimately, Bazin's apparatus was hired to direct divers for a new salvage attempt on the famous Vigo Bay Galleons in northwest Spain. Though many fortunes had already been swallowed up, 166 years of general failure only encouraged new ventures, and, in the spring of 1868, Paris would see the formation of still another enterprise called the Vigo Galleons Salvage Corporation.

Not surprisingly, investors all over France could still be found to sink money into the elusive treasures of Galicia. The corporation would peddle 250,000 francs worth of stock, with a single investor named Hippolyte Magen buying another quarter million and taking command of the grand scheme. Along with his interest in sunken ships, Magen also got a lot of free publicity. The stories, in fact, were so enticing that, as Verne proceeded with his manuscript, he couldn't resist including the Vigo Bay history.

The inclusion was reasonable since the notoriety of the Spanish galleons had really grown up alongside the state of the art in diving. The same Rouquayrol Denayrouze diving apparatus that Verne conscripted for Nemo was now going to be employed at Vigo Bay – without much more success than previous devices had achieved. In the real world, salvors Magen and Bazin would have little to show for all their efforts and equipment. Author Verne, of course, had no concessions to make. In *Twenty Thousand Leagues*, Professor Aronnax would easily view Vigo's floor as the *Nautilus* cruised over the wreck site. Nemo's men would salve the treasures at will, while impeded, surface-based workers toiled in vain. Ironically, Verne took the chance of predicting Magen and Bazin's small return by having Nemo clean out the site. His novel would be well into circulation by the time the salvage corporation decided to abandon the project.

Back on the Brittany coast, before Bazin ever decided to gamble in Spain, the ocean floor was evolving into a fashionable pastime. There, the wealthy Alexandre Leopold, Marquis de Folin, had taken a keen interest in undersea research. Presiding over a series of summer cruises, he explored the sea bed with a dredge in preparation for his book, *Les Fonds de la Mer*.[28] The treatise would later help him persuade the French government to establish a commission for marine exploration. In the years 1867 and 1868, in fact, Neptune's realm was a good publishing bet all around, and books other than Leopold's filled the stalls. Still a second *Fond de la Mer* was authored by Leon Renard. It, in turn, shared space with new works like Fletcher Bassett's *Legends and Superstitions of the Sea*, Louis Figuier's *The Ocean World*, and Arthur Mangin's *Mysteries of the Ocean*. Any one or all of these could have logically dressed the *Saint Michel*'s cabin during those two formative years. Lacking hard evidence of this, it is still reasonable to insist on Verne's many debts. He was a chronicler as well as a visionary and his research techniques are common literary knowledge.

As for his own undersea book, discarded titles included *Voyage Under the Oceans*, *Voyage Under the Waters*, and *Journey Under Sea*. With every correspondence to Hetzel, the name changed, as did entire concepts. In fact, the novel itself underwent countless revisions, but, through it all, its place of creation remained the *Saint Michel*. Verne's attachment became somewhat extreme and when Hetzel called for a mid-manuscript meeting, Verne insisted on taking his boat through the Somme and Seine canal system in order to reach Paris. This was in the face of a drought that had lowered all the inland waters to dangerous levels. Nonetheless, the undaunted shipmaster Verne got in and out of the city without being grounded. By mid-August, he was back in Le Crotoy and the Somme estuary – the body of water where, ironically, his country's first submarine experimenter, Jean Petit, had lost his life some 33 years before.

Through the fall, Verne continued to carve the waters of the estuary and the English Channel. Face down on the deck or seated in the cabin, he threaded Aronnax, Nemo, Conseil, and Ned Land through the labyrinths of the Atlantic and the Pacific. "What a book it will be if I pull it off," Verne wrote his father; "What incredible ideas I have while sailing . . . ." And incredible they were, because by this time, Verne had transcended the existing technology that was his starting point. Not only were his undersea crew viewing kelp forests and salving gold, they were now mining minerals, harvesting nutrients, and extracting vegetable fibers and dyes for their clothing. Verne had developed the *Nautilus*, and its men, into a concept for living entirely from the sea. It was a mobilized capsule of lives existing both within and off an infinitely larger form of life – the way Verne viewed the ocean. After a fishing expedition, Nemo says:

> Professor, is not this ocean gifted with real life? It has its tempers and its gentle moods. Yesterday it slept as we did and now it has woke after a quiet night. Look . . . it wakes under the caresses of the sun. It is going to renew its diurnal existence. It is an interesting study to watch the play of its organization. It has a pulse, arteries, spasms; and I agree with the learned Maury, who discovered in it a circulation as real as the circulation of blood in animals.[29]

By October of 1867, a serial began in *Le Petit Journal* that carried men through that watery plasma to far zones of the globe. Their submarine penetrated the Sargasso Sea, navigated the Cape of Good Hope, and even slipped under the icy canopy of the Antarctic. At the helm, however, was a man who answered not to the name of Nemo. Nor was his ship called the *Nautilus*. The captain's name was Trinitus and his vessel was christened *L'Eclair* (*The Lightning*). In the glitter of Louis Napoleon's great exposition, or in the news of the *Hunley* – or perhaps in just the atmosphere of a science club – someone other than Verne had seen the literary possibilities of submarine exploration. Ironically, after four decades of inspiring events to draw from, suddenly there were two competing books in gestation. As it happened, the story of Trinitus beat Verne's story to the publishers by a number of months and Pierre Hetzel would have to risk the expense of extra promotional clout to insure his investment in Verne's manuscript.

In 1868, while Verne was still immersed in his labors, the firm of P. Brunet published the bound version of *Voyage Sous Les Flots* (*Journey Under the Waters*) by one Aristide Roger.[30] However, as "Capitaine Merobert" had been a pseudonym for Clement Briois (*Journey to the Bottom of the Sea* in 1845), so "Aristide Roger" was the nom de plume for a P. Jules Rengade. Like Briois, Jules Rengade was a physician as well as a writer,[31] and for both men, a pseudonym was a necessity. Youth books were considered a frivolous undertaking for professionals like doctors or stockbrokers – even if they meant revenue. Verne was an exception, but then, so was the quality of his work when compared to other youth market writers of the day.

Just a few years out of medical college, Rengade had already authored two other children's books aligned with science and, in particular, medicine: *The Invisible Monsters*, about microbiology, and *The Human Machine*, a layman's guide to the wonders of anatomy. Later, he would go on to write dozens of professional works ranging in subject from epilepsy to pneumonia, and he further popularized medicine by creating two comic operas on medical themes. No matter what one's profession, in the Second Empire everyone seemed to try a hand at comic opera.

Journey Under the Waters was, by no means, up to the intellectual caliber of *Twenty Thousand Leagues*. Rengade directed himself specifically to young children and he maintained a juvenile and fanciful style throughout. The submarine was employed to find a shipwrecked family and the crew of three included a man who was in love with the inventor's daughter.

Meshed with legitimate sea creatures was a unicorn, and often, the crew rode on a swing which hung from the sub's exterior. In contrast, *Twenty Thousand Leagues* was a mature statement on human rights. As well as praising science and the sea, Verne had a penchant for moralizing and the bridge of the *Nautilus* served as his pulpit. His Nemo was a philosophic outlaw who raided despots, salved lost gold for the benefit of oppressed peoples, and accepted no restraints on his autonomy except moral ones. Cruising the world undersea, he lectured his guest, Doctor Arronax, on art, world history, and corrupt governments. In *Twenty Thousand Leagues*, the solitude of the undersea was a cultural and political freedom as well as a cradle of life. *Journey Under the Waters* treated it only as a geography and a quasi-scientific adventure.

In Rengade's story, Doctor Trinitus is an inventor from Calais. Receiving word that his wife and daughter were aboard a ship lost in the Coral Sea, he launches a copper submarine to find them. It is the stubby little *L'Eclair* and the product of ten years labor. Trinitus' gardener, Nicaise, and the gardener's nephew Marcel, then accompany their master on a voyage that will supposedly get them to the area faster than any surface ship of the day could – a voyage down the western coast of Africa, across the Indian Ocean, and up into the New Hebrides. Needless to say, the journey is eventful – and also cramped. Their submarine is a modest one and has little room for comforts. Aside from this, the state of industrial arts is well represented – though not on the same scale as Verne. The sub has electricity, batteries-only lights, an oxygen regeneration system, and an air lock with diving suits. Protruding from the bow is an iron rod that reverses the engines if it strikes an obstacle. Those features were basic. However, *L'Eclair* also sported a photographic and chemistry lab, a means for fishing which included an "electric arrow," and a sea water distillation system. Futurists to the core, the crew ate concentrated food, meat extract, and bouillon cubes.

Rengade, however, did not have the expansive imagination of Jules Verne. The *Nautilus* of *Twenty Thousand Leagues* would not allow that confinement was a necessary lifestyle – or, indeed, that undersea duty was more than slightly restricting.

Verne's Nemo dwelled in palatial fashion, amidst art treasures and a library and the captain's table was graced with culinary delights. Similarities between Rengade's *L'Eclair* and Verne's *Nautilus* were slight; however, the similarity in their respective occupants is amazing. In the first place, like Nemo, Trinitus is a didactic scholar of the sea and free with his opinions. Like Aronnax, the gardener Nicaise is filled with admiration for his teacher, and, in *Journey Under the Waters*, a running dialogue between the captain and his guest serves as the vehicle for disseminating knowledge of the sea – just as it does in *Twenty Thousand Leagues*.

Even more striking is the similarity in areas they both travel through and the things they encounter. In distance, of course, the voyage of Trinitus is no match for the voyage of Nemo. The *Nautilus* traveled the full length and depth of all oceans and *L'Eclair* remained in the Eastern Hemisphere; however, within its limited scope, the little *L'Eclair* may just possibly have influenced Verne's journey. Its individual encounters are all mirrored in the epic novel that would follow almost a year later.

Rengade's adventurers find an extinct volcano rising out of the sea near the Azores. Through an undersea canal, they gain access to its internal lagoon where they disembark, climb the periphery, and marvel at its geological wonders. Verne would employ such a volcano in his book. Located in that same East Atlantic region, it, too, would be penetrated by way of a submarine tunnel, and there Nemo mined coal to extract sodium for his electrical system. However, where Verne's men would depart in orderly fashion, Rengade's crew were driven out by an eruption.

In *Journey Under the Waters*, *L'Eclair* reluctantly enters the cold prairies of the Sargasso Sea where the heroes study the incredible vegetation that thrives there. Later, the *Nautilus* would also pass through that isolated carpet of kelp while Nemo lectured his passengers on its dynamics and the geography of the waters surrounding it. As usual, the *Nautilus* would pass through undeterred while the more fantasy-prone *L'Eclair*, entangled in seaweed, made its escape by following in the wake of a whale herd as they penetrated the barrier. Later, the crews of both the *Nautilus* and *L'Eclair* go ashore on an island in the Coral Sea, and, there, they both run into cannibals.

Trinitus and his men encounter the Atlantic telegraph cable and so would Nemo. *L'Eclair* rides out a storm on the surface and so would the *Nautilus*. Rengade comments on the needless slaughter of whales and Verne would express the same concern. Instructional throughout, both books discuss the formation of coral, the dynamics of the Gulf Stream, and the migration of fish. Operating strictly from Matthew Maury's hypotheses, *L'Eclair* is ultimately driven under a portion of Antarctica. Likewise, Nemo would lead his men through the thick, liquid undercarriage of that icy continent in order to reach the South Pole.

Trinitus declines the Pole journey, but, in the Victoria sector, he does find an icebound shipwreck and, in it, a message. This leads him up the Straits of Cook, into the tropics, and closer to his lost family. With *L'Eclair* in western Pacific waters, Rengade then made his best attempt at describing the undersea experience. It was, in fact, a journey through coral embankments. The images and metaphors were valid enough; unfortunately, they were devoid of the water element itself, the play of light, and other visual sensations. As with Verne, it indicated a knowledge gap. The good doctor did his homework, and he also showed commendable vision, but, in all probability, he had never gone into the depths of the ocean.

> They had entered a fairy-like world where, for millions of years, a multitude of zoophytes had worked towards building a continent in the middle of the sea. Surrounding *L'Eclair*, huge and majestic as the oaks of a dense forest, gigantic trees of stone stood tall, white and hard like ivory.

> The dimensions of these colossal pillars were beyond computation. Their base, as wide as the ones of the pyramids, rested on the entire surface of an underwater plateau. Their cavernous flanks, detailed in the way of a Middle Age church's steeple, comprised a mass of curious animals, enshrined in iridescent mother of pearl, or in crimson coral reefs, like diamonds set in gold.

L'Eclair was slowly moving forward through the meandering paths of the corals; as it was going deeper down in the ivory vaults covered with live enamel, the undersea scenery was changing and was becoming more imposing. The pillars and columns took colossal dimensions; the arches, porches, balustrades, and flying buttresses multiplied themselves to infinity and interlaced in a thousand of fashions; the gigantic polypes's boughs joined together to form vast porticos, and gradually this boundless forest of madrepores was turning into a magic palace.

Chance had combined, in this extraordinary architecture, the most audacious lines as well as the most extravagant forms; and yet, wonderful harmony resulted from such. Nothing was shocking to the eye; nothing stood out by its smallness. Every detail of this work of art – which had begun at the origin of the world and which would perhaps last until its end – charmed Trinitus's observing mind and astonished him.

From all around, the scientist caught sight of adornments and embroidery work of stone in all proportions and styles. Every prominent edge had been graciously sculptured. Every anfractuosity [winding, curving passages or channels] had been hollowed out as if such work had been performed by the most clever artist. And yet, the authors of these unrivaled marvels had worked by no guide, no rule, no law. The gelatinous mouth of the polyd, the dissolvent kiss of the water, the rubbing of the wave had alone accomplished this prodigious work! . . .

But these underwater edifices were not just inhabited by their hard-working craftsmen who continued, as each day passed, their endless construction. All the zoophytes, annelida, molluscs and rare fish that inhabit the Indian Ocean meet in the meanders and madrepore-like arcades of the Coral Sea. That is where the animals, which are welded to the stone by their head and body altogether, reside.

There, the sea-anemones spread out their brightly colored tentacles and bloom in the polypes's excavations like magnificent dahlias in large flower baskets. There, the branched "lithophytes" and the "caryophilies" erect a thousand arms and the "retipores" cover with a netting of lace "flustres," "astreas," and sponges. There, halysites prosper and shaded gorgons settle their large fans.

At times, these motionless tribes of lively flowers quiver and seem to extricate themselves from their mysterious torpor. The unknown spell ceases as by miracle and all these creatures awake and shiver. Life seems to spurt at once from their translucid and immaterial bodies. Pencils of rays, phosphorescent halos shine from all around.[32]

Such was the passage of *L'Eclair* through undersea architecture. Rengade confined himself to either the shapes or colors of solid forms, and, in all truth, his material could have easily been lifted from Darwin's *The Structure and Distribution of Coral Reefs* or a dozen other such books that preceded *Journey Under the Waters*. His imagery was a matter of simple configurations, and for that kind of description, most scientific texts of the day were more than adequate – some even achieved poetry. After four intense decades of adventurers and scientists piercing the depths, fiction writers were crippled from a lack of first-hand exposure. Only poets functioned well without it.

With respect to Rengade, it's safe to assume that he was one of the deprived. In descriptions fashioned since the mid-twentieth century – easily the product of personal experience – authors have invariably felt compelled to include the quality of natural light and shadow. They write of reflections and diffusion. They write about the play of moving shapes against more inert ones and the visual transformation that matter goes through when viewed from within a liquid element – not just matter in and of itself. Rengade didn't feel a need for such imagery; however, on occasion, neither did Jules Verne.

As Verne toiled at his own manuscript, he painted awesome undersea panoramas, but, in fact, he often succumbed to the same lack of experience that stifled Rengade. Whether in the forests of the Sargasso or the pearl beds of Ceylon, Verne infused his narrative with so much biology that it frequently crowded out the dream-like vision of his pictures. It's possible that he never descended in Ernest Bazin's contraption or any other device that would allow him to see his water world from beneath the surface. In coral reefs and other spectacular settings, Verne often avoided any extensive comment on daylight conditions. This he did by sending his crew to extreme depths and lighting their way with electric lamps – an atmosphere he could easily visualize in the theatres of Paris – and more clearly comprehend. Thus Aronnax records his journey into a coral kingdom to watch Nemo bury a dead crewmember:

> The light from our lamps produced sometimes magical effects, following the rough outlines of the natural arches, and pendants disposed like lustres, that were tipped with points of fire. Between the coralline shrubs I noticed other polypi not less curious, melites, and irises with articulated ramifications, also some tufts of coral, some green, others red, like seaweed incrusted in their calcareous salts, that naturalists, after long discussion, have definitely classed in the vegetable kingdom.
>
> . . . We occupied, in this place, the centre of a vast glade surrounded by the lofty foliage of the submarine forest. Our lamps threw over this place a sort of clear twilight that singularly elongated the shadows on the ground. At the end of the glade the darkness increased, and was only relieved by little sparks reflected by the points of coral.[33]

Only on rare occasions did Verne indulge himself in descriptions of sunlight when submerged. Perhaps from a residential pool or the Paris Aquarium, he had acquired some limited knowledge of its properties when viewed from under water. However, he wisely kept such descriptions at a minimum. The most lengthy occurred when Aronnax walks on a submarine plain northwest of Hawaii:

Truly this water which surrounded me was but another
air denser than the terrestrial atmosphere, but almost as
transparent. Above me was the calm surface of the sea.
We were walking on fine even sand, not wrinkled, as on
a flat shore, which retains the impression of the billows.

This dazzling carpet, really a reflector, repelled the rays
of the sun with wonderful intensity, which accounted
for the vibration which penetrated every atom of liquid.
Shall I be believed when I say that, at the depth of thirty
feet, I could see as if I was in broad daylight?

. . . It was then ten in the morning; the rays of the sun
struck the surface of the waves at rather an oblique angle,
and at the touch of their light, decomposed by refraction
as through a prism, flowers, rocks, plants, shells, and
polypi were shaded at the edges by the seven solar
colours. It was marvelous, a feast for the eyes, this com-
plication of coloured tints, a perfect kaleidoscope of
green, yellow, orange, violet, indigo, and blue; in one
word, the whole palette of an enthusiastic colourist![34]

And later that same day:

For one hour a plain of sand lay stretched before us.
Sometimes it rose to within two yards and some inches
of the surface of the water. I then saw our image clearly
reflected, drawn inversely, and above us appeared an iden-
tical group reflecting our movements and our actions; in
a word, like us in every point, except that they walked
with their heads downward and their feet in the air.

Another effect I noticed, which was the passage of thick
clouds which formed and vanished rapidly; but on reflec-
tion I understood that these seeming clouds were due to
the varying thickness of the reeds at the bottom, and I
could even see the fleecy foam which their broken tops
multiplied on the water.[35]

It was rather practical to ration such daylit dramas. Even with their scant allocations, both Verne and Rengade produced some wild romances about what could be seen underwater. One of the biggest misconceptions they ever propagated, in fact, had to do with visibility. In the central Pacific, Aronnax is the herald of enviable water conditions, as Verne has him comment:

> [At thirty feet,] I clearly distinguished objects at a
> [lateral] distance of a hundred and fifty yards. . . .
> [And later] We were at a depth of a hundred and five
> yards and twenty inches . . . At this depth I could
> still see the rays of the sun, though feebly; . . . but we
> could see well enough; it was not necessary to resort
> to the Ruhmkorff apparatus [lamps] as yet.[36]

Even when Verne – through Aronnax – stated that "the penetrating power of the solar rays does not seem to cease for a depth of one hundred and fifty fathoms [900 feet],"[37] he wasn't entirely erroneous. He simply took spectroscopic sensitivity and translated into a visually unencumbered vista. And the reasons for such visibility? Aronnax explains: "We know the transparency of the sea, and that its clearness is far beyond that of rock [spring] water. The mineral and organic substances, which it holds in suspension, heightens its transparency."[38] Any modern diver who has groped through the pea-soup of richly organic northern waters would wince at that reasoning. However, although he didn't deal in depths-of-field, Rengade exceeded Verne's imagery by having the undersea come visually alive *at night* – on the mere strength of some phosphorescent plankton:

> And when night spreads out on the surface of the sea, the
> depths of the sea, together with the celestial infinity, light
> up with a thousand sparks. . . . the whole underwater
> world bustles about as if to greet the world of the stars,
> the splendors of the sea, and those of the sky which will
> only fade out at sunrise.[39]

Illuminated seascapes were harmless fantasy; Rengade's

book was immature. Verne's was to be thoroughly mature, but would miss the ingredient of his personal experience. It also lacked some of the visceral emotion that would have accompanied such experience. Interestingly enough, in the decade of Verne's novel, some of the finest undersea images in history came neither from *Journey Under the Waters,* nor *Twenty Thousand Leagues.* The imagery came instead from a novel so intense and studied in its descriptions that one would swear its author had somehow experienced free diving during the book's gestation. In tribute, Verne could not help but allude to this work in his own. Shaken from seeing the giant squids attacking the *Nautilus,* Aronnax tried to record his feelings "under the influence of violent emotion" but finds his writing inadequate. "To paint such pictures," he says, "one must have the pen of the most illustrious of our poets, the author of *The Toilers of the Deep.*"[40]

Two years before, as Verne completed his synopsis for *Twenty Thousand Leagues,* Victor Hugo had published his own controversial book. Hugo was Verne's acquaintance through Dumas, but his story was not about a submarine or a renegade captain or even a scientist. It was, in actual fact, an elevation of honest labor as presented by a wrecker named Gilliatt. The tale had to do with Gilliatt's salving the wreckage of a ship from an isolated and treacherous island-reef called the Douvres. Tackling the job single-handed, the salvor free dives night and day on the open reef, fighting currents, cold, and even an immense octopus that resides there. Certain modern-day critics find Hugo's narrative cumbersome and tedious, but, by whatever literary standards it may have failed, *The Toilers of the Deep* could not be easily surpassed in its vivid portrayal of the undersea experience.

Hugo was intrigued by the concept of a reef in open ocean, and, like Verne, he had a fascination for the sea's secret places – perhaps more. He often took far greater literary pains to romanticize the subject than did Verne. With the sea's underside, he was meticulous in affixing descriptions. As in this passage on the illumination of a submarine cave, he mandated that the descriptions be poetic as well as profuse:

It was through this submerged porch that the light from
the open sea entered the cavern. A strange daylight, given
by engulfment. This light spread out under the water like
a large fan, and was reflected from the rock. Its rectilinear
rays, cut into long, straight bands, on the opacity of the
bottom, growing lighter or darker from one crevice to
another, seemed as if refracted through layers of glass.
There was daylight in this cavern, but an unknown daylight. There was nothing of the earthly in this brilliance.
One could fancy that one was in another planet. The light
was an enigma; one would have thought it the glaucous
light from the eye of a sphinx. . . . The ray of sunlight, as
it traversed this porch, obstructed by a vitreous medium of
sea water, became as green as a ray from Aldebaran. The
water, all filled with that liquid light, appeared like a
melted emerald. A shade of aquamarine of unprecedented
delicacy, gently tinged the whole cavern.

. . . It softened down all lineaments into a sort of visionary diffusion. Each wave was a prism. The contours of
things beneath these rainbow-hued undulations had the
chromatic shades of optical lenses made too convex; solar
spectres floated beneath the water. One thought that
one beheld fragments of submarine rainbows floating
in this auroral pellucidness. Elsewhere in other corners,
there was a kind of moonlight in the water. All splendors
seemed amalgamated there to accomplish some unknown
and hidden deed of darkness. Nothing could be more
disquieting and more enigmatic than that sumptuous-
ness in that cave.

. . . That which illuminated this crypt was like the light
of the Apocalypse. One was not quite sure that the thing
existed. One had before one's eyes a reality stamped with
impossibility. One gazed at that, one touched it, one was
there; only, it was difficult to believe in it.

Was it daylight which came through that window
beneath the sea? Was it water which trembled in that

gloomy basin? Were not those arches and porches the celestial clouds imitating a cavern? What stone was this under foot? Was not this support on the point of becoming disintegrated and turning into vapor? What jewelry of shells was that of which one caught a glimpse? At what distance was one from life, from earth, from men? What was this rapture, mingled with these shadows? Unprecedented, almost sacred emotion, to which was added the gentle uneasiness of grass beneath the water.

What Hugo did for the undersea's architecture and light, he also did for its living creatures. Even non-divers – those who have studied only the treasures of a tidal pool – can appreciate passages such as this:

> Beneath this vegetation, the rarest jewels in the casket of the ocean were both hidden and displayed; mitre shells, helmet shells, purple shells, whelks, struthrolaria, and turreted murexbrandaris. The bell-shaped limpets, resembling microscopic huts, adhered to the rocks in every direction, and were grouped together in villages, in whose streets roamed ascabrions, those beetles of the sea. As pebbles could enter this cavern only with difficulty, shell fish took refuge there. Shell fish are the great lords, who, all bedecked with embroidery and gold lace, avoid the rude and uncivil contact of the populace of pebbles. The shining heap of shells formed beneath the waves, in some spots, ineffable radiations, across which one caught a glimpse of a throng of azures and pearly tints, and of golds – of all the shades of the water.

That image was a familiar one to visitors of the French coast, but Hugo ran into a credibility problem when he graduated from limpets to an octopus. The picture he then painted was born out of his own worst nightmares rather than observations. It assumed that the animal's size could be as limitless as that of a squid, and its temperament as aggressive. From what we know today, Hugo's text was fear-mongering of the highest order – unless one identifies with the octopus' natural prey. It even incited critics of his own era; but one thing is certain, those who read the appropriate chapters never forgot the nightmarish image that they evoked:

> No grasp equals the embrace of the cephalopod. It is the pneumatic machine attacking you. You have to deal with a vacuum furnished with paws. Neither scratches nor bites; an indescribable scarification. A bite is formidable, but less so than a suction. A claw is nothing beside the cupping-glass. The claw means the beast entering into your flesh; the cupping-glass means yourself entering into the beast.

> Your muscles swell, your fibres writhe, your skin cracks, under the foul weight, your blood spurts forth and mingles frightfully with the lymph of the mollusk. The creature superimposes itself upon you by a thousand mouths; the hydra incorporates itself with the man; the man amalgamates himself with the hydra. You form but one. This dream is upon you. The tiger can only devour you; the octopus, oh horror!

That man-eating octopus was Hugo's small indulgence in either fantasy or uneducated zoology – depending on what one thinks of Hugo. Considering the length and breadth of his novel, however, it was rather excusable. His exaggerations weren't half as numerous as Rengade's. They also weren't a tenth of what Verne's unintentional, yet definite, miscalculations would be.

As *Journey Under the Waters* was being distributed, Verne was drawing the voyage of Nemo and Aronnax to an end, and he brought the *Saint Michel* to snug harbor. Though he had not rhapsodized the undersea as Rengade, it was not important. The rhetorical style of *Twenty Thousand Leagues* completely eclipsed its competitor. Both the scope of its science and the quality of its storyline were vastly superior to the undersea novel gracing bookstalls in Paris. Far more than a children's book, it was a work of great and lasting magnitude.

With his own sub-ocean epic, Verne had drawn upon a life influenced by literature as well as science. The writings of Scott, Cooper, and Poe had not only shaped his literary attitudes, but were, in fact, directly applicable to his literary technique. Cooper had taught him the very mechanics of an adventure tale. Even the near impossible heroism in *Twenty Thousand Leagues* was a device instilled by Cooper. In pushing himself to the edge of unknown worlds, Poe had given Verne his haunting visions. From Poe, Verne acquired a feeling for inner space – the love of hidden treasure, cryptic meanings, and secret societies such as the *Nautilus* crew. Verne had even produced an essay on Poe for the *Musee des familles* some four years before, and, as a way of concluding his story, Verne would have the *Nautilus* dragged into the Norway Maelstrom; an idea first utilized by Poe in his *Descent Into the Maelstrom*. From across the Channel, Walter Scott taught Verne a special set of priorities where action and background could compensate for a lack of character analysis. Both Scott and Cooper showed the former stockbroker how to enhance a simple narrative with studied renderings of seascape, landscape and weather. Their French editions were faithfully produced by the same translator. In short, *Twenty Thousand Leagues* had a good foundation of author-craft, and it was a substantial and well-written book whereas *Journey Under the Waters* was not.

In the waning months of 1868, Verne put the final touches on his manuscript and Nemo's voyage emerged truly unparalleled within the adventure genre. For that reason, it is rough conjecture to assume that Rengade had an influence on Verne. Nevertheless, the similarity in their two tales is astounding. It is a fact that *Journey Under the Waters* came out in 1867 and that Verne did not hand over his own manuscript until December of the following year. Possibly Rengade or an associate got word of Verne's story early in its writing. The quality of *Journey Under the Waters* suggests a goal of quick publication. However, the prospect is somewhat diminished considering that Hetzel was shrewd enough to keep silence and that Verne was isolated on the *Saint Michel*.

After Hetzel received the manuscript, he needed time to mold *Twenty Thousand Leagues* into a physical masterpiece – a book design befitting Verne's vast horizons and tenacious research. No doubt, he also wanted a visual format that would knock the wind out of *Journey Under the Waters*. However, Hetzel had waited two years for the material and he needed to make the story earn its advances. He decided to move ahead and publish it first in the *Magazin d'Education et de Recreation*. During March of 1869, the children of France were thus introduced to Nemo's domain and through June of 1870 they read the story in installments. As it turned out, the text was cut for the medium, Verne was upset over it, and *Twenty Thousand Leagues* wouldn't regain its original glory until its publication in book form which began seven months after the introduction.

To insure absolute success in the youth market, Hetzel had a second element to develop. Before the serialized version was typeset, and probably before the manuscript was even finished, Hetzel commissioned a staggering amount of illustrations. In all, there were some 110 of them – more than one full-page engraving for every three pages of text, and their importance to the book was unquestionable. More than any work Verne had written – or perhaps would ever write – *Twenty Thousand Leagues* cried out for graphic interpretation. Readers would want help in visualizing the mysterious lands under the sea. As it turned out, the expenditure was also sound economic thinking on Hetzel's part. Rengade's publisher had made a minimal investment in artwork, and that oversight would help Verne's tale to eclipse *Journey Under the Waters*.

Verne's undersea tale became part of a great age of illustrated books – children of the illustrated magazines. The magazine pictorials were part of a new technology in plate reproduction, and in both London and Paris, editorial illustration was growing around this technology. Metal plates were being cast from hand-engraved boxwood and then mass-produced by an electroplating process known as "galvanotype." For the first time in history, multiple copies of the same engraving could be easily circulated to publishers all over the world. Thus a work became universal even before the translations were complete. As were Verne's other novels, *Twenty Thousand Leagues* was a natural beneficiary of this new art form. His themes had no national boundary, since armchair adventurers were the same in England, Germany, or anywhere else. They all understood pictures.

The timing was historically perfect. Just as Verne was entering into literature, elaborate drawings became reproducible "en masse" – and with almost the same ease as simple drawings. With such freedom, publishers started competing to issue the most abundant illustrations, and it soon became characteristic of the nineteenth-century book. It certainly became characteristic of Verne's books, because Hetzel was in the forefront of the movement. Even before his current journal, *le Magazin d'Education et de Recreation*, Hetzel had launched *le Nouveau Magazin des Enfants* – one of a half dozen brilliantly illustrated tabloids which had emerged in Paris by 1843.[41]

Later, the increased demand from Hetzel's firm and from others spawned a new group of craftsmen. By 1857, there were some 200 wood engravers in Paris and at least that many commercial illustrators. They perfected their skills and grew into a regular café society like their counterparts in painting. The illustrators hawked romantic realism and their engraver companions translated it into an ever-increasing clarity and depth – two great virtues of "standing" wood over other mediums of the day.[42] Before long, this new elite had their own audience. The illustrations of a novel became indivisible from the text and Verne's followers grew to regard his "Voyages Extraordinaires" as denuded if missing their graphic commentary. It was a stimulus to young dreams of geographic conquest.

In *Twenty Thousand Leagues*, Pierre Hetzel now had a very special geography for youth to dream about. It was the land beneath the sea, and, for Hetzel, the best person to visualize such strangeness was Edouard Riou, a disciple of the great Gustave Dore. Since only the extraordinary attracted Dore, the master himself would have seemed more desirable, but Riou had a better relationship with Hetzel. Though he was less imaginative than his mentor, Riou was more realistic and he had already illustrated the four previous Verne novels. However, Riou got only as far as the eleventh chapter. After the frontispiece, his pen never left the surface of the water or the interiors of the *Nautilus*. As the *Illustrated Geography of France* had once delayed Verne's writing of *Twenty Thousand Leagues*, so it now permanently severed Riou from the undersea tale. Hetzel needed his realism on "the Geography." It was much nearer publication and the present illustrator, Hubert Clerget, was taken ill and fell behind schedule.

In Riou's place, Hetzel installed Alphonse-Marie de Neuville, who was a student of Delacroix. As it turned out, de Neuville was not a poor second. His renderings of the undersea emerged as a spiritualized dream.[43] With a gift for creating dark interiors and many degrees of translucency, he fashioned a phantasmagoric world. His pictures mainly utilized the available biology of the time, and yet he carpeted the sea-floor in such a way that the drawings for *Twenty Thousand Leagues* became as haunting as Dore's creations in *The Rime of the Ancient Mariner*, published five years later. Oddly enough – except for some later contributions to *Around the World in Eighty Days* – de Neuville would never work for Hetzel again. He, instead, went on to become a painter of battle scenes.[44]

Before the serialized version was concluded and before the illustrations were finished, *Twenty Thousand Leagues* came out in two small volumes between October of 1869 and June of 1870. There would be a later edition wherein the works of both Riou and de Neuville were beautifully engraved by Theophile Hildibrand, and Verne's and Hetzel's faces recorded in the forms of Aronnax and Nemo, respectively. That edition, however, would wait for eighteen months. In July, book printing and distribution suddenly came to a standstill when war broke out between France and Germany. On the tails of that conflict, a second war then surfaced within France itself. Hetzel stuck it out through the Franco-Prussian tribulations, but he left Paris in despair when a degrading armistice was agreed upon. When he finally decided to return, he was prevented by a communard government which had taken control of the city. It was months before Hetzel could reenter, and, by then, the trades were all on strike. Verne was no help during this period since he had been drafted into the coast guard and ordered to command his *Saint Michel* as an armed patrol boat.

Only after France began a reconstruction was the book on its way again. In November of 1871, the elaborately illustrated edition was finally delivered to a war-weary but anxious public. When 1873 arrived, *Twenty Thousand Leagues* was printed in English, but, by then, it had suffered still another wound – this time on the battlefields of interpretation. The Reverend Lewis Page Mercier, a theologian and translator, cut more than 20 percent of Verne's narrative and made hundreds of trans-lingual errors. His cuts were ideologically rooted, but his errors were the result of rushing. As a consequence, many English readers thought Verne's text was jerky and amateurish. Nevertheless, the substance of the book came through, and, within another two years, *Twenty Thousand Leagues* was a world-wide success. It prevailed despite Rengade's novel, the war, the commune, and even Hetzel's difficulties, which, for a while, were economic as well as political. After the English translation, Nemo and Aronnax soon walked the ocean's floor in a dozen or more languages.

And so, with the distribution of his undersea masterwork, the die was cast for Verne's literary life. In all of his stories to follow, Verne used his skills to actually novelize both the scientific and industrial revolutions. He made a hero of the scholar and created high adventure out of the quest for knowledge.[45] But, of all his efforts, *Twenty Thousand Leagues Under the Seas* is of particular stature. In the 125 years since its first publication, rarely if ever has the true educational and historic importance of this book been adequately stated. It was far more than a portent to submarine navigation and untethered diving. It was a sympathetic portrayal of the sea's ecology – dramatized and made palatable for inquisitive young minds, and, in the final analysis, for all levels of intellect.

Starting with Cooper, Marryat, and Sue, life at sea had been novelized for almost half a century. The geography of the sea was part of the storytelling and so, it too, became novelized. Its imagery, however, had almost never left the surface, and, in literature, it took poets like Hemans, Tennyson, and Shelley to share a subaqueous vision with the public. Yet, the poets could only embrace a small aspect of the ocean experience. It was Darwin, Maury, and Milne-Edwards who dealt with the ocean on a broader scale. But these men were scientists. Their discussions rarely addressed the general public.

Amidst these and other involvements, Jules Verne emerged as the great amalgamator. He brought all the threads together and fused them into a drama. In doing so, he gave the average land-dweller a new consciousness about the sea and its relationship to the rest of the earth. Ocean science was carried from laboratories and admiralty bureaus and delivered to the masses. Thus, the modest seeds of a new attitude were sown – one where society would someday see beyond the sustenance it could reap or the transport it could set afloat. To this end, going beneath the surface had justifications beyond mere adventure. Because of Nemo and the *Nautilus*, children everywhere were suddenly viewing the ocean without the baggage of mercantilism, immigration, or navies. They were, instead, penetrating its skin and watching its life rhythms as they could never do from above. They weren't just *under* the sea. Thanks to Jules Verne, they were now *inside* the sea.

The Man Who Painted
Under the Sea

(1886–1937)

IN MOST HABITATS OF WESTERN MAN, THE SEA IS REACHED BY extremely divergent terrains: rocky cliffs or sandy beaches. Either way, the journey terminates with a spectacle, as waves roll and burst into the confines of land. In southeast India, however, the sea is the Bay of Bengal and it simply touches farmers' fields as if it were another field. It is warm, smooth as glass, and, out to the limit of vision, there are no ships because there is no depth. For that reason, Walter Howlison Mackenzie Pritchard had first conceived of the sea as neither alien, foreboding, nor navigable for commerce.

Walter Pritchard was born in the coastal city of Madras in 1866 on what was called the "Edge of India." Although Madras was built on ancient Dravidian foundations, it became the resplendent fief of the British East India Company and the product of two hundred years of English dominance. Its princely esplanade was equal to anything on the Riviera. Young Walter would sit in the unmenacing ripples and envision an ancient local myth: that the world was a plate and that people sat on its rim with their feet dangling over the edge – if one never fell off, there was always the "pleasant" feeling that, someday, perhaps one just might.

The marina where Walter daydreamed was one of the places that had smooth access – two hundred glistening yards deep and with no surf to fear. The only danger was invisible from above, but real enough to keep Walter up to his waist and no further – a total infestation of sharks.

For this Irish child of India, the sea was more for dreaming and less for immersion. But, all that changed when he was ten years old, for in typical colonialist fashion, Walter was shipped back home to attend school. The academy was in

Edinburgh, Scotland, and it wasn't warm, placid water that he found there. But then, the sea didn't boil with primal killers. He and his friends could swim and dive as long as their blue-chilled bodies would let them. Since the world had once been a steaming, flat place, the cold, rolling ocean would now test Walter's adaptability.

East of the city and along the southern shore of the Firth of Forth, he found his aquatic playground – a modest indentation called the Bay of Portobello. It was portentous that Jules Verne had stayed there and written of it some seventeen years before. The area, however, was not noticeably picturesque. Portobello was a seedy resort with gray-brown sand, yet its sea breezes were a relief from the stench of coal fires and brewer's malt in Edinburgh. Here, Walter discovered ship watching. On the lifeline to Scandinavia and the Baltic, there was an endless traffic of coal and whiskey outbound from the port of Leith and endless manifests of grain and timber coming in.

When spring arrived on the firth, so did water tag. Walter and his friends had a robust version that declared you "safe" when under the surface and "fair game" when you were catching a breath. Racing around on top and free diving underneath, Walter became all legs and lungs very early in life. One day, he ignored the salt sting and fully opened his eyes underwater. Through the blur he could see the wonderful blues and greens that tinted the bodies of his playmates as they thrashed around, and in that instant, young Walter acquired a lifetime obsession with everything under the surface.

As far as his friends were concerned, it was Walter's energies that led him to suddenly modify the routine: everyone was to now jump in carrying rocks to see who could stay under and hold his breath the longest. As heads broke the surface, however, Walter was never the "rotten egg." The Scottish boys adopted his game because it was reckless; but, in reality, Walter had contrived it so he could spend time looking about in those mysterious surroundings. Clinging to his weights, he saw another world – one landscaped with its own vegetation and peopled with its own creatures. Their blurred and pastel appearance was out of fairy-tale books, and, even without air space for his eyes, he was aware of all the delicate tints that direct sunlight would have made garish. The young artist-to-be ultimately left his game and struck out to find other images in other places.

He soon discovered a group of fir trees that spring rains had washed down from the mountains. They lay in shallower water and had become the catalyst for a new crop of vegetation. Young Walter swam around them, fascinated by what happened to form and color under the water's surface. He retained the image of those trees all of his life. "The greens of the firs were so modified and blended with the diffused sunlight," he later wrote, "and the sunlight so broken by the waving mass of growing weeds, that a thousand and one colors and new harmonies were revealed."[1]

After a contrivance he saw in travel books, Walter fashioned a set of goggles out of cowhorn and padded them with leather. Once he could see with clarity he returned day after day to the submerged trees to study the changes in form created by the changes in light and weather.

When he was four years old, the English language edition of *Twenty Thousand Leagues Under the Seas* had come out and Walter spent his childhood perpetually entranced by Verne's descriptions and de Neuville's haunting illustrations. However, he quickly discovered the first of Verne's optical mistakes when he tried to watch the sky from under the surface. In the novel, Nemo and his companions could shoot most any creature for sustenance, including skyborne ones. Pritchard found it was "impossible to shoot birds from the sea bottom . . . since the sky is rarely glimpsed by the diver, and then only by looking directly upward; for at an angle, the surface becomes a gigantic silver mirror, reflecting the shapes on the bottom and the lone, grotesque figure of the diver."[2] Later, the young artist would also learn about refraction and just how impossible Verne's shooting alignment would be.

As a matter of practice, he began carrying his cowhorn goggles on every outing, and, as the months and years followed, Walter Pritchard could be found bobbing about in firths, lochs, rivers, ponds, and even rain puddles if he thought there was a new underwater image to witness.

Summers in Scotland recurred and so did Walter's visual experiences – below and above the water. School years also accumulated and by the mid-1880s the Irish boy from India was in college as an art student. It was a good time and a good place to be an art student. Edinburgh folk drank their ale amidst some of the finest libraries, museums and galleries in the world. The university was ancient and, next to whiskey-making, the printing trades were the second largest industry. Wedged between the Georgian terraces and the crow-stepped gables of this grey city, Walter studied design and decoration and graphic arts.

Yet his early rendezvous with the sunken trees and rocks was prophetic. He loved both nature and landscapes, but, when not committing them to paper, he'd occasionally sketch some of his underwater visions from memory. Then, in the spring, Walter could be found at the seashore renewing his childhood explorations. The water was cold and dark – the green and brown of northern waters – but it offered some awesome shapes. Scotland's undersea terrain was an amalgam of mammoth rock clusters, as was the land above the sea. Even through the dense water, Walter could delineate the forms easily. His problem was the 30 to 40 immersions it took to sketch a picture. Each time he dived, he had to then swim to shore and record on paper a portion of what he had just seen.

Before his academic days were over, Pritchard had finished a half dozen undersea pictures for his portfolio. Among them were rock and sea grass studies done near the west coast island of Staffa and also some pillars of the Giants' Causeway, which rise up from the northern entrance to the Irish Sea.

After almost twelve years in Scotland, Walter Pritchard then tied up his schoolwork – including the subaqueous drawings – and left for the south and whatever career London could offer him. He didn't know it, but he was taking a fourteen year absence from the undersea and embarking on a period of urbane applications. Only once in that time would there be any interest in his submarine sketches, and that one spark would be of far-reaching significance in returning Pritchard to the ocean.

It was fortunate that Pritchard left Scotland with a diverse port-folio because no one liked his undersea pictures. Not even the novelty of the subject had appeal. London's stolid art trades thought the imagery was lacking in human reference and some thought it downright grotesque. Nor did they appreciate the spirit of adventure in trying to capture such a subject. For them, the intrepid methods required to sketch a submarine picture made the whole prospect rather arrogant. On the other hand, decorating was somewhat governed by rule and book, and was an acceptable pursuit. Pritchard needed to eat, so he started odd-jobbing as a decorator.

One night in 1890 – two years after his arrival in the city – Pritchard went to see a performance by the grande dame of eccentricity, Sarah Bernhardt. In later years, he would romanti-cize the story by saying that his last shilling got him there. But poverty-stricken or not, he sat and watched the tragedienne in an historic dramatization of Cleopatra – a cameo created for her by her near-exclusive collaborator, Victorien Sardou. It was not as good as some of his other plays, but it gave Sarah two theatri-cal elements she loved the most: violent acting and elaborate costumes. About the latter, Mme. Bernhardt was a fanatic. On any tour she carried 45 costume crates, 75 trunks of off-stage attire and 250 pairs of shoes. She and Sardou always worked long hours together on the authenticity of whatever she wore.

That evening, Pritchard would have departed with the usual infectious admiration had it not been for Sarah's sudden appearance in the costume of a sea sorceress. At that moment, no one in that theatre, and possibly no one in England or the world, knew more about borrowing undersea imagery than Walter Pritchard; and he had immediately decided that the cos-tume was all wrong. The following night, with his submarine pictures under his arm, he bounded backstage to stand in line. Not only did Sarah's undersea themes fall into his field of knowledge, but Pritchard wanted to pursue costume design. If he could get even a trifling commission from the spendthrift actress, it would be a passport to other theatre jobs.

Along with the poverty aspects, Pritchard liked to further embellish his tale by saying that he either stood in line for days or that he was repeatedly bumped by one of her suitors. He might well have had some difficulty, but, in fact, Mme. Bernhardt used to make herself as available to the public as she possibly could. Even had she been besieged with appointments, Pritchard figured that any woman who dealt only in gold coins, who pistol-shot birds before breakfast, cohabitated with an Andean wildcat, kept live snakes everywhere, and slept in a coffin, would certainly like to hear opinions from an artist who had drawn pictures under the sea – and he was right.

Pritchard also spoke Sarah's native language, French – the only language she knew – and that certainly helped. The lady who had such a gift for fascinating the public now herself sat fascinated by Pritchard's vivid descriptions of the underwater world. She watched intently as he sketched out his own version of Cleopatra's ornamented sea-gown. Considering herself a rather supernatural creature, she especially liked the supernatural quality of everything she saw. Before the visit was over, Pritchard not only received an advance on the costume, but sold Bernhardt two of his pictures and acquired a lifelong friend.

The Bernhardt endorsement was eminently valuable to Pritchard. For twelve more years he was able to parlay that sea sorceress gown into a great deal of work for the stage. Ultimately, he designed costumes and accessories for other theatre greats including Ellen Terry, Henry Irving and Beerbohm Tree. Then his talents for interior design and murals became marketable and he made his own patterned hangings, cushions, and portieres to go with his concepts of decor. Some notable projects included a "Temple of Music" for a Comtesse de Bearn and a huge and regal boathouse in Paris called "The Lotus." In short, Pritchard had evolved from an aspiring seascape painter into a graphic dandy – a craftsman of all the indulgent furnishings and gewgaws of a pampered society.

Whereas Bernhardt's commission for the costume launched Pritchard's design career, her purchase of his two undersea pictures did nothing. People everywhere worshiped the things Sarah wore, but they couldn't have cared less about her taste in art. Her surroundings were a hodgepodge of the admirable and the awful, with a million potted palms to bridge the two. Everybody knew it, few people liked it, and Pritchard's pictures were lost in the sea of her million other novelties.

Occasionally, he would dust off his early underwater experiments and show them to companions, but the reaction was always lukewarm. As completely virgin as the image was, somehow its unfamiliar properties and the popular notions of art didn't correlate. So Pritchard shelved the pictures in a far corner of his mind, and they would have remained there had it not been for a physically devastating occurrence – one responsible for changing the whole nature of his artistic pursuits.

As the retelling process occurred in later years, either Pritchard or his interviewer tended to generate stories that were widely at variance concerning this period. Some had him living on cocoa and a penny loaf a day before he met Bernhardt, and others had him near suicide over the rejection of his submarine pictures. It was all pretty harmless artistic license in documenting the life of an artist, but at least two stories need to placed in common agreement with the facts.

First of all, it is not likely that a nabob of India who sent his child to Scottish academies would let him experience poverty. Besides that, when Pritchard later came to the United States of America, his immigration sponsors were both listed as stockbrokers by profession and after his arrival he managed to travel and to build himself a home before he ever sold another picture.

The second story had Bernhardt as the causal agent for Pritchard's immediate departure to America and the subsequent resurrection of his undersea art. But her endorsement only led him into more cosmopolitan vocations – for a dozen more years, at that. In fact, his exodus from London had nothing to do with art, but with ordinary human frailty.

Shortly after the turn of the century, when everyone had sobered up from the centennials, expositions, and parties, Pritchard woke up one day gasping for breath. The next day he was on the brink of death. He had contracted a vicious form of pneumonia at a time when few people survived the illness. He ultimately recovered, but not before his lungs were severely and permanently damaged. As a result, his doctors told him to get out of London's dampness and off to warm, dry Egypt or else he could hang up his brushes for good.

As far as Pritchard was concerned, he had served enough time in the colonies and he countered with the comment that he "was not ready to paint Egypt therefore not ready to see Egypt."[3] The suitable alternative was to strike out for California which, among other things, was already gaining a reputation for its recuperative climate.

Pritchard was nearing middle age. The idea of starting over in a place like the United States had more of an adventurous ring to it than cranking out watercolors of a fossilized land dominated by a near-fossilized empire.

So on December 13, 1902, Pritchard bid farewell to London and Paris society, boarded a ship called the *Columbia*, and steamed off for the States. His new beginning in a new world could not have been better synchronized with classic measurements of time for he arrived at the port of New Orleans on New Year's Day, 1903. From there, he made his way by train to California and a rendezvous with friends who lived in Santa Barbara.

After some twenty-six years in two of the largest cultural playgrounds of Europe, California must have felt like a wilderness to Pritchard. The total population was a million and a half people and most theatres, colleges and newspapers were no more than thirty years old. Southern California's first fine arts society was celebrating its eighth birthday.

Pritchard might have preferred Boston or New York, but their weather wasn't much improved over London's and the first order of business was for Pritchard to stay alive. Little did he know that, instead of being a hindrance, California would soon turn out to be his artistic El Dorado and the incubation of a new undersea involvement that would last the rest of his life.

The United States had snatched California from Mexico only

fifty-odd years before Pritchard's arrival, and, excepting San Francisco, it certainly looked it. The southern part of the state, where he dropped his bags, was basically an agricultural empire; blessed with Mediterranean weather and dotted with little Spanish-style buildings. As he once did from India to Scotland, the natty Victorian designer went through another passage of environment and time.

The state also had at least one additional attraction besides blue ribbon air to breathe. It was the spectacular natural wonders, and though he'd been decorating for fourteen years, his first love was still landscapes. The majority of artists who were migrating to the state were landscape painters; all now contentedly replicating the forests, deserts, and coastlines for publications and private sales.

Pritchard took up residence in Santa Barbara and being a mild-mannered Briton, he fell in quite easily with all those engaged in California's quest for Arcadia. He also fell into landscape work and crafts just as easily. The spectacular California coastline was all around him and he dabbled in land- and sea-scapes and commingled with the dune-and-driftwood-school of painters and sculptors.

But in all of this activity, Pritchard wasn't content. His life was pleasant enough but he was really more of a goal-oriented craftsman than his environment seemed to promote. Pritchard also had an acceptable level of egotism and along with feeling "out to pasture," there was the anonymity he experienced in such a vast geography as California, and indeed all of America. In short, he was an artist entering middle age, feeling he still had a destiny, sitting on the edge of a wilderness, and having little distinction in his field.

It is always surprising, however, the way people come by, and are returned to, certain stations in life. As a pair of weakened lungs, and not a lust for travel, had caused Pritchard to be in California, so was his realization of an old dream caused, not by another painter, but, of all things, by a poet.

Robert Cameron Rogers was his name and his style ran from naturalist to classical to romantic. His subjects were anything from apple trees to unrequited love and it all came out thick with the sentimentality of the era. But Rogers knew and loved the sea. He had written a fictional sea yarn about the War of 1812 and he frequently laced his verse with metaphors from the water's edge. That characteristic was his common link with Walter Pritchard.

One day, after the two of them had been walking about the tidepools, Pritchard dragged out his old undersea sketches. Rogers was ecstatic. From that moment on, he never stopped trying to reinstill in Pritchard what had once been the artist's own enthusiasms. After years of apathetic reactions to the work, however, Pritchard was hesitant to renew any strong feelings and Rogers knew he had a challenge.

Over the weeks his rhetoric accomplished nothing, so Rogers finally lured Pritchard away for an orientation beneath the California coast. As early as 1894, Charles Frederick Holder, a naturalist author, had formulated plans for a glass-bottom boat while on Santa Catalina. Since that time, the island had become probably the first tourist mecca in the United States to capitalize on its underwater attractions.

Rogers and Pritchard boarded a steamer at San Pedro and when they arrived in Avalon harbor, they were met by entire fleets of glassbottom boats; all constructed on the island and ranging from glorified dories to big side-wheel steamers. For the next few days, the two men boarded one or another of the boats and sat before the windows to watch plants and creatures pass in review. It was Pritchard's first experience in such a vessel. The sensation was like descending into a darkened puppet theatre and watching a blue-lit stage while a long painted backdrop was cranked from one side to the other. As the boat moved slowly along the shallows, the scenery changed as if manipulated by a submarine stage hand. The hull carved a fluid path through the kelp beds and Pritchard watched as the green and ochre ribbons folded and unfolded to reveal countless animals. Many of them like starfish, sea urchins and sea cucumbers, reminded him of the Scottish coast, although the water had a little more clarity than in Scotland.

In those days before the popularizing of science for tourists, Avalon skippers had their own fanciful names for everything under water. On Santa Catalina, their line of patter informed viewers that they were seeing "The Yosemite" or the

"Grand Canyon" or "The Great Divide."[4] But Rogers hadn't intended the trip for scientific explorations. He wanted to kindle a fire in Pritchard's heart and excite him with a fresh exposure to the world of light and shadow under the sea.

The trip had its desired result and in the weeks that followed, while Pritchard sat defenseless and impressionable, Rogers regaled him with every vivid description he could muster. He wasn't selling California. Certainly the water was more enticing than Scotland's, but Santa Catalina was merely to set Pritchard up for greater geographies. Rogers wanted his artistic companion to see the tropics. He wanted to send him where the clarity of water was such as he'd never imagined and where coral formations were like canyons and castles and forests – or anything an imagist could make them. As yet, no undersea photographs existed of those regions, so Rogers could only create pictures with his words and enthusiasms.

Pritchard brought up his current frailties, but Rogers was ready for the argument. As far as chill factors, the waters of the tropics ran up to eighty degrees as compared with a range of fifty to seventy degrees in California or forty to fifty degrees in his boyhood Scotland. As far as the rigors of swimming back and forth to complete a sketch from memory – well, Rogers had an answer for that as well. He came up with the outrageous theory that a color rendering could be done under the water – looking directly at the subject, not relying on memory and not coming to the surface except to breathe.

Pritchard accepted the temperature story, but scoffed at the possibility of sketching something while under water. Rogers, nevertheless, hammered away on the possibilities and before long, Pritchard was reading travel books and sitting in his bathtub with every drawing vehicle he could buy. He never resolved the problem in Santa Barbara, but he saw enough in his experiments to tell him that Rogers was probably right.

Some twenty-three years later, he would ascribe the whole inception of the submarine painting to Robert Rogers: "who persisted in urging me – despite my conviction that his idea was not possible of achievement – to paint the sketches in full color below the surface of the sea so as to [later] render the scenes perfectly from the best point of view."[5]

Hearing South Seas tales convinced Pritchard to once again re-locate his life, and he made plans to ship out of San Francisco. Rogers had convinced him that in Tahiti he would find "the most beautiful submarine scenes in all the world."[6] Of course, marine science could not determine the absolute superiority of undersea landscapes from one equatorial region to the next – at least, not enough for anyone to say: "most beautiful . . . in all the world."

Pritchard could have chosen from any number of areas in the Pacific and he might have sensed that probability. What attracted him to Tahiti, however, were the same literary and historical associations that had drawn so many others – and romanticized Tahiti out of all proportion with respect to the rest of the South Pacific.

Ever since Bougainville found Tahiti, only the picturesque and voluptuous aspects of the culture had been circulated. See-ing a profound similarity between the worship of Aphrodite and the Tahitian love rites, he called the island "New Cythera" after the birthplace of the Greek goddess. His expedition's nat-uralist, Commerson, furthered the image with lines like these: "Born under a most beautiful sky, nourished on the fruits of an earth which is fertile without tillage, ruled by patriarchs rather than kings, they [Tahitians] know no other god but Love."[7]

With that kind of promulgation, the followers of Jean-Jacques Rousseau then decided that Tahiti would be a good proving ground for their leader's theory: that man is noble only if severed from society's corrupting laws and left alone to live in a natural state. They, of course, made the process easy on them-selves by choosing a place like Tahiti rather than a more demanding environment.

A year after Bougainville's landing, there began the voy-ages of Captain James Cook and twenty years after that, the mutiny on *H.M.S. Bounty* occurred; the islanders first hosting Bligh's loyalists, and later, the mutineers.

By the time Walter Howlison Pritchard sailed for Tahiti, its reputation as paradise was full blown. Herman Melville had decided to mutiny there. Even when thrown in the poky, he enjoyed it so much that he used the time to scribble a humorous recounting of it for his novel, *Omoo*. Then Robert Louis Stevenson dropped by for a stay and after that, Paul Gauguin arrived to begin a ten year residence. Gauguin had, in fact, relocated to the Marquesas just two years before Pritchard's arrival in Tahiti.

Pritchard reasoned – and rather pragmatically – that if he could find his submarine dream-world, there would be no harm in leading a pleasurable life on land. Underwater panoramas aside, there was already an artistic rationale for being domiciled in Tahiti and the island was now beginning to attract monied folk from the States – the sort who bought paintings.

In short, if you were an artist in the United States around the turn of the century and you just wanted to "get away from it all," Tahiti was in vogue.

Sometime in late 1904, Pritchard said his goodbyes in Santa Barbara and a few days later he steamed away on the four thousand mile journey to the Society Islands. Bearing southwest through the Japanese current, the water at first looked no more inviting than the North Sea. It was cold for days and the dense blue ocean registered no enticing changes.

Pritchard, however, had plenty of romantic propaganda to complement his deck chair and, considering his rakishness, probably a romantic someone to complement the adventure. He read Melville's *Omoo*; *The Marriage of Loti*; Courtet's *Autour de l'ile de Tahiti*; and Pallander's *The Log of an Island Wanderer*, then in its second year of distribution. By the time both the sea and the air started warming, he was consummately prepared.

Finally, the day came when Pritchard sensed the voyage's end. When he got on deck, it was all there: the stillness either real or imagined, the flotsam, the birds; proclamations that some abused heap of steel and rivets had mothered another gang of humans and their burdens through purgatory.

When the green cone of Mount Orohena appeared, Pritchard also noticed that the water was changing color. The island was getting closer and the sea floor was gradually rising up to meet its volcanic termination. As the ship slowed its engines, he caught the very first indications of the sea floor's presence. In that moment, buried deep in a dark blue field, the first mottled patches of aquamarine started slipping past the bow waves.

Orohena was coaxing clouds over to its peak and everyone on board watched as its warm foliage drew in the white fluff and threw it back out as waterfalls. Everyone watched, that is, except Pritchard. He was staring over the rail and down onto other peaks – forty feet below the ship. The patches of light blue had now become so numerous that they merged into one great variegated field. It was just as Rogers had described – liquid air. Because of this clarity, the water had now acquired its own space and dimension apart from anything that existed above its surface.

Pritchard wanted to be down there. He wanted to be off the ship – penetrating the smooth interface and sitting in those vast interiors. Most of all, he wanted to belong to that world – painting what he saw and having his presence accepted by the strange creatures around him. As he walked down the gangway and onto the town docks, the eccentric designer from London was about to slip back into the earth's watery placenta in order to induce his own artistic rebirth.

French was the official language and Pritchard spoke it fluently. That one skill hastened his orientation and he soon discovered that, considering both his needs and expectations, the southwest corner of the island was where he should be.

In one of the wettest places of its size on earth, this particular area had only a third the rainfall and was protected from the strong, often violent eastern trade winds that battered the opposing side of the island. More importantly, offshore, the most pronounced and continuous barrier reef of any other area occurred, and, as a result, the largest sheltered bodies of water; the lagoon of Maraa beside the village of Paea, and the lagoon of Papara beside a town of the same name.

In modern times, the southwest shore is crowded by Europeans who shuffle government papers or who work at a local nuclear facility. The Tahitians themselves must live in the surrounding hillsides. However, at the turn of the century, the beach belonged to the natives and the area was an amalgam of thatched roofs and fishnets. Somewhere along the twenty mile stretch between the sheltered hamlets of Paea and Papara, Walter Pritchard made himself a home near the water's edge – with the over-generous blessings of the local people.

No one knows exactly what day or week the Irishman first saw a tropical underseascape from within. One morning, however, Pritchard walked out of his home to penetrate that boundary, having some premonition of its mysterious relationship to his own aesthetic drives.

The ocean's horizon looked out toward the lands of New Zealand, Tasmania, Antarctica, and a hundred other islands like the one he stood upon. But Pritchard wasn't interested in lateral horizons anymore – nor what lay beyond them. His only horizon was straight down through the reflective skin of the water that pressed against his waist.

Wearing a pair of cowhorn goggles – much like the ones he had fashioned in Scotland – Pritchard slowly lowered himself through the looking glass and into a new world of visual treasures. He held his breath and looked all around. What he had seen from the ship and accepted as a clear image had been, in fact, only a muted image – frosted over by the patterns on the surface and compressed into two dimensions by his overhead vantage point.

This time, however, he was looking from inside the crystal element, and with his feet still planted on the white sand bottom, he gazed straight out into the deeper water instead of down on it. Beyond the sand shallows, the forms he had seen before did indeed now have three dimensions. There were grotesque mountains of coral and clusters of sea plants and gardens of sponge. There were the moving formations – fish that lived and traveled as one giant animal in and out of the other, less kinetic images. All of these planes and forms were staggered like props on a dark and surreal theatre stage – many of them in motion and all of them sprinkled with a million reflections and shadows that came from a million other sources. The scene before him was a blue-tinted inner chamber of life. It undulated and soothed. It was indeed that silent, half static–half buoyant dream world he had envisioned as a boy.

During the day, Pritchard gradually ventured out and floated over progressively deeper water. As subsequent days passed, he began modest free dives in an attempt to close the distance between himself and the magic life clusters that lay on the bottom. Although he could see them from just past the shoreline, they were always faraway and filtered through the compounding blue density that even perfectly clear water will produce. He wanted to see truer colors and he wanted to touch objects and swim through and around them and to be a part of their life motions instead of an awkward alien.

What Pritchard needed was the aquatic agility of his youth, but he was now in early middle age – his body the result of a sedentary manhood spent in Victorian London. With ten thousand coal fires in his blood and the physical inertia of his past professions showing, Pritchard suddenly felt deprived of his right to observe and experience anything he chose. And, of course, foremost among his problems was his near fatal bout with pneumonia. It had weakened his lungs to the point that it was an effort to submerge himself more than a few feet.

In the lagoon of Papara, Walter Pritchard faced a sobering fact. He had determined to revive his own unusual art form – one where physical stamina would be a prerequisite for seeing and recording an image. Before he could ever execute an undersea picture, he had to first rebuild a weakened body – a prospect his art academy professors would have never entertained.

Pritchard's new home made this physiological renaissance easy to initiate. He hiked, he sunned his white frame, and he swam many times a day – each time trying a few brief strokes under the surface. Despite the frequently high moisture in the air, every movement and breath slowly started to heal the scars of his sedentary former life.

He then acquired some guidance and encouragement

from another source; a group of gentlemen who were also shaking off society's golden chains – although for what was presumably a more philosophical reason. Sporting beards and long hair, they were the tropical precursors of the hippie generation – latter day disciples of Rousseau called Tahiti's "nature men."

What with his resurrected ties to the outdoor world, Pritchard became acquainted with the most famous of them, Ernest Darling. Darling lived stark naked, slept on the ground with his head pointed north, and produced an endless stream of literature about the virtues of nudism, vegetarianism, pacifism, christian socialism, and phonetic spelling. He also advocated complete abstinence, but most of his friends, including Pritchard, ignored that philosophy, putting their disagreement into tangible practice.

Nor was Pritchard inclined to practice nudism. In fact, his exposure to the water was becoming so cumulatively long that he started covering himself with more clothing to help retain his body heat. In due time, he evolved a somewhat consistent outfit that featured cut-off trousers under a knee-length skirt, heavy long-sleeve workshirts, cloth shoes and a number of brilliant bandannas around his neck. The costume looked like some gypsy had collided with a medieval blacksmith.

Despite all this paraphernalia, his submarine mobility increased with every excursion into the lagoon. His breath-holding improved and he was descending to fifteen and twenty foot levels – gaining the vantage points he wanted among the undersea growths. Gradually, he reached a point where he could pause a moment, ignore his pulmonary discomfort, and begin to truly study the things around him.

What he saw was an immense display of poetic shapes; a world of slow spatial conquests by slow moving creatures – a place where light rays were liquified and shadows had a static darkness yet a pulsing luminance. Years later, Pritchard would deliver a series of lectures about the undersea experience and this is how he phrased it:

> Beneath the water is a world completely different from
> that of the air. It is a territory of quivering light and shade, of
> a profusion of strange colors, of plants of extreme delicacy

and beauty, of sea-creatures gorgeous and mysterious to the eyes. The coloring is all in the lowest keys, merging from deep indigo and purple into the lighter delicate tints of pale greens, grays, and yellows. Rocks and cliffs in the dim light assume an appearance of inconceivable size due to the magnifying power of the water.

Many times I have been surprised by what seemed to be rivers flowing between the coral buttes and would listen for the sound of water. But as I approached these rivers I found that they were only clean sand washed down by the action of the tides. In some instances, where the sand had been washed near the top of a pinnacle, with the diffused sunlight upon it, the effect was that of a wonderful waterfall.

When beneath the water, one is amazed to find that the surface of the water has become a mirror, reflecting everything below it and shutting out the whole upper world. The absolute silence is thrilling. On land we see the foundations of every object, no matter how large or small its bulk, but when one looks into the depths of the huge coral formations under water, they seem to be resting upon deep, blue air.[2]

Descriptions like these sounded otherworldly to an armchair traveler of the early twentieth century. In later years, Pritchard would combine the exclusiveness of such experience with his gift for speech and entertain audiences all over the world. However, it was 1904, he was in tropical waters for the first time, and he had yet to determine a method for sketching the undersea landscape – much less produce a painting to lecture about.

Between the periods of deep breathing and physical resurrection, Pritchard continued the quest he had started in his bathtub back in Santa Barbara – finding a way to record the scenes of his new world. He had shipped a steamer trunk of all the liquids, pastes and solids that he and Robert Rogers theorized might work. Now, he sat in the shallows each afternoon, submerged to his chest, experimenting with every combination of materials he could think of – as if paper and paint were ever intended to interact while immersed in water. Some mediums dissolved, some floated away in beads, and if any adhered, it was not for long. His boards and papers came out in shambles.

The idea was not to create a finished oil painting while under the surface, but to execute an intermediate picture in some other medium; one that could be translated into a more exacting image back in his studio. The persistent Irishman finally crossed his frontier one day with some items that were as unorthodox as the images he pursued: glass, coconut oil and surgeon's tape.

First he took a heavyweight drawing paper and flattened it against a sheet of glass. Then, with wide surgeon's tape, he secured the paper to the glass all the way around. Glass was the smoothest surface to be had, and, for that reason, it insured that no water would creep between itself and the tape. Of course, the water could have penetrated the paper, but that problem was solved with the oil. Pritchard applied it to the surface of the paper in degrees, each time draining off the surplus so that it would not completely penetrate.

Now he had a textured paper, fixed to a hard working surface – waterproofed from the front and protected from the back so that it wouldn't warp and buckle. As it turned out, his hand tools were not so complicated. After the idea of brushes was discarded, Pritchard hit upon Raffaeli crayons – then a commonly used medium. They adhered beautifully to the oiled paper and their semi-solid oil points were a perfect substance for anyone with the insane idea of creating pictures under the sea.

It wasn't long before Pritchard began his pursuit of that goal. With the aid of a helper and a small boat, he would swim ahead of his escort using a "window" he inherited from his free-diving Tahitian neighbors. A cumbersome ancestor of the face mask, the "window" was a glass-bottom box with a semicircular section cut into the top on one side. Hunting a shellfish dinner, the natives would lift their heads up and into the box and grip the cut-out section with their teeth, leaving their hands free to swim. When they made a dive, the box would stay afloat on the surface. The artist started using it to search for his subjects. Unlike the goggles, it allowed him to breathe without lifting his head and it didn't fog up. When he found the garden spot he wanted, he'd switch back to the goggles and make his descent.

If Pritchard's materials were as bizarre as his paintings, the method for reaching his subject and setting up his work was necessarily even more unusual. Certainly, he could now swim a bit underwater and even engage in small explorations when submerged. But his weakened lungs still forced a limitation on his travels.

It soon occurred to him that, once he started sketching, the real key to extended periods on the bottom would be to immobilize himself as quickly as possible and not waste time fighting his natural buoyancy. As with his boyhood days in Scotland, what he now needed was weight and plenty of it.

On any morning over the sunlit half of the world, artists of the time would sequester themselves in studios to start sketching – often with a hot pot of tea by the taboret and Caruso on the gramophone. There were heartier souls out painting nature's green earth, but they still operated on terra firma, had warm clothes, and took breathing for granted.

By the time these artists were asleep, Walter Pritchard was arising in Tahiti to start his own particular ritual – but it certainly wasn't within the same framework of comfort. After using the water "window" to find a desired spot, he would swim to the boat's gunwale and his assistant would lower a forty pound lump of coral over the side with a rope. Pritchard had a large hook on the back of his belt and a ring embedded in the coral was dropped over the hook. At that point, Pritchard adjusted his goggles and took a deep breath. His helper would then let go a rope, sinking the artist like lead on a fishing line. It all happened so quickly that Pritchard had to start adjusting the pressure on his inner ears before he even left the surface.

Also hooked to his belt were the oil-point crayons – all

strategically separated in bandoleer loops, their placement memorized so that no time would be lost hunting for colors. When Pritchard and his weight hit bottom, the coral quickly became a seat and then forty five seconds of frantic sketching would ensue before he had to unhook himself from the coral and shoot back to the surface. The boatman would pull the coral up by its rope, and, as soon as the gasping artist regained his breath, the entire process would be repeated – again and again, until Pritchard had finished his picture.

In this way, and with breaks for rest and warmth, it often took days to complete a single sketch. Practice or not, with his damaged lungs Pritchard could never increase his time on the bottom beyond a minute. At the day's end, he would return from the lagoon, wrapped in coats and totally exhausted.

Through the centuries, artists have spent their physical well-being in pursuit of æsthetics and paid with malnutrition, chemical poisoning, and marble dust in their lungs. But some-where in the annals of artistic sacrifice, Walter Howlison Pritchard should be recorded. He loved his subject so much that he worked – at least for that first year abroad – in an environment where he couldn't even breathe.

Pritchard theorized that most of his physical aggravation was unavoidable given the place but not necessarily the times. A number of closed-dress diving suits had been developed and the Siebe helmet was already eighty-five years in use. But the painter was thousands of miles from an industrialized shipyard, and even had a commercial suit existed in the islands, the logistical problems were fierce for those not in the salvage or dredging business. In addition to a tender for your air line, it took two more men to turn the manual compressor, which weighed hundreds of pounds. Moreover, Pritchard had never been schooled in the use and potential hazards of the diving suit.

Finally, even had he acquired the knowledge and equipment, such a diving operation was against the law outside Tahiti's commercial harbor. The French had a good grip on ecological balances even back then, and the government, to protect the pearl-oyster beds, didn't allow any advanced diving gear in the lagoons.

So, over the months, Pritchard produced his crayon paintings with the same rigors inherent in free diving for food. As a result, it became important for him to embark on a few daily excursions – limited trips that were free from the stress of creating an entire underseascape. Denied the luxury of casual observation in his larger pictures, he began to accumulate smaller but still relevant images. His observation dives allowed him to simply stop a moment on the sea floor and take note. Quickly, he would sketch little light and shadow phenomena that he couldn't always sense in the frantic – and often myopic – process of recording a broader scene.

Back in his terrestrial studio, every thumb-nail sketch was then stored away, and as larger works emerged from the ocean, they were enhanced by using the reference file of imagery. This way, Pritchard could tell what he had missed when his lungs were bursting, and, in the solitude of a Papara bungalow, his undersea vision was sharpened and trained to anticipate the forms of his new world.

During that year in Tahiti, however, the affable Irishman didn't entirely isolate himself under the sea or in his studio. Though obviously consumed with deep and mysterious elements, Pritchard was neither a brooding nor a reclusive man. A combination of nabob gentility and unusual artwork carried his reputation around the island and he filtered into the society of Tahitians and Europeans alike.

There was an added advantage to Pritchard's living in Papara. It was home to one of the most interesting families in the South Pacific – the nine children of Alexander Salmon, an English merchant, and Arii Taimai, whose exalted lineage of Teva chiefs had ruled the island federation sporadically since time immemorial. Of these, a daughter Marau became the last queen of Tahiti, and later, a chronicler of South Sea legends and histories. Another daughter, Moetia, married American Civil War hero Dorence Atwater – a key prosecution link in the Andersonville prison trial, and later, U.S. Consul to the islands. A son, Tati, was chief of Papara and translated his business acumen and political ambitions into an impressive financial standing.

UPPER LEFT: Jules Verne at the height of his literary career. UPPER RIGHT: Charles-Marie Brun, co-builder of *Le Plongeur*. BELOW: A model of *Le Plongeur* and an artists' conception of Brun's boat at sea.

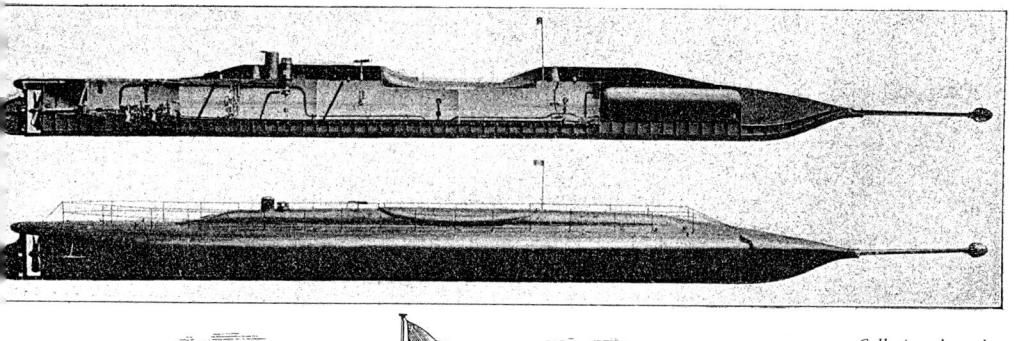

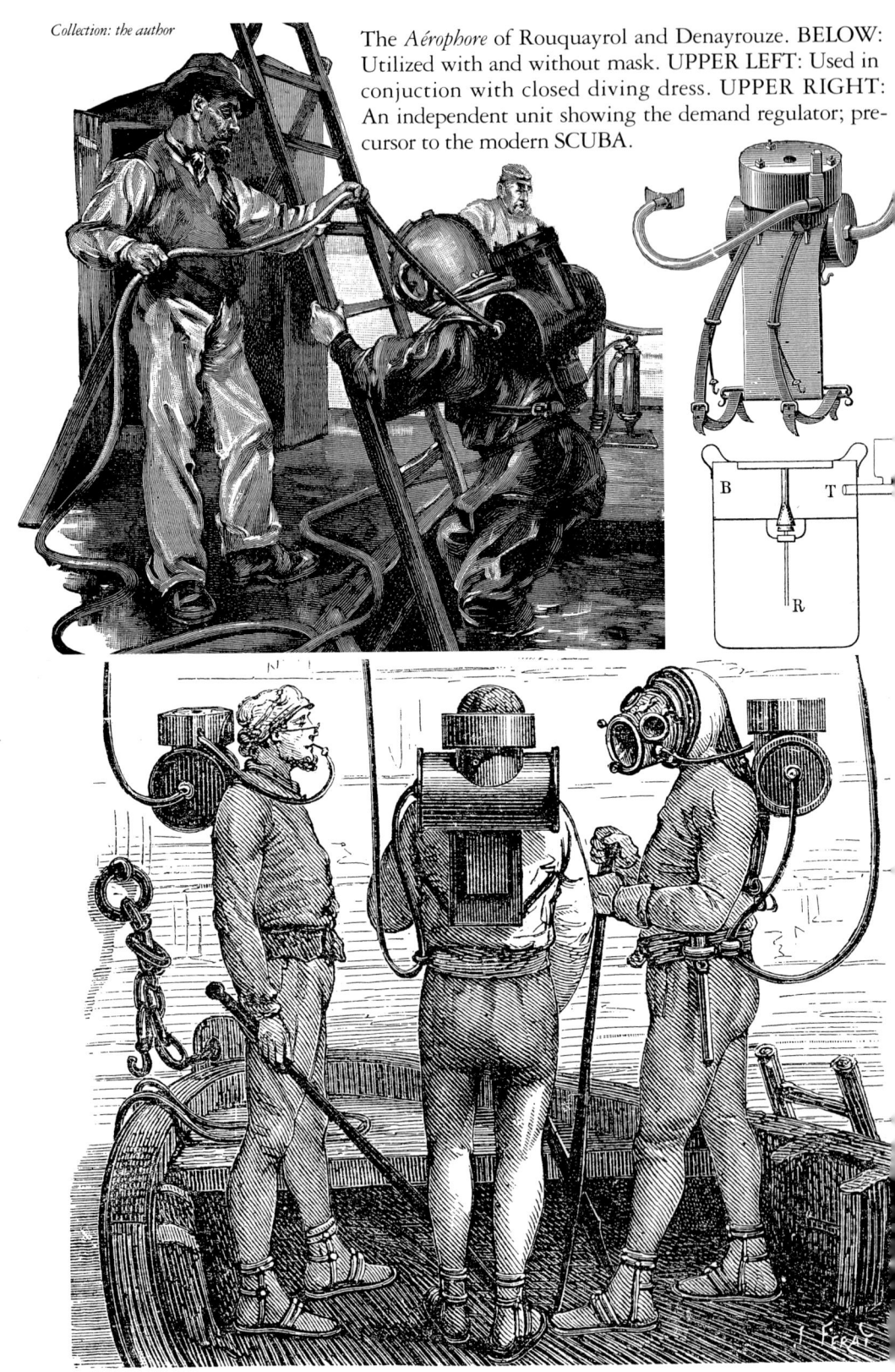

The *Aérophore* of Rouquayrol and Denayrouze. BELOW: Utilized with and without mask. UPPER LEFT: Used in conjuction with closed diving dress. UPPER RIGHT: An independent unit showing the demand regulator; precursor to the modern SCUBA.

B   T

R

The Mystic Imagery of the Undersea; de Neuville's illustrations—Hildibrand's engravings.
TOP LEFT: Nemo lectures his guests at the viewport of the Nautilus. TOP RIGHT:
Engaging a monstrous sea-spider. BOTTOM LEFT: Nemo battles a shark off Ceylon.
BOTTOM RIGHT: A coral cemetery—the burial of a crewman.

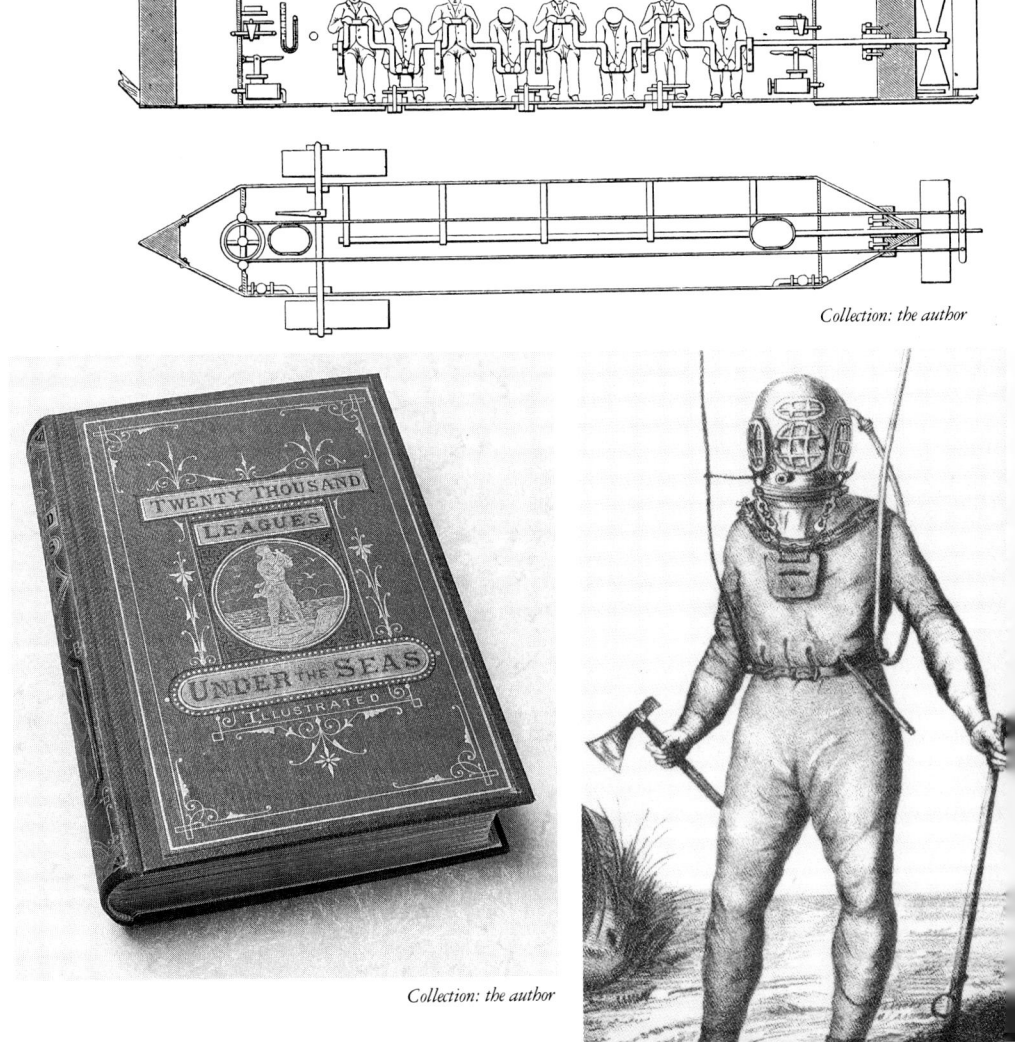

... vou la Coanza...

— Mais aura-t-il cette idée? demanda Negoro.

— A coup sûr, puisqu'il est intelligent, répondit Harris, et ne doit ~~pas~~ soupçonner le danger. Dick Sand ne peut prétendre revenir à la côte par le chemin que nous avons suivis ensemble. Il se perdrait au milieu de ces immenses forêts.

Jules Verne

Culver Picture

Collection: the author

TWENTY THOUSAND LEAGUES UNDER THE SEAS ILLUSTRATED

Collection: the author

OPPOSITE PAGE; TOP: A typical Verne manuscript revision, sent to Hetzel in letter form and signed. MID-PAGE: A diagram of the C.S.S. Hunley which made naval history's first successful submarine attack. LOWER LEFT: The 1873 English-language edition of *Twenty Thousand Leagues*. LOWER RIGHT: The French *Cabirol* suit — worn in 1844 by Henri Milne-Edwards, academia's first diving researcher. ABOVE: Frontispiece of the initial illustrated edition of Verne's undersea masterwork in 1871.

ABOVE LEFT: Zarh Pritchard. ABOVE RIGHT: Pritchard in his free-diving costume of 1904—near the Lagoon of Maraa, Tahiti. BELOW: Pritchard about to descend in diving dress. Tahitian entrepreneur, Narii Salmon is in the foreground.

Cleveland Museum of Natural History

Undersea Impressionism: Four of Pritchard's early paintings of the type actually executed on the ocean floor. ABOVE: "Dance of the Seaweeds." LEFT: "Coral Cavern with Sunbeams." TOP RIGHT: "Blue Depths —Coral Pinnacles." BELOW RIGHT: Coral Shrine—

...eland Museum of Natural History

Neg. 2A 19959. Photo by J. Beckett, Courtesy Department Library Services, American Museum of Natural History

ABOVE: Coral Pinnacles in the Lagoon, 1922
Negative No. 2A 19956, Photo by J. Beckett, Courtesy Department Library Services, American Museum of Natural History

BELOW: Pritchard's transition to featuring fish life; "In the Coral Garden in (only) 10 feet of water" Maraa, Tahiti, 1910.

ABOVE: Pritchard places himself in the picture—beneath a coral arch in 1922. BELOW: A coral garden in Tahiti.

Clockwise from top left: Negatives No. 2A 19961, No. 2A 19962, and No. 2A 19960. Photos by J. Beckett, Courtesy Department Library Services, American Museum of Natural History

LEFT: Work-Bell attachment for the Williamson Tube; its original function as designed by Captain Williamson. ABOVE: The Williamson's first still photograph, Hampton Roads, 1913. BELOW: The special addition that helped to launch the first expedition.

Virginian Pilot

| SPECIAL FEATURES | **Virginian-Pilot.** AND THE NORFOLK LANDMARK | SUNDAY, JUNE 22, 1913. |

Submarine Movies to Reveal
the WONDERS OF THE DEEP

SECTIONAL VIEW of PICTURE TAKING CHAMBER

ERNEST WILLIAMSON DESCENDING INTO TUBE TO TAKE UNDER-WATER PHOTOGRAPHS

How the Submarine Movies Will Be Obtained

"CROAKERS" AT THE BOTTOM OF HAMPTON ROADS—HOOK AND LINE IN BACKGROUND

WHEN Ernest Williamson went into a barber shop a month ago to have his blond locks shingled he did not know he was going to come out with a "big idea."

But he did, and thereby hangs a tale which probably will revolutionize the scope of the present worldwide activity of the motion picture people, as well as open up to the eyes of the whole world, layman and scientist, the wonders and beauties and mysteries of the deep.

For be it known that three-fourths of the world's surface is covered by water and up to this time only the patched-up replicas of divers have been had to furnish us mortals with any idea of what lies beneath the shimmering waves. With one exception, however, and that is part of the singular chain of coincidences that gave Ernest Williamson his idea.

Some years ago a young artist by the name of Z. H. Pritchard was told by his physicians that he would soon die unless he went away from his English home and lived in some temperate climate, so he hiked off to the far South Pea and landed in Tahiti. There he sketched and painted and watched the "native

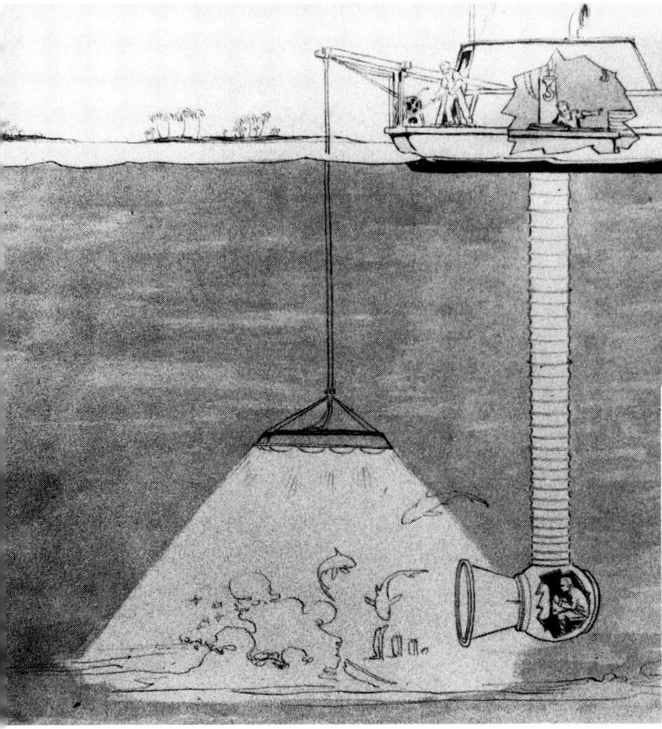

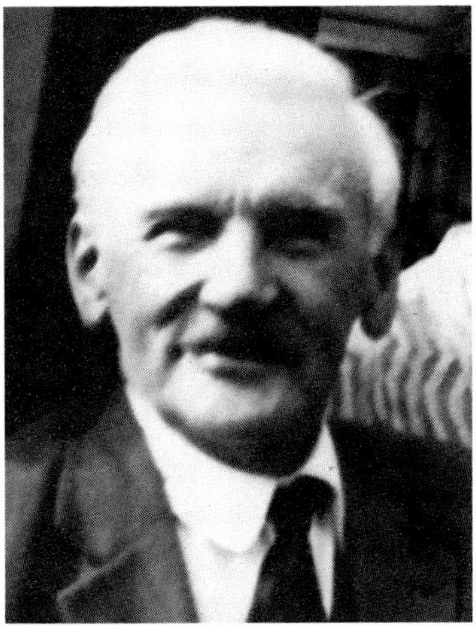

ABOVE: Ernie's drawing of the photosphere in operation. LEFT: Captain Charles Williamson. BELOW: The photosphere with cutaway showing the cameraman in position.

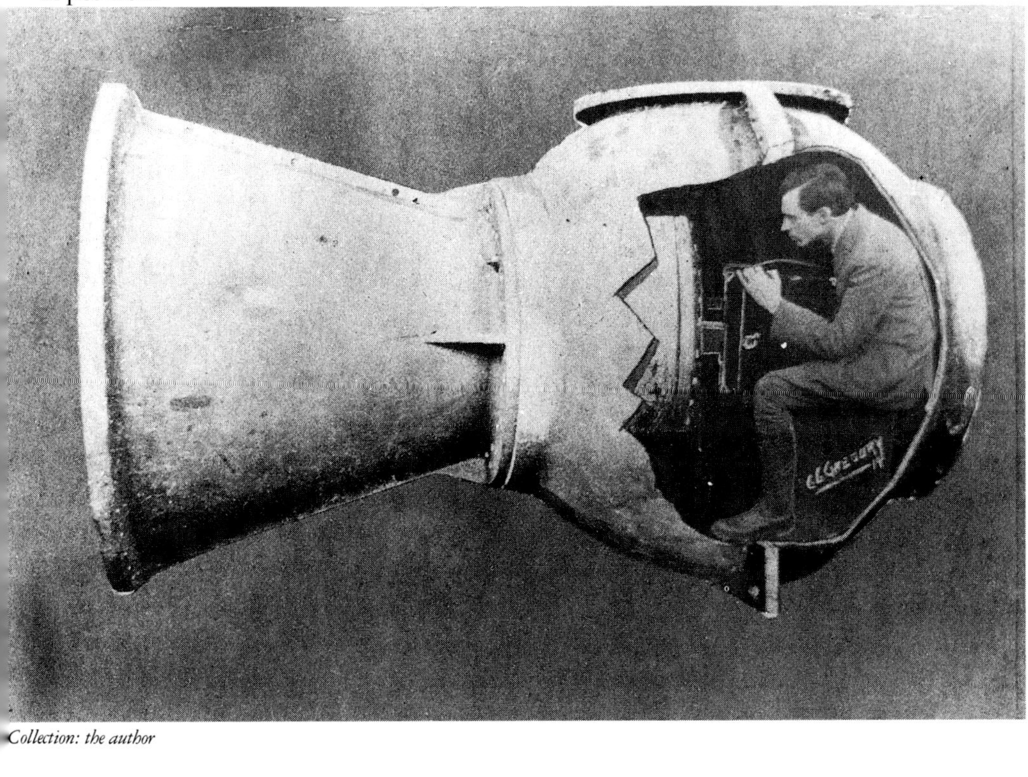

Collection: the author

LEFT: The Williamson's and Gregory's experiments using Bahamian divers. CENTER: One of Carl Gregory's first test shots in Bahamian waters. BELOW LEFT: George Williamson in diving gear about to descend for an acting sequence in the 1914 expedition film. BELOW RIGHT: The Williamsons and Carl Gregory aboard the "Jules Verne." Carl is starting to descend the tube as George transfers their camera.

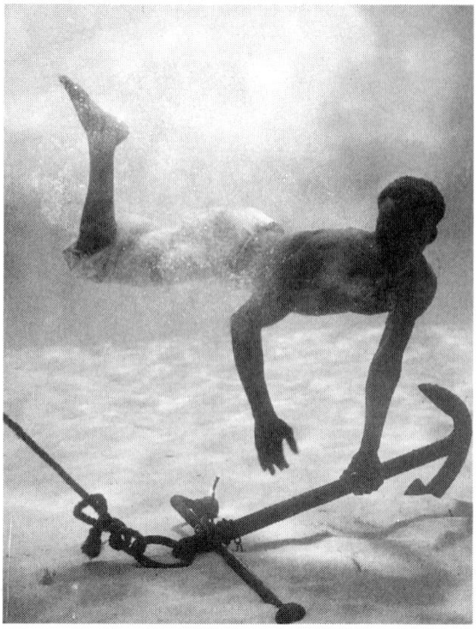

Collection: the author

Collection: the author

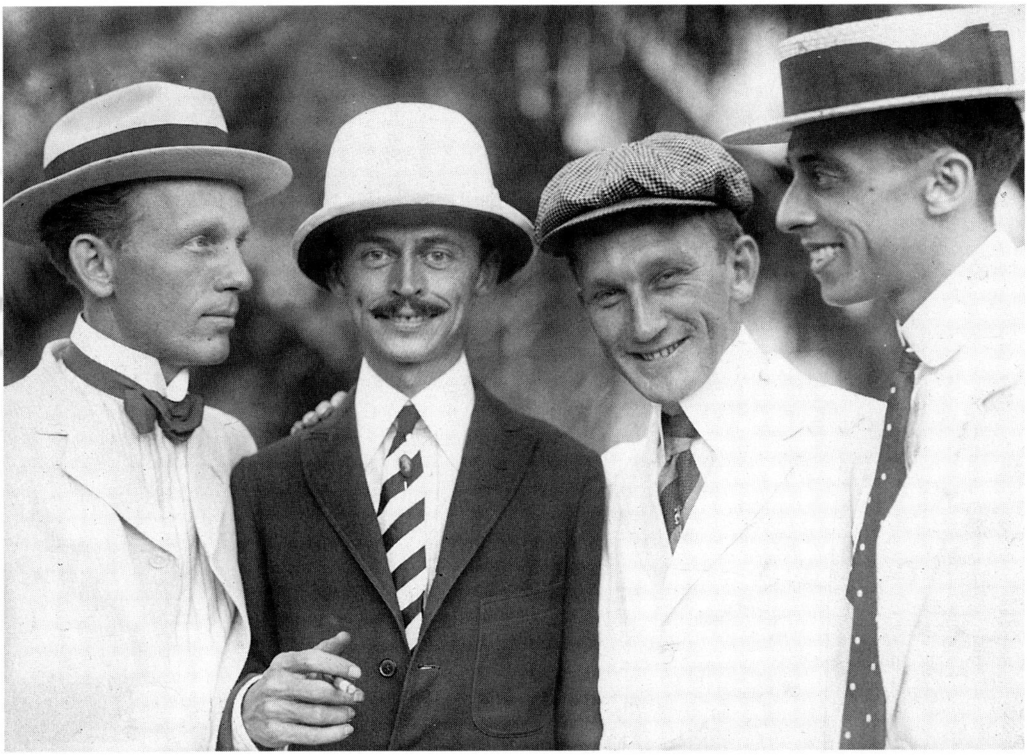

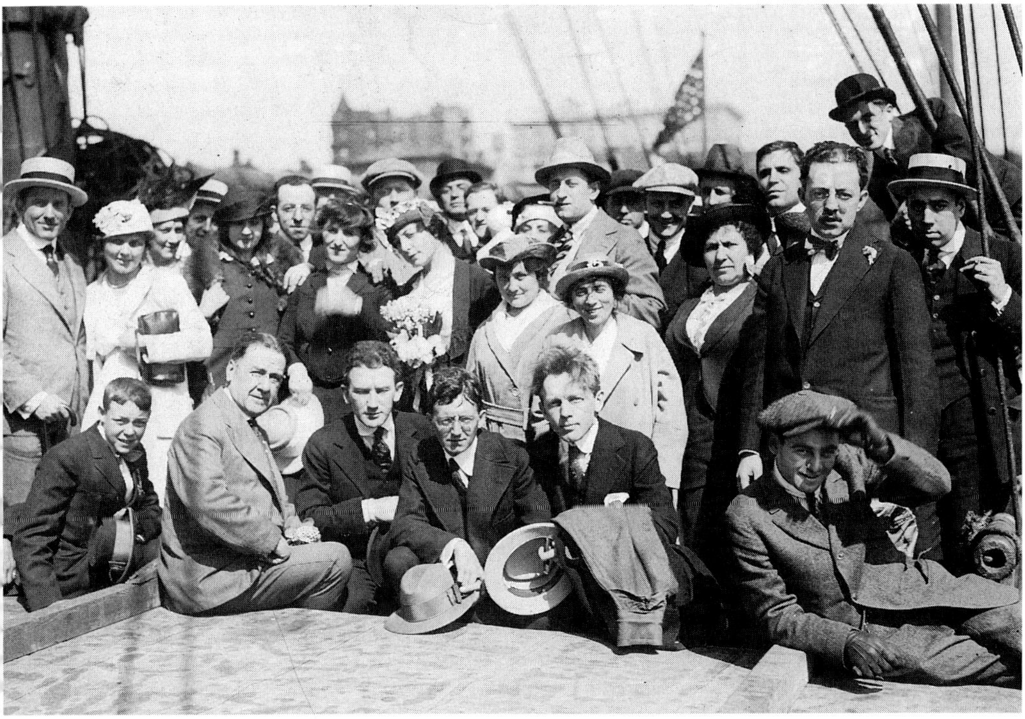

ABOVE: John Ernest Williamson, Carl Gregory, George Williamson, and a friend: Fred Ambrister. BELOW: George, John, and some of Universal's cast, crew, and management on board a steamer bound for The Bahamas, 1916.

Library of Congress

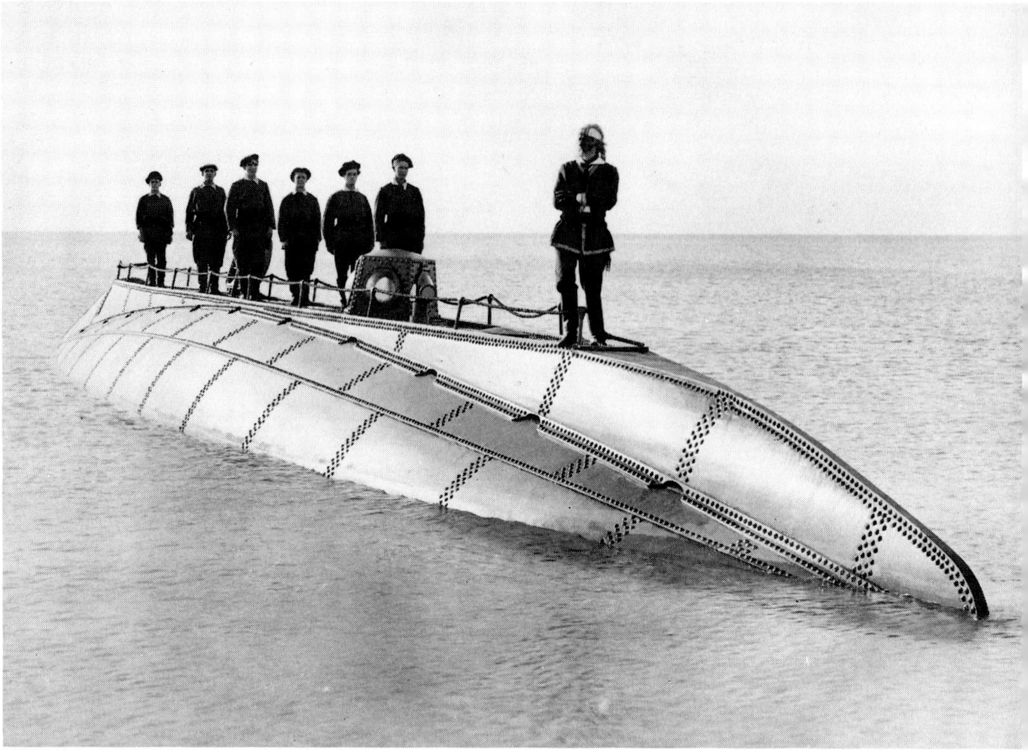

ABOVE: Captain Nemo and his crew aboard the Nautilus, 1916 production.
BELOW: Divers of the Nautilus "discovering" a shipwreck as filmed through the Photosphere.

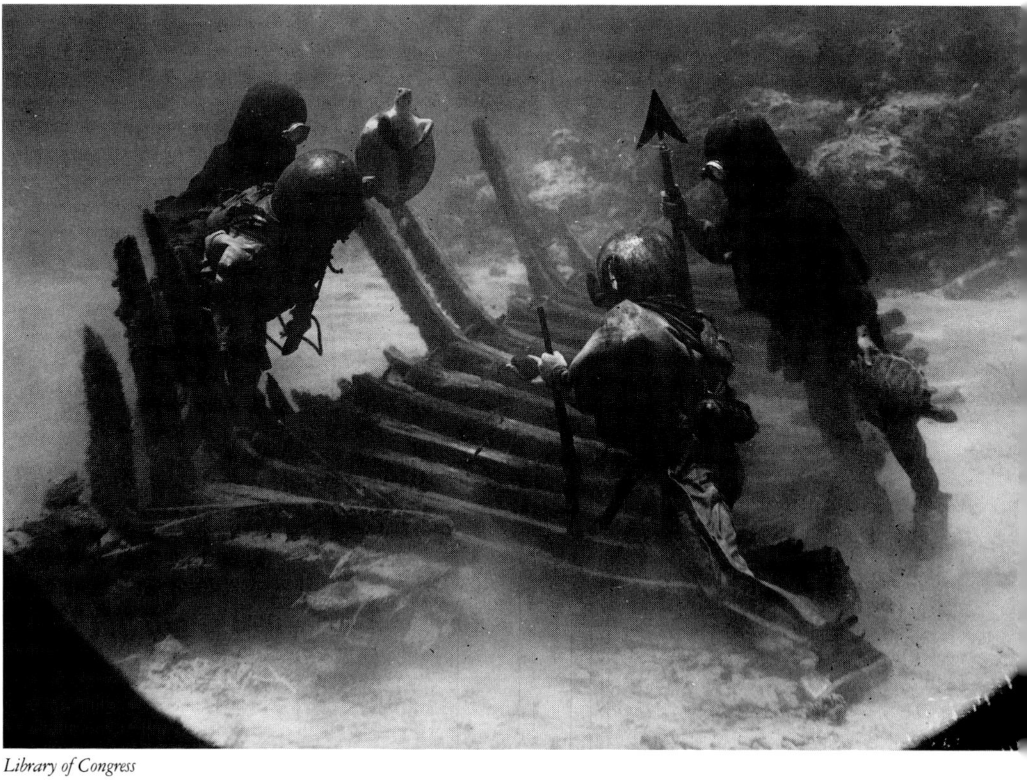

Library of Congress

Library of Congress

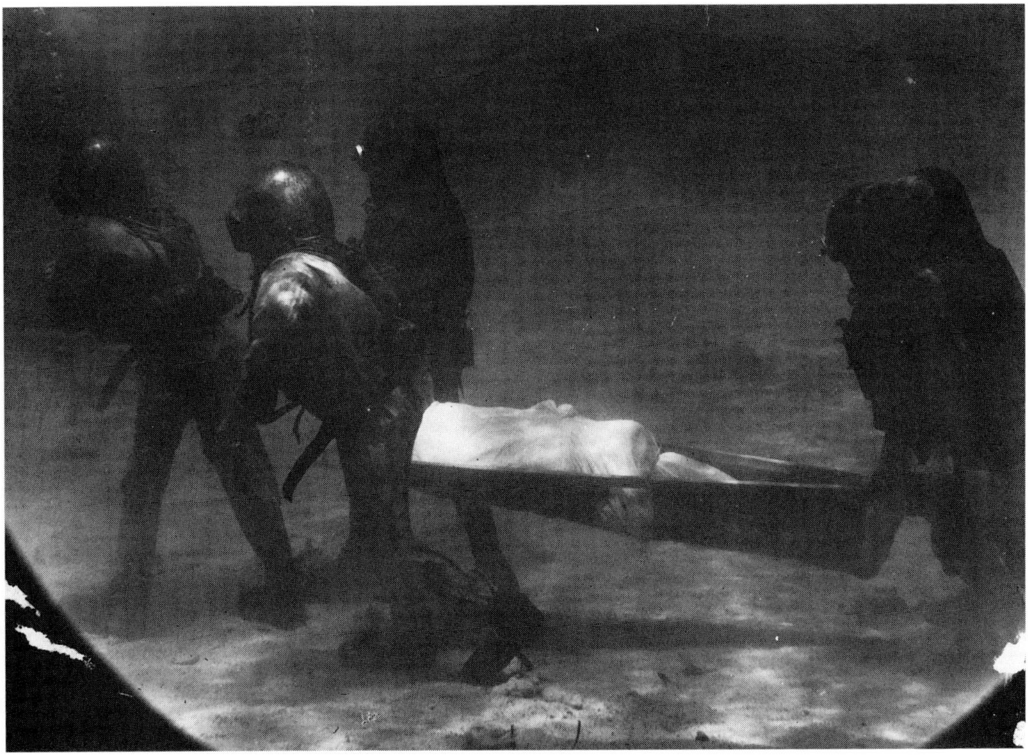

ABOVE: Men of the Nautilus bury their captain.
BELOW: Nemo and his crew launch a torpedo in the Universal epic of 1916.

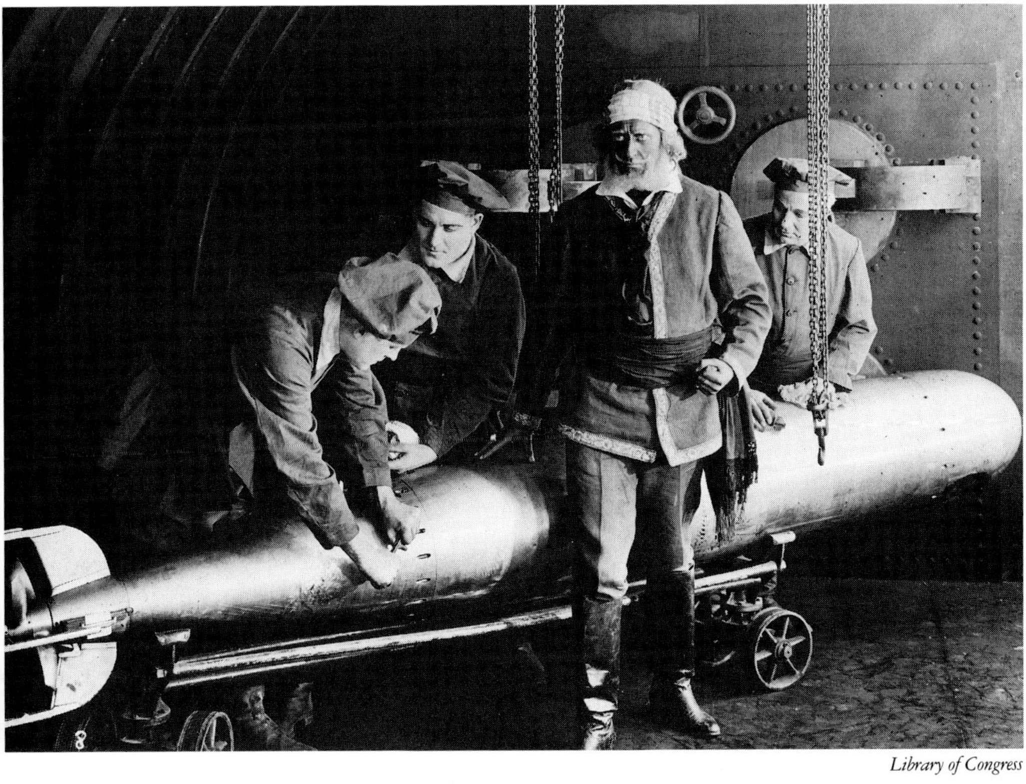

Library of Congress

Library of Congress

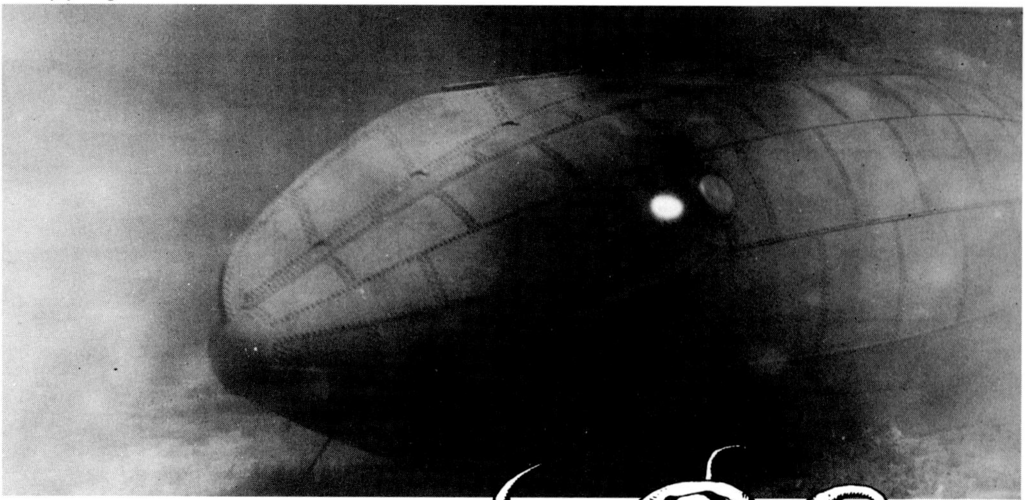

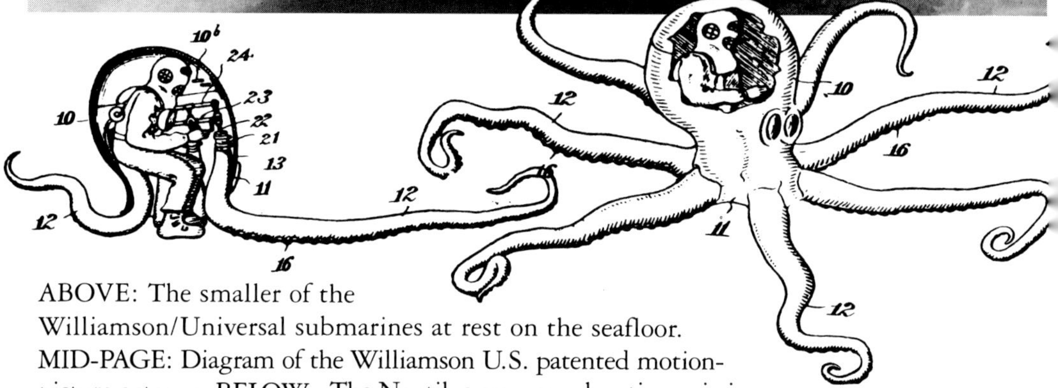

ABOVE: The smaller of the Williamson/Universal submarines at rest on the seafloor. MID-PAGE: Diagram of the Williamson U.S. patented motion-picture octopus. BELOW: The Nautilus crew on a hunting mission.

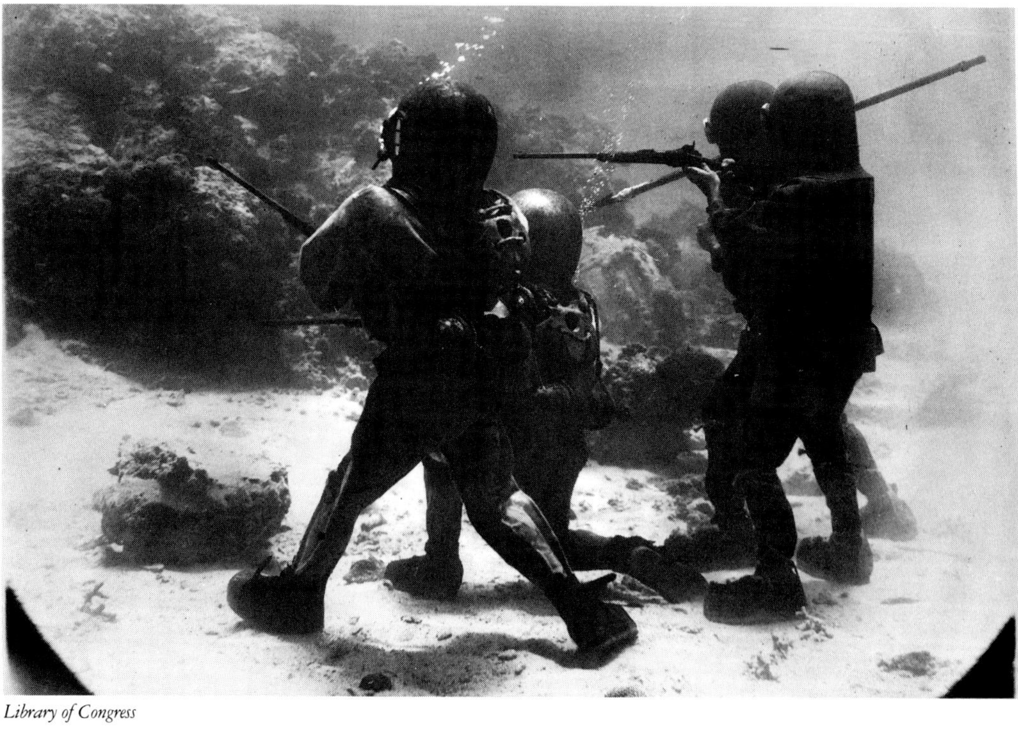

Library of Congress

But of all the brothers and sisters, it was gregarious, mischievous Narii Salmon who became the most frequent friend to Pritchard. Narii had been educated in England and he loved to socialize. He later moved north to the more lively town of Papeete which was also closer to his interests: partnership in a coconut oil empire called the *Societé commerciale de l'Ocean.*

In addition to that, Narii had a share in the harbor maintenance facilities, and, quite by accident, Pritchard discovered that the enterprising Tahitian had purchased a full diving rig for one of his service barges. From that moment on, Pritchard was obsessed by the prospect of sitting on the ocean floor and breathing – calm, relaxed, and with all the time he needed for observing and recording the images around him.

Now occasionally, Pritchard was invited to one of Narii's dinner affairs to help fete the landed gentry and on one such heady evening in December, he decided the time was right to bring up the subject of diving gear. Champagne was flowing liberally and the artist had an ally in the lady he escorted. Apparently, Narii had never really seen Pritchard at his labors, and, at some point in the evening, he slapped the table and declared that pictures could *not be* created underwater. "Now is your chance," said the feisty Mrs. Arthur Cornwall of San Francisco. "Get him. Get his diving suit."[8]

On that cue, Pritchard was beside Narii Salmon delivering a challenge; the use of Narii's equipment to prove he could do it, or five hundred dollars if he couldn't. Narii quaffed another glass of champagne and took up the gauntlet. His artist friend could use the diving barge for the rest of his stay in Tahiti if he did indeed emerge from the drink with a painting. However, Narii was explicit about the definition of painting. He wanted to see oil paints on canvas – not crayons on paper. Luckily, Pritchard had been experimenting with oils and knew they could work if certain preparations were made. The only hitch was that he had never actually done it. The free-diving and breath-holding had made paints unmanageable, but now, with the diving rig and plenty of time, he was positive he could win the bet.

These inebriated agreements, however, were still contingent upon getting the local government's approval. A nod from

Governor Jullien was needed before taking the rig out of the commercial harbor and into the lagoons. Shortly thereafter, with a little more champagne and a song and dance about nature's relationship to art, Pritchard engineered that deal as well. The important thing was to convince the old pooh-bah that he was going down to paint and not to wreck the colonial oyster beds.

Recalling those dinners, Pritchard later remarked: "This was the only diving suit in all those wine-cheered islands. Strange . . . that a few bottles of champagne should have opened up to me and a whole multitude of sea lovers, those amazing underwater coral lands."[8]

Some forty-five years later, an entire generation of undersea enthusiasts would thank France for more than champagne, as a navy captain named Jacques Cousteau entered the arena.

In a state of sobriety, Mister Salmon was reminded of his commitment and it took a little persistence by Mister Pritchard to make him honor it. A few weeks after their wager, and many reminders later, Pritchard received a reply down in Papara:

My Dear Pritchard:

Don't be anxious. I will give you ample time to get in town and drown yourself.

Yours sincerely,

Narii[9]

True to his word, Narii arranged it. On an afternoon four days before Christmas, his barge set out for the closest lagoon to Papeete. It was the height of summer and the barge had no steam propulsion. As a consequence, the trip was pleasant only if you were not one of the eight men required to row the thing.

After they anchored in what appeared to be thirty feet of water, Pritchard discovered the truth about Narii's much heralded diving suit. The "suit" was a discarded old sou'wester – stitched up the front, smeared with breadfruit tree sap to waterproof it, and attached to a breastplate. It was open at the bottom, and although the waist was cinched and the cuffs tightened with rope, one accepted the reality that, despite the tree sap, water was going to creep in and fill the jacket up to his neck – only the air pressure in the helmet holding it back.

After the jacket was on, a lifeline was tied around Pritchard's waist, a signal line tied to his wrist, and some breast weights hung over his shoulders. Pritchard was almost ready to show the white flag when he found there were no shoes to help stabilize him. As Narii slammed on the helmet, he gave Pritchard a few pointers on signaling and told him how to work his exhaust valve. That was the sum total of Narii's instructions. The glass was screwed on, and, since there was no ladder, Pritchard jumped off the deck. For a few moments, he bobbed around like a cork, and then, as his air was adjusted, he sank under the surface.

The brief preparations were just a mild form of humor for Narii. The playful Tahitian had his biggest joke waiting under the surface. Pritchard had never seen areas over forty feet in depth and had never settled himself in water over fifteen. On this occasion, however, Narii had let him off on the seaward side of a "fathomless" drop off, and, the tender fed out just enough slack to allow his new diver to start sinking without support. Despite the disorientation, it didn't take Pritchard long to figure out how to slow himself down – closing his exhaust control to blow water out of the jacket. Soon he was hanging by his own buoyancy in mid-water and this maneuver – essentially a critical one – quickly turned into a sensual state of being. "Never before had I known this freedom from the power of gravity that so dogs us on earth," he later wrote. "As though I were a sphere and capable to be accosted thus, closer about my body, the invisible, pleasant water molded itself, permeating every fiber and making me one with it."

Pritchard then took his first look downward and experienced the visual impact of being suspended over a yawning undersea chasm:

> My vision, focused to perceive the coral garden at a
> distance of some thirty feet, . . . suddenly dropped to
> a bottomless, vast space of indigo, in which there was not
> one smallest object. When we gaze at night into clear
> skies, there are always arresting stars on which we can
> anchor our sight. But here I was completely lost.[8]

But Narii had underestimated Pritchard's comfort with
this new world. His efforts to scare the artist were quickly can-
celled out by Pritchard's total fascination for the images he saw
all around him. In recalling the sensory events of this – his first
undersea experience with the means to breathe and the time to
observe – Pritchard exhibited an eloquence reflecting intense
love for his adopted territory:

> Quickly I gazed above. I was astounded. Many times
> before, beneath a sea absolutely calm, as on this
> morning, I had marveled as I looked upward to the
> surface. For that surface is a mirror, its under side
> more amazing than the face it reveals to human beings.
> Now, not an object on the shallow bottom was reflected
> from above. Over me was the same vast depth as the
> unfathomable depth below, translated into far-reaching
> distance by the mirror of the surface. The whole great
> sphere was held together by horizontal, blending bands
> of color. Deep indigo shaded into a complete circle of
> ultramarine and that, in turn, into azure, which merged
> into the clear emerald of the surface water. Above this
> came the reflected circle of emerald-azure, ultramarine
> and the indigo of the bottom. In other words, I was an
> atom suspended in the center of a limitless, horizontally-
> banded sphere of translucent color. I was moving forward
> and, as I moved, the sphere traveled with me, a great
> ethereal form.[8]

Walter Pritchard's recollections revealed not merely a love
for the undersea, but a love that was all-inclusive of the undersea; a love for the liquid element itself and not just the seascapes
it grows or the sea life it supports. But, that fact aside, the diving

painter was about to see those very seascapes and sea life in spectacular forms. It took him a while to realize, but Narii was terminating the puckish tricks and commencing some nice surprises. At first, he had weighed anchor and both barge and Pritchard drifted across the six-hundred-foot-deep Passage of Papeete. Now, as the barge crept shoreward on a one-knot current, the depth was gradually decreasing. Narii was setting Pritchard up for an incredible revealing of deep but visible forms that would soon loom ahead of him and yet rise from underneath him. Pritchard continues his vivid descriptions:

> Again I looked upward. Suddenly against the blue gloom appeared a pendant of brightest azure, illumined on its extreme points, which were descending toward me, by shining emerald light. Like stalactites, the tapering emerald points approached nearer to me. Others began to appear. They came closer, closer, a perfect coral structure, pinnacled, fretted, carved, hanging from the dome above.
>
> Then I knew what had happened. They were, of course, reflections, and at once, to my delight, I saw what I had always longed to see – resting on the submarine bottoms, the coming up of coral substance to meet its reflection. Gradually, the longest spire descending from above had joined its fellow rising from below in a slender, beautiful pillar. To the right, more pinnacles were rising. They seemed to be attached to no substance, to have no foundation, so dark was it below.
>
> Walls rose on my right and on my left. I was entering a wide chasm, its sides rising in pinnacles, with lonely pillars toward the center. Then I found myself at the portals of a cavern, its ceiling hung with carved ornament, its spaciousness divided by stately columns. But this was illusion; it was the reflected blue of the bottom that gave a sense of the vaulted roof of a cavern terminating in a bright entrance.
>
> Soon I was above depths of seventy-five feet, then of sixty and less. Blue forms were reflected dimly, as in moonlight. Then the blue mystery above was again filled with

121

forms, clearer and brighter, until I rested, thirty feet below
the surface, on a strip of sand, rippled as sand is when the
tide recedes from the beach. Around me were magnificent branches of living madrepore and at least ten other
varieties of coral growth. Thus, gently, noiselessly, from
the great banded sphere, I had crossed the Passage of
Papeete – carried from the undersea chasm to the shallower part of the lagoon. It was as if I had been watching
the working of the mind of a creator – spirit, shaping,
out of glorious color, forms that might be permitted
to remain substantial.[8]

From these intense verbal pictures, one could imagine the
artist had submerged not only into the deep, but into another
existence. It would seem that, of all his submarine experience
so far, this was Pritchard's most profound – the day when his
fascination with the undersea transformed into an æsthetic
commitment that would last the rest of his life.

For the longest time, Pritchard had been levitated over the undersea valleys like a stage angel on a wire and now he was
standing atop an overlooking shelf. There were coral monu-
ments below and around him, but only thirty feet of water left
above him. Narii Salmon knew his reefs – and his theatrics.

After indulging himself in so much environmental worship, Pritchard was reminded of why he had been dropped on
such a panoramic location – his wager with Narii. The artist
looked up and discovered the barge directly over him. There
was a little "window" in the water and someone's dark eyes
inside it looking down at him. With a signal from Pritchard,
the legs of an iron easel broke the rippled undersurface, and
then the rest of his painting paraphernalia followed with lead
weights attached.

Soon Pritchard was seated before his easel, bubbling and
painting away. His strategy was simple enough. He defied the
elements by literally isolating his entire medium – everything
he used – in oil. Of course, the oil-based paints would hold their

ground against the water. However, every surface the paints would contact had to be made just as impenetrable. Days before, Pritchard had saturated his wooden palette with oil and then applied segregated patches of his most frequently used colors on it. He pre-soaked the brushes in oil and impregnated the canvas with oil as well. In this way, all surfaces rejected the water and received the paints. He squeezed the tubes onto their corresponding color patches and the brushes transferred the paint to his canvas.

Ironically, a hindrance wasn't so much the sea but the sea life. As tiny threads of paint broke away from the brush and into the water, they were caught by curious little fish. This wasn't a problem until they tried to rid themselves of it by rubbing their mouths against the coral – or on the canvas which was closer.

Pritchard finished his undersea painting and ascended in triumph. Narii accepted defeat like a gentleman, accepted the painting with gratitude, and in the weeks that followed, made good his offer of the barge. Pritchard took advantage of it, using far more discretion than he wanted and doing far less of painting than he was capable. To continue in such comfort – and at those depths – it was obvious that he would somehow have to acquire his own equipment.

With the time that remained in Tahiti, Pritchard spent longer periods in his studio. When he wasn't diving for new subjects, he was working with still different media, experimenting with what best imparted the undersea image. His practical side was also at work: determining how best to present this imagery to art patrons back home. What finally went into the shipping trunk was a variety of techniques and mediums. Many of his crayon drawings were refined enough to show in their original form, but larger adaptations were in crayon, ink, or chalk. There were oils on canvas he had done using Narii's equipment and also about 100 small renderings of tropical fish.

Months before, Walter Pritchard had established himself as the first free diving man to render a sketch while under, and in, the sea. Later, in a diving suit, he had created the first paintings ever painted under the sea. Despite this exclusivity, he had been preceded by at least one utilitarian craftsman. Some thirty-five years before, a French expeditionary artist named Durrand-Brager had sketched some shipwrecks while inside a diving bell. His drawings were aids to a salvage attempt at Vigo Bay in Spain. Also, just three years earlier, Father Otta Blundell, an abbey dropout, had amalgamated a bit of diving and sketching. Blundell was a champion of Scottish archæology, and in full diving dress, he had descended into various lochs to study and sketch the composition of ancient man-made islands called "Crennochs." Continually there were copperplate "interpretations" of the undersea by both technical and creative illustrators who had never seen that world.

But, as a free-diving youth, Pritchard predated Blundell. He had not rendered from his imagination and he no longer drew from memory. Neither was he encased in the safety of an iron bell, using bone-dry materials. On the contrary, Pritchard was the first solitary diver to ever sit and paint with his tools, his mediums, and himself all submerged in – and exposed to – the water. Also, what he was shipping home was neither a salvage survey nor an archæological sketch, and, except for the fish drawings, it wasn't biology. It was evocative and expressive. It was art. It was the mood and feeling of his adopted world. Walter Pritchard had created undersea painting and he was going to try making a life's work of it.

Around March of the new year, Pritchard sailed back to California and a rendezvous with art enthusiasts there. After his departure, Tahiti was hit by a cyclone which flooded Papeete and caused much destruction. When he heard of it, Pritchard figured he and his paintings had outrun the devil, but, as it happened, this was 1906 and the devil was waiting for him in San Francisco.

In the western United States, San Francisco was the art market of substance. Even with that standing, Pritchard knew it was limited in many respects. Most artists who lived there relied on exhibits and sales out of their own studios or homes. There were a few dealers and also *Gumps*, which held auctions, but most of these firms were caught up in the Nob Hill hunger for eastern painters and European masters. The only gallery that significantly helped California artists was Paul Elder, then at 238 Post Street. Through their Santa Barbara branch, Robert Rogers was able to arrange an exhibit in Elder's precious space in the big city.

By the first week of April, the undersea pictures were having their first exposure to the American public and their first gallery showing ever. Just how they were received will never be known – there wasn't time to find out.

Pritchard was in town helping the gallery to mother his exhibit when, at 5:30 on the morning of the eighteenth, he woke to find his bed moving violently back and forth. He suddenly realized that his room, his building, and the entire city was moving as well. The massive tremors lasted the longest seventy-five seconds of his life and the noise was like a North Sea storm hitting Scotland.

When the rumbling stopped, Pritchard looked out on a city that was littered with bricks and concrete yet still relatively intact. And it would have stayed intact except that when downtown firemen attached their hoses to a hydrant, no water came out. Most pipes had been snapped by the moving earth, and many others had not even been hooked up to the water system because of city hall's negligence.

By mid-morning, the entire northeast of San Francisco was burning. When the last flames were extinguished three days later, almost five hundred people were dead and five hundred city blocks were destroyed – including 238 Post Street, the Paul Elder Gallery, and every one of Pritchard's pictures.

It was the culmination of many travails. Not only had the work in Elder's gallery been strenuously produced, but, considering Pritchard's lung condition, some of his undersea accomplishments had been nearly Herculean. In his quest for this imagery, he had traveled thousands of miles and the work had been produced to signal a new creative orbit. Pneumonia denied him Europe and encumbered his present life; one maintained in a strange and precarious new country. After the smoke had cleared from the great San Francisco earthquake, Walter Pritchard decided that for him the twentieth century had begun in a rather laborious fashion.

Despite everything, Pritchard's bank account was intact and he immediately did what most craftsmen would do to stay sane. He started all over. There were artists less resilient. Carleton Watkins, for one, was a pioneering photographer whose stereo views had captured the West and helped influence the federal government to establish national parks such as Yosemite. He lost nearly all of his plates in the fire and the destruction of a life's work finally sent him to an insane asylum.

Joining others who had lost their work, Pritchard left the burned-out capital of the north for its rival city in the south. His journey, however, was part of a greater exodus of artists. In addition to San Francisco victims, the southern California climate had started attracting both ailing and retired artists from the east coast. About five years before, a beneficent fellow named Frederick W. Blanchard had erected a fine arts building in downtown Los Angeles where they could all go to set up shop, organize clubs, and hold exhibits. Following the April disaster though, the Blanchard Building grew into a kind of artists' refugee camp. After picking up his gear in Santa Barbara, Pritchard threw-in with the rest of the displaced from San Francisco and all the coughers and hackers from the east. The Blanchard Building became "home."

Considering the crowded accommodations, he was able to put forth a surprising amount of work. By the third week of May – just one month after the San Francisco fire – he had doctored up enough scraps saved in Santa Barbara to have a small showing at a festival in Venice, California. As it turned out, his old friend Sarah Bernhardt was there on the the tail-end of a southern and southwest tour. She and her young renegade producers, the Shuberts, had bucked a powerful theatre trust and Sarah was exhausted from playing the whole circuit in skating rinks and circus tents. She, in fact, was so glad to see a comrade from home, she bought another undersea painting for friendship's sake.

In all probability, the painting Sarah bought wasn't created from scratch. During Pritchard's first few months in Los

Angeles, almost nothing was. He had retained his preliminary crayon sketches in Santa Barbara, and, this time, his graduated method of producing a picture worked to an advantage. With a little inventiveness, probably the entire exhibit could have been recreated in his studio – allowing for a few representational liberties to which the public would have been oblivious. Like the stories of deep sea divers, in those days no one had a comparative frame of reference to check his accuracy. Nevertheless, Pritchard did steam back to the islands for a couple of months. By the autumn of that same year, he was back with a wealth of new material to complement what he had begun reworking.

Through all this chaos, Pritchard was prodigious. He had doubtless become the world's first undersea painter, but, he wanted to cast the image as quickly as possible and earn a reputation that would allow him to work and live with a pre-eminence in the field. Accordingly, he lost no time in escaping from San Francisco, setting up in Los Angeles, getting back to Tahiti and then back to the United States. He lost no time in making money and he also lost no time in spending money to get himself permanently settled. That latter process was now manifesting itself in a studio-home he designed and contracted for in the town of Pasadena. Hopefully, he could occupy it in the spring and be ready with enough pictures to hold a reception.

As in his first – and cremated – exhibit, there was a combination of mediums: oils on canvas that he did using Narii's diving suit and the crayon renderings that were executed half under water and then finished on the surface. This time, however, Pritchard was working to perfect an entirely new approach.

The crayon work was faithful to undersea moods, and well-suited for impressions. Fully oriented to Impressionism, society was certainly ready to live with its diffusion, but in his pictures, Pritchard wanted a more refined and permanent image.

Oils had not been sufficient for this purpose; not when used underwater. In the studio they were limitless, but Pritchard had still other problems with oils. Early in this new approach, he was quoted as having uttered some gobbledygook about oils "losing the delicate blue" or that "oils on a canvas would not adequately express the exquisite gradations of color."[10] Of course, the classic and wonderful medium of oils had, for centuries, supplied any degree of delicacy or blending the artist could want – provided the artist knew how to use oils. One gets the feeling that Pritchard's facility with oils simply wasn't that good and that he needed an easier medium to record his undersea world the way he felt it – and perhaps as rapidly as he wanted to express it.

In all of this however, Pritchard had an argument that sounded more valid and raised an issue that few people probably contemplated. It was that, whether his materials heretofore had been physically wet or dry, varnished or unvarnished, he felt they were "wet mediums" that always "looked wet."

On first examination, Pritchard's problem with "wetness" seems totally ironic considering the scenes he was depicting. But by 1906, he had made an astonishing observation – one that may since have been visually expressed but never consciously stated by an undersea explorer or photographer. It was that if a person, once submerged in water, could separate his visual sensations from the sensation of water on his skin and separate what he saw from the knowledge of where he was – he would realize that few objects, unless enhanced with bubbles or currents, appear to be wet or covered with water – at least not by the visual conditioning man has acquired on the surface.

When he was in a mood to be concise, Pritchard would simply say: "There is no feeling of wetness when one is below the surface."[10] And the statement was essentially correct because the harsh, shiny reflections of wet objects on land rarely exist in an undersea world that appears powder dry – oddly enough, due to the complete enclosure of light-diffusing water.

The new medium that Pritchard developed to attain that same matte, dry appearance was, of all things, leather instead of canvas. It couldn't be taken underwater as could his other materials and so any image rendered upon it had to be copied from a preliminary crayon drawing. But it always looked powder-like regardless of how much paint was applied, and as long as his pictures didn't exceed the length of a steer – or a chamois, which was really his preference – he could stretch a frame as large as he wanted. Additionally, since he was now in the American West, leather was just as available as, if not more available than, canvas.

He used it in the rough, untanned state and his vehicle turned out to be a number of dried, pulverized pigments or powdered chalk – both mixed with spirits of resin to varying degrees depending on the effect he wanted. Once brushed on, his formula had the effect of coloring the rough surface and not just lying on top of it. In fact, a sort of dying process took place. Combined with the matte finish of the liquid when dry, the end result gave "the veil-like aspect that lies over everything submarine."

When responding to the technique, art editors would later comment: "With what perfection the medium adapts itself to the subject, one must see to realize. It is almost unbelievable how the surface of the leather holds the pigments . . ."[1] But then, as was the fashion of art criticism, something just had to be said about authenticity – and, of course, the critic would assume an authoritative posture with remarks like: ". . . gathers light and depths perfectly interpretive of deep water."[1] At that point, with the smallest possible percentage of mankind having ever seen the undersea, one wonders how the evaluation process took place.

Shortly after 1907 arrived, Pritchard moved up to his newly completed studio and home in Pasadena – one he would occupy for many years. Pasadena was a bucolic town – tucked into a corner of the San Gabriel Valley and thriving from its horticultural expertise. It had been settled only thirty-two years before by orange-growing, teetotaling immigrants from Indiana.

It may seem odd that a man who had determined to spend his life painting the undersea world should install himself in the middle of a valley – surrounded by orange groves instead of pounding surf. But it must be remembered that, for Pritchard, bronchial weaknesses dictated it. He was stronger now than when he first arrived in the United States, but he would always be flirting with potential ailments every time he went beneath the ocean. To live beside it as well would have been pushing his luck. California's coast was often cool or foggy and Pritchard needed warmer, dryer air to subsist on. For the rest of his life, his body chemistry would always work in opposition to his aesthetic persuasions. That's why the valley and Pasadena came to be home.

But Pritchard had company. Around the time Pasadena was established, a book entitled *California for Health, Pleasure and Residence* came out, and it compared the weather of Southern California favorably to that at many international spas and health resorts. After that, trainloads and boatloads of tuberculin, asthmatic and bronchitic people continuously arrived in Los Angeles and the area was becoming the national sanatorium. Then special attention was drawn to Pasadena; not because of any outstanding hospitals, but because of one G.G. Green who built a resplendent hotel there. "Colonel" Green was a patent medicine mogul and the inventor/originator of Green's "August Flower," "Ague Conqueror," and "German Syrup." His backyard formulas were popular all over America and when he built what ultimately became an opulent 360 room tourist palace, it was interpreted as further endorsement of the area's healthful properties.

But there was another reason why Pritchard wanted Pasadena as his home. In a word, it was money – not his own but other people's – and there was an abundance. Predictably, both the healthful climate and scenic location had combined to form an enticement for the Easterners and Midwesterners who could afford to come out as often as they pleased on the cross-country railway. The severe weather back home evidently made them almost half as uncomfortable as the people who worked in their factories and so Pasadena became a "rancho town" – a winter playground for millionaires.

When these industry captains started building sumptuous homes, their wives started building a sumptuous social life so that Pasadena could be yanked up from orange grove status to that of a Newport or an Easthampton. The town was starting to draw retailers, craftsmen, and artisans to cater to the ever increasing whims of these people. From the practical point of selling his work for the best price, Walter Pritchard intended to ease his undersea paintings into that capricious system of supply and demand.

Considering his rather special needs, Pasadena gave Pritchard everything he required. Initially, it had furnished a climate for his physical well-being, and, in the second place, it would be a market for his painting. But the town supplied yet a third element in his equation for a home. That element was a direct and fast umbilical to the coast whenever he wanted to paint. For the bathers there were, of course, train routes to the beaches of Los Angeles and most particularly a Southern Pacific line direct to Santa Monica. But for Pritchard, the best of all possibilities was right in his lap. As it turned out, the most popular summer place for Pasadenans was none other than Catalina Island, where Pritchard had renewed his faith in the beauty of the undersea. Many of his fellow citizens had even built second homes on the island, and, as a consequence, the Santa Fe gave service every half hour to San Pedro where the boat for Catalina could be boarded.

Some time after he settled in his new studio, Pritchard either purchased or made arrangements to use a diving outfit in Avalon, the harbor of Santa Catalina, and from that day on, his undersea world was one short train ride and one short boat ride away.

In addition to his standing as an artist of unusual environments, Pritchard should also be recorded as an archetype of inverse commuting. He was not able to live by the ocean, but he had to have his work there. Then, although he worked in the ocean, he had to return home to make a living. These inversions would earn Pritchard a reputation for being eccentric – something his Pasadena customers would love.

This author may have a desire for biographic surrealism, but surely there is something surreal about the image of a man ritualized thusly: getting up in the morning and leaving a neighborhood of sumptuous valley homes, passing through the aroma of orange groves, boarding a train, later a boat, arriving at his destination to slip into a diving suit, painting pictures all day on the ocean's floor, and later returning to his valley home to finish his work and aggregate with a few wealthy patrons. All of this, of course, taking place in the time of Gibson Girls, stereoscopes, and Teddy Roosevelt. It's hard to imagine a more bizarre juxtaposition of environments and yet it well could have been a normal work day for Walter Howlison Pritchard.

Pritchard had obviously assembled a life style that would best suit his endeavors. But there remained an obstacle to any wide recognition – certainly by the Eastern establishment of the day; one that even his unusual paintings would have trouble surmounting. It was the fact that he was now a *California artist* – a subject of enduring discrimination.

The problem was that California and the Northeast didn't care for each other's frames of reference. The original colonies thought the West was interesting as long as primitives recorded the wilderness experience. Once the railroads were completed, however, Yankees assumed it was the end of frontier mystique, and, consequently, the end of Western art.

That assumption was entirely wrong, but not so wrong was an idea that the West had begun to worship itself – creating a brand of regionalism for which the East had no identity. Much like an oversized *colony*, it developed infatuations with its terrain and, yet, in an area of such vast geographies, the subject matter was becoming repetitious to the extreme. At the turn of the century, it was not unusual to attend an exhibit and see fifty to a hundred renderings each of the Grand Canyon, of Yosemite, and of wind-swept coastlines; most of them sporting wild, untempered colors, having an aggressively obvious point of view, and depicting not a dash of human involvement.

It could be said, of course, that New York, Philadelphia or Boston had their own insular qualities, what with their adaptations of Old World styles and motifs. But defining American art was their privilege. They had the museums, the galleries, the critics, the schools and the publishers – and they had more money. All this made them arbiters of whose name got chiseled in stone and whose didn't. Also, at that time, much of California painting remained there because, back east, cosmopolitan life was in the ascendent and pure nature wasn't that popular. In New York, urban residents had paid in blood to escape nature, the agrarian ones who had nature saw it as hard work, and the wealthy class sought access to nature only if it was groomed and manicured to accommodate gazebos and statuary. Nature needed plenty of cultural baggage to sell in the eastern markets. The few natural landscape painters who kept working – even those who painted terrain more familiar to the Eastern eye – were usually relegated to the art colonies of New Hope, Pennsylvania or Provincetown, Massachusetts.

Added to the problems of subject matter was one of quality. The dilettante painters of Southern California were soon to become legion and that vast number of untrained and ill-trained caused the general standards to slide. In the warmth of a non-competitive environment, it was the tendency of the retired and the expatriates to congratulate or at least tolerate each other in most anything they did. With all this pleasantness abounding, there was less criticism; less of the constructive bite that prevailed in places where painters would metaphorically kill themselves and each other in a race for recognition.

In addition to the non-professionals, there was also an abundance of *misdirected* professionals. Like Pritchard, they were former decorative craftsmen. They came by their situation because the art academies of the world refused to realize that the machine age would cut, shave, rout and die-stamp tens of thousands of applied designers out of work. Like Pritchard again, these displaced people gravitated into painting though it might not have suited their talents. By the time Pritchard settled in Pasadena, there were fifty painters in America to every worker in applied design. Consequently, painting became compromised with artists who did not belong in painting and many of them migrated to California to start cranking out landscapes.

The state, of course, rightfully claimed a number of masters like Thomas Hill, Charles Nahl or Thomas Moran and there were newer talents yet to replace them. Still another noteworthy group were the photographers of the region. But the greater number of competent artists in California were those with a modest statement to make; the flower painters, china painters, printmakers, miniaturists, and commercial folk – craftspeople who were able to retain their intended trades instead of tackling an upright canvas. It was a reality that finally took the form of a crafts movement right in Pritchard's adopted town of Pasadena a few years later.

As to executional qualities, Pritchard was a well-intentioned painter. As far as being faithful to his subject matter, there simply were not many people in 1908 who could dive under the ocean to check his accuracy. But with his expertise unchallenged, Pritchard could still be easily identified with the general California art scene. By Eastern standards, his imagery was extreme and repetitious, he dealt in unreal color ranges, he painted vistas that excluded human interaction, and quite often, the amalgam of his shapes resembled Western terrain. Although immersed in water, the outrageous formations of coral and calcium often had a similarity to the outrageous formations of a Bryce Canyon or a Monument Valley.

Pritchard was going to need help in avoiding the potential anonymity that lay before him. Since he couldn't change his location, he would seek patrons who easily traveled from east to west and back again. These patrons also opened and closed their pocketbooks independent of any art critics at home. Not only could they keep him solvent, but they would carry their purchases back to the money capitals of the country and act as *de facto* publicists for his fantasy-like and fanciful art.

When the elements of his new existence were aligned, Pritchard cut the ribbon. On a Saturday night in March of 1907, he gave a reception at his new studio. A reviewer for the *Los Angeles Graphic* didn't quite understand what he was looking at and wrote that Pritchard's work "belonged to the curiosities of art."[11] But it was no matter. The guests were fascinated, some enough to make a purchase, and the affair spawned articles in a number of publications including a foreign journal, *Atlantisches Tageblatt*, and also *The Scrip* which quoted someone as saying "no painter save one who had beheld the deep through a diver's helmet could represent so truly the hills and valleys of the underworld."

Afterwards, Pritchard attracted all manner of solvent visitors to his studio on Oakland Avenue. He made a good bet in his choice of towns because Pasadena was turning into a bloated little plutocracy in the middle of the orange groves. Its tree-lined streets were also lined with those of national prominence. The railroad sidings were continually filled with glistening private cars that became an integral part of the scenery.

Hand in glove with all of this, of course, the social functions became larger and the affairs more brilliant. And when society ladies weren't lolling in flower-laden parlors, they were out with their guests stalking the artists and strolling through their studios. Pritchard kept a directory and over the next few years, his undersea atelier collected some impressive names – and comments. One can imagine a robber baroness cooing to her friends: "you absolutely must see this incredible English gentleman who goes under the water in one of those diving suits and paints pictures."

The ladies liked Pritchard. He was an even six feet and had steel blue eyes. It's reasonable to assume they were intrigued with his bachelor status and his English accent as much as with his paintings. The characteristics could only enhance his undersea mystique.

We can also assume that Pritchard liked the ladies. One, who had met him in Tahiti, later decorated his guest book with this suggestive string of metaphors: "Your pictures certainly look familiar and remind me forcibly of the days I went below the surface and struck bottom with you in the lagoon of Tahiti."

Regardless of his amours, Pritchard had material reasons for keeping company with women – men didn't do much of the buying. It was the normal function of a society woman to spend money in decorating her family's life and as the first few years of his painting progressed, the fair sex consistently remained Pritchard's most frequent customers.

Also of value were their activities. Traveling regularly and extensively, they were his best means of promotion. The social life of these *beau monde* ladies and the parties they gave assured that Pritchard's work would get exposure. It was a self-perpetuating system for generating patrons.

With all of this, Pritchard played an endorsement game which also was perpetuating. He knew that in their purchases, the socialites were imitative of royalty, theatre personalities, and then each other – usually in that order. So when he introduced himself into society, Pritchard had in his hand the perfect catalyst to start a high-bred chain reaction – his friend,

Sarah Bernhardt. Once the first Pasadena patron heard about Sarah, she then figured it was quite alright to own something as otherworldly as a painting of the ocean's floor. After that, one notable led to another.

Pritchard settled into a ritual for the next five years. He was working and the social machinery was in motion to keep him working. Regularly, he would go out to Catalina Island and there, he'd employ a couple of strapping locals to fairlead his manual compressor into a dory and row him out to a good spot at low tide. Having a full diving suit now gave him the time he needed to draw and it also kept him warmer in waters where, for him, the temperature would have been prohibitive.

Usually he placed a thirty foot limit on his dives. That way he could stay down as long as his tenders could crank the pump – often as long as two hours without decompression problems. Not an odder sight could have existed than Walter Pritchard as he sat on the sea floor off Catalina. He was encased in mankind's most grotesque anthropomorphic tribute to the machine age and yet he was engaged in one of mankind's most gentle pursuits – a brass and canvas monster stroking delicate lines on an easel. Enhancing this image, it's both pleasant and realistic to imagine him humming some Scottish ballad to accompany the droning hiss of air inside his helmet.

Occasionally, he painted with oils on canvas, but more often, his procedure started with the same materials he had developed for free diving. He would render a scene as tightly as he could in his oil point crayons, making additional sketches for detail on plants and fish. Each piece of paper – having the ungainly name of "double elephant" – was pre-mounted on its own sheet of glass. He then would take his crayon pictures back to the valley and recopy the entire scene onto a large sheet of leather which he had stretched like a canvas.

Although Pritchard's paintings were abundant with both hard and membraneous forms, he never neglected the liquid element itself. Viewers might have assumed that a seemingly transparent field required no imaging, but Pritchard painted water environments with the same diligence that he painted solids. Nothing ever looked "wet," but the presence of water was always felt. In more masterful landscapes, the air was present – its density always diffusing objects and muting colors depending on their distance. Pritchard knew that, regarding density, water was a magnification of air and its effect on undersea objects would likewise be magnified. No attempt was ever made to sharpen or refine images that were naturally softened. As a result, the inbuilt haze and delicate blur of his edges caused his work to resemble a pastel rather than a painting.

On the other hand, though his delineation of objects was soft, Pritchard wasn't beyond the occasional enhancement of color. In one sense it was cheating and in another way it wasn't. In real life, the colors were all there, but to the eye of a person underwater, they became progressively muted as their host objects receded into the background. This veil of the sea was employed in Pritchard's pictures, but his tendency was to be honest and forthright only about depth-of-field limitations and optical resolution. He would, however, compress his picture so that saturated colors were more consistently distributed regardless of distance. When he chose to introduce fish into the foreground, they were the epitome of this practice – an exercise in razor sharp clarity and even more brilliant with color. It was frequently the ruination of his already saturated backgrounds.

On a few occasions, Pritchard went back to Tahiti to wash his eyes with the tropical sea floor and accumulate new images. For the most part, though, he stayed close to home as his reputation quietly but definitely grew. His receptions and gallery shows were generating new friends who were entranced by his work and who then went out into the world to extol the virtues of Pritchard the Undersea Painter. On a visit, Jack London once commented, "Your beautiful work has made me homesick for the South Seas. Beautiful it is and full of wonder."[12] Later, John Burroughs, the naturalist, wrote to him, "These submarine views are positively enchanting. My seventh view of these pictures confirms my first impression. They show us a true wonder-world."[13]

Another of Pritchard's friends was David Starr Jordan, a noted ichthyologist, geologist, historian and Unitarian "prophet of democracy." Along with other diverse auguries, Jordan was telling the world about the future of aquatic resources; literally decades before the terms "aquaculture" and "mariculture" became popular. Reacting to Pritchard's work, he once said that, for the first time, he was seeing the undersea "as an intelligent and thoughtful ocean creature must see it."[14] – a statement that surely anticipates the emotional qualities attached to the scuba experience of later generations. Also a regular visitor was Charles Livingston Bull, one of the most highly regarded natural history illustrators of the day. Bull was an intrepid personality and wanted "beyond anything to go down with Pritchard and paint there (on the sea floor) with him."[15] Whether Pritchard ever extended an invitation is not known. He may have enjoyed his carefully fashioned exclusiveness too much to share it with another artist.

Finally, there was an acquaintance that was right in Pritchard's philosophical camp and whose involvements were at least as exotic and unorthodox as his own – Percival Lowell. This heir of a great Boston family had spent his young manhood and his familial money in Japan, writing about its art, religion, and occult. When he met Pritchard, however, he was completely dedicated to the possibility of life on Mars and was building the observatory at Flagstaff, Arizona to try proving it. It's easy to see why Pritchard's otherworldly scenes attracted Lowell since Lowell himself was in the otherworld business.

Around this time, Pritchard also developed two new and intriguing monikers – one acquired and one devised. In an article about Pritchard's work, Anthony Anderson, art critic for the *Los Angeles Times* and a founder of the Art Students League, repeatedly alluded to a poem by Tennyson entitled "The Merman" and later he affixed the title to Pritchard. From that time on, Pritchard was often referred to as simply "The Merman" and he enjoyed the pseudonym immensely. It reflected exactly what he felt he had become.

The second name was his own invention. Possibly, there was another Walter Pritchard circulating in the art world, but one day, the *diving* Walter Pritchard simply became "Zarh" Pritchard. The origin of the name is unclear. There are the approximations, Zared, Zarah, and Zara – all of Hebraic or Old

Testament origin, yet, strangely enough, all found in distant corners of England and Wales. Obscure origins aside, if Pritchard felt that his name had been confusing or commonplace, it certainly was commonplace no longer.

When 1912 arrived, Zarh Pritchard's life picked up momentum. In May, he received an ornate piece of paper that said he was now a citizen of the United States of America. Then, the seeds of all his painting and socializing seem to flower all at once – at least in the gardens of high society. The acceleration was due largely to two of his newest patrons: Miss Helen Gould and Mrs. Russell Sage, a widow. After having each purchased two of his undersea paintings in Pasadena, the exuberant ladies decided they would sponsor a whirlwind Eastern trip for the Merman. Actually, the tour would last well into the following year, but Pritchard assumed he could withstand one northeastern winter as long as the dampness did not equal London's levels.

It was mid-summer when Zarh took off for his first stop which was an exhibition in Evanston, Illinois. After that, he arrived in New York City, and, counting smaller sketches and crayon drawings as well as paintings, Pritchard had several hundred items to offer the public. He also carried his diving outfit along, occasionally putting it on display with the pictures. With Pritchard's work, it often helped stimulate the uninitiated to show them just how he gained access to his subjects.

As to the support of his hosts Gould and Sage, Henry Frick had once remarked, "Railroads are the Rembrandts of investment" and of those old masters, the women had many. Miss Gould and Mrs. Sage were both the beneficiaries of railroad manipulation and they were also neighbors in the residential display of wealth along Fifth Avenue. Each occupied a mansion on the lowest end of the "gold coast" – Mrs. Sage on the west side of the street and Miss Gould on the east.

Although the "Mauve Decade" was gone, the money in New York was definitely not. The conquest of Newport just made things a little less conspicuous in Manhattan. Zarh

Pritchard still got a healthy taste of all the extravagance he had heard about. After all, Pasadena was just a vacationing place. Although New York papers no longer covered the affairs of the rich by printing their guest lists and menus in full, society's "four hundred" were still throwing two hundred thousand dollar parties.

Baiting a gallery owner here or there, Pritchard helped as best he could with the wholesale dissipation of riches. He was still very much a Briton at a time when America's bluebloods loved emulating the British and it's quite possible, in fact, that his reception in the art community was a modest one whereas his social value to Mrs. Sage was much greater. Wealthy women stretched their wits to mount an entertaining ball and that necessitated having a few unusual guests. Conversations about painting under the ocean could have been useful in keeping people occupied.

Society aside, it was an interesting and inspiring time for an artist to be in Gotham. As the new year arrived, Pritchard desperately wanted a reputation in the art world beyond Fifth Avenue wealth. Outside of society, however, Pritchard's art wasn't the kind to attract widespread attention. Actually, in 1913, the majority of public awareness was focused on commercial illustrators like Maxfield Parrish, Charles Dana Gibson, and N.C. Wyeth. As to fine arts, the city was in an upheaval over the transitions taking place.

About the time Pritchard came to these shores, the United States was still being supplied with refined realism from Whistler, Sargent, Homer, and Eakins. But these men were now passing from the scene and the country was looking for something or someone to replace them. Later, just four years before Pritchard's New York pilgrimage, a controversial teacher named Robert Henri had fallen out with the National Academy of Design. With seven other artists – four of them ex-newspaper illustrators he had nursed into painting – he organized a controversial show that coined the name "Ashcan School." These robust natives, which included Sloan, Glackens, Luks and Prendergast, were all realists as well. But unlike their quiet and dignified predecessors, they dealt with bawdy street scenes, prize fights, or religious revivals – all the glorious insanity of

America-in-the-raw. Their now classic work wasn't accepted at first, but it drew much attention over the next few years. Ultimately, it helped establish day-to-day American life as a valid theme in American art.

Finally, at the very time that "Pritchard the Merman" was slipping in and out of drawing rooms and hawking his submarine pictures, there was another landmark event about to jostle the populace. It had started with Mabel Dodge, a wealthy lady who lived, not on upper Fifth Avenue, but down in Greenwich Village. She championed Freud, female suffrage, and modern painting and generally made a habit of telling the rest of the wealthy class to stuff it. Together with the mavericks from the "Ashcan School" she organized a colossal exhibit at the Sixty-Ninth Regiment Armory that went down in history as simply "the Armory Show." In all, there were twelve to sixteen hundred pieces by new and innovative American artists either of the "Ashcan's" persuasion or less orthodox still.

The highlight, however, was the first all-inclusive representation of late nineteenth and early twentieth century Parisian artists – Cézanne, Gauguin, Van Gogh, Picasso, Matisse and others. One look at all the cubism and expressionism and many citizens were ready to tear the Armory down. Enrico Caruso satirized the show with his own cartoons, newspapers flared up in outrage, and Teddy Roosevelt called the participants all "lunatics." Nevertheless, not too many years after the smoke had cleared, a point would be made that graphic beauty was not always in natural forms, but also in the exotic areas of the human mind.

Robert Henri preached the dramas of day-to-day life as a motive for painting, but Pritchard didn't paint that kind of life. The anti-establishment was challenging prevailing standards, but Pritchard didn't provoke anyone. The modern movement saw him as a simple landscape man, but the landscape people of Provincetown and New Hope couldn't easily relate to his world.

Between European-style realism, the new American realism, and finally the moderns, Pritchard had passed through three major periods of art in just nine years and not one of them could accommodate his work – not even J.H. Twacht-man's belated Impressionist school that had developed in America five years before his arrival. Being from California was only part of the problem. Being the only man in the world who painted what he painted – that was the problem.

In fact, being this particular only man almost excluded Pritchard from the whole of art history. As much as the world likes to see its artists as solitary people, artists are necessarily as social as anyone else and history finds it convenient to record them as such. They do work as individuals, but usually the *growth* of their work occurs in concert with their peers – the impressionist *school*, the realist *movement*, the New Hope *colony*. Ideas grow when artists socialize, but, even among the nature painters, Pritchard's work was considered anti-social. He shared no common frames of reference because few had seen his world, no one else had painted it, nor thought it worth painting.

Yet, though no movement – popular or unpopular – could include Zarh Pritchard in its ranks, he was still selling his paint-ings. His audience just wasn't extensive. The people who re-sponded emotionally to his paintings were of a naturalist bent. They saw his undersea as a cradle of life and could feel the bio-logical peacefulness that the work projected. The people who actually bought his paintings were the wealthy, and, whether or not they had emotional responses, their purchases were for other reasons – mostly decorative. For them, the Merman's paintings were "pleasing."

To a degree, there was justification in both responses – in the categories of either "naturalist painting" or "decorative painting." When he became "studied" in his approach – when sea creatures became a dominant element, then in fact, Prit-chard's pictures *were* nature studies. Then again, his work was design-profusive and when his creatures became part of the entire composition, one could often see the decorator instinct emerging. When he departed New York, the "naturalist" label had not quite taken hold, but he had definitely acquired the label of "decorative." Neither title would give him a place in history and although "decorative" was a suitable category for supplying the whims of the rich, it wasn't suitable to Pritchard when he felt he had exposed a whole new range of poetic feeling from a world beneath the ocean.

Regardless of which label he wore or how little he attracted the rest of the art world, Pritchard had a number of private showings that winter. In New York, February and March of 1913 were especially successful months, and just before the Armory Show, he had rewarding exhibits in Chicago and Boston, as well. After that, he passed back through Gotham to say goodbye to Miss Gould, Mrs. Sage and their friends and then he boarded a southbound train. Having heard that the continental United States possessed its own coral reefs, he headed down to the Florida Keys with his helmet, suit, and easel.

After his sojourn in the East, Pritchard went home to start developing some of the scenes he had rendered in Florida. But this time, as he settled-in with his "decorative paintings," a change began to take place – not in the artist, but in his clientele. Ranks of the landed gentry had started making room for a more serious group. Having lived off the bon ton crowd for five years, Pritchard was getting more attention from the scientific community. The term "decorative painter" would give way to "naturalist painter" – a label that, oddly, he would keep for the rest of his life, though he often maintained his fanciful techniques.

In a way, this turn of events was predictable. Although Pritchard was infrequently mentioned in art journals, the scientific and general interest publications had begun to pick up his story. Three years after the earthquake, *National Geographic* had given him mention, and later, as he left for New York, there was an article in the *Literary Digest*. Then, just before he departed New York, both the *Scientific American* and *Technical World* had come out with feature stories. Mrs. Russell Sage, who ultimately acquired six of his paintings, was also a factor. She had channeled a lot of money into higher education, and, even after Pritchard had left town, she was using her influence to develop his image.

The first upshot of all this publicity was a new exhibit in New York for September and October of 1913. Instead of a private gallery, however, it was held at the aquarium of the New York Zoological Society. Another lady, who no doubt helped swing the exhibit, was Ella C.B. Fassett. She had seen Pritchard's paintings some years before in Pasadena and she was now married to the director of the aquarium, Charles H. Townsend. The exhibit was a small affair, but it led to a much larger one three years later. Director Townsend would write of the show:

> You must have the field of submarine landscape and
> marine life all to yourself, as I know of no one else who
> has ever tried it. You are painting a world that artists
> know nothing about, and I believe portraying it faithfully
> . . . I shall be glad to talk to anyone you may send to
> the Aquarium while your wonderful pictures are on
> exhibition and hope you will not be in a hurry about
> taking them away.[16]

This second exhibit led to further ones and also sparked a number of lecture requests. In December of 1916, for instance, Pritchard gave a talk at the Scripps Institute and one official later replied:

> I have told you several times my notion that artists and
> scientists are really fellow workers in the interpretation
> of nature . . . talks like this of yours, about the methods
> and materials used by both artists and men of science are
> a high public service . . . I wish everyone in the United
> States could see your underwater pictures and hear you
> talk about making them."[17]

The public service aspect wasn't exactly what the Merman had in mind when he became an artist and the response – though well intentioned – was as clinical as any scientist could materialize. But it didn't mean that all scientists would overlook the poetic aspect of his painting. In fact, the most artistically gratifying statement Pritchard ever received was from a man of science who responded to his lecture and exhibit at the California Academy of Sciences the following December. In one short letter, an official of the Academy was able to crystallize the whole emotional and æsthetic reason for Pritchard's work – more than any artist, art critic, or wealthy patron could have ever done. The letter also hinted at Pritchard's eloquent facility with words.

My dear Pritchard:

It has been for many weeks my desire and purpose to try to tell you my pleasure in your paintings of the undersea. The memory of them lingers – a very distinct impression of the strange, subtle beauty of a realm little known.

The achievement has been not in painting the bottom of the sea, merely, but in conveying in so great a measure, a sense of its mystery and poetry. This you have done. One becomes conscious of its silence, its tranquility and utter remoteness from the everyday terrestrial.

One knows too that you were not only able to see, but to feel. And you have succeeded in telling what you feel – the rarest success in any effort or expression, whatever the means.

It is difficult to express my enjoyment and appreciation of your talk at the academy. Aside from the unusual character of the experiences you described, it was inter- esting and graphic to the highest degree. You do with words what you do with paint and I doubt if better could be said.

Truly, next to the interest there would be in having the actual experience was that of hearing you tell of yours; and while I was eager to hear the lecture, I'm yet more eager to hear it again – which I believe you will admit is a rather unusual frame of mind in regard to a lecture.

Seasonable greetings of the most cordial sort.

Sincerely,

Charles B. Hudson[18]

145

Pritchard's ascent into scientific circles wasn't the only change. In the summer of 1915 – a year before his second New York Aquarium exhibit and the resulting lectures – the mammoth Pan-Pacific International Exposition was running at full pace in San Francisco. The city had rebuilt itself and local business wanted to show other capitalists that the earth didn't really move around that often and that it was quite alright to invest there. In the California pavilions, although there were some sixty-five artists represented, they all bore the strict responsibility of telling visitors what the West was all about. Also, in contrast to something like the Armory Show, the forces at work in San Francisco wanted "internationally palatable" pictures and they certainly got them. Titles read: "Monterey's Blue Bay," "Fisherman's Quay," or "Tree and Seashore" – all harbingers of a tourist economy to come.

The directors, no doubt, assumed there was no percentage in showing California's underwater side, so Pritchard wasn't hanging in the exposition. But it was no matter. Like so many other artists and craftsmen, he set up a temporary studio-gallery to entice the overflow crowds in the city. That included an overflow of dignitaries.

One afternoon in July, the studio was suddenly and coincidentally occupied by two influential gentlemen. One was Jiro Harada, Japan's commissioner to the exposition. The second was none other than Jean Guiffrey, Curator of the Musée de Louvre. Guiffrey waltzed around the place uttering all sorts of astonished reactions. He concluded his visit by asking Pritchard to come to Paris and show his people ". . . all the beauties of a new domain – incomparable through its grandeur and the force of its colorings."

Harada had his own favorable impressions. But in a letter to Pritchard, he only described how he perceived Guiffrey's reactions. This was important for Harada because he was going back to Japan to make recommendations to his government on future exhibits of Western art. For Pritchard's sake, he couldn't have had a better endorsement than Jean Guiffrey. That afternoon in San Francisco finally added "international" to the Merman's status of "naturalist." Harada and Guiffrey departed for their respective homes – each in the opposite direction – and the name of Zarh Pritchard, the world's first undersea painter, was simultaneously carried east and west.

The first tangible result was from Harada. In 1919, Pritchard toured Japan with his work, giving lectures at each opening. Japan was one place where the design consciousness of his paintings certainly didn't alienate him from the art community. Æsthetic Nippon was deeply impressed by his work and Pritchard repeated the performance a year later. Between the cities of Tokyo, Yokohama, and Osaka, he sold over sixty paintings, and, as in the United States, his patrons were from the upper reaches of society – including the crown prince, Fushimi. Later, Harada authored a review in which he verbalized an Asian's response to the tranquility in Pritchard's paintings – and also alluded to a world crisis which, even then, was in its incubation:

> In this age of turmoil and confusion in which unrest
> is as rife in the art world as in political and economic life,
> the work of Zarh Pritchard deserves to be more widely
> known. For in his paintings are to be found that tranquil
> peace and soothing restfulness of which the world is in
> so much need today. And this peace and restfulness arises
> not merely from the negation of all those worldly actu-
> alities which are the cause of the turmoil, but from a
> positive revelation of an unknown world of beauty that
> quickens the imagination and stimulates it to wander
> in the spiritual realm.

About the spiritual aspect, he was quite serious. As an example, when Mokusen Zenji, one of Japan's most revered Buddhist priests, heard Pritchard speak on the physical and optical sensations when underwater, he exclaimed "Those are the experiences in the realm between life and death of which the founder of the Soto sect of Zen writes." Harada continues:

> What an amazing world of utter silence, in which noth-
> ing gives the impression of being wet, self-contradictory

147

though it may sound. What marvellous iridescence of
specks of colour through which gleam myriads of fishes
disporting themselves with exquisite grace among the
brilliant-hued coral growth. What a world of colours,
the brightest and deepest of which melt into the illusive
harmony of an ethereal music in the silence of night –
the colours not to be seen, nor the music to be heard,
but both to be felt, rather, in the soul.[19]

It seems as though no one had difficulty being poetic
about what they saw and felt in Pritchard's paintings. There
is no record of Jean Guiffrey getting that verbose, but, like
Harada, he was sincere about the visitation. By 1921, after
Pritchard's second tour of Japan, Guiffrey had arranged an
exhibit for him at the posh Galeries Georges Petit in Paris. The
show opened in July and the resulting success was a near dupli-
cation of what had happened in Japan. His purchasers were of
the same drawing room variety and included four members
of royalty; industrialists like Henri Guerlin, the perfume king;
and also a few "statesiders" like Mrs. George Plimpton and
Mrs. W.K. Vanderbilt.

The crowning achievement, however, was the sale of
eleven paintings to Albert I of Monaco. Albert spent practically
the whole of his rule on the sea. He was known as the "oceanographic prince," and, when there wasn't a street lamp to repair
or a police payroll to meet, he saw to it that the profits of the
Monte Carlo casinos were regularly funnelled into the ocean.
With all that gambling money, he hosted scientists aboard his
research ship, built two marine research facilities, and was now
furnishing his famous oceanographic museum. Pritchard's pictures were to hang as part of the museum's permanent exhibit.

This was really Pritchard's first "institutional sale" but it
certainly would not be his last. The Paris show initiated a chain
reaction. Taking her acquisition home to New York, Mrs.
Vanderbilt then infected Arthur Curtiss James with her enthusiasm and James purchased two paintings. The significance lay
in the fact that James was a trustee and benefactor of the
American Museum of Natural History, and more importantly,
he was also on a committee for the design, construction, and

furnishing of the immense Hall of Ocean Life. This new wing was to be a veritable cathedral to the glory of the sea – the largest exhibit hall of its kind in the world. It had already been in progress for some fifteen years and the public would have to wait still another ten years before they would ever see it. However, this didn't stop the committee from stockpiling everything they wanted to exhibit, and soon the museum's director, F.A. Lucas, was looking for subscriptions to buy a dozen of Pritchard's paintings. Pritchard's old friend from the New York Aquarium, C.W. Townsend, also helped move the deal along, for he was on the museum's committee as well. Describing Pritchard's evolution, Lucas closed a letter to sponsors by saying:

> The wonderful views of coral arches and marine growths
> which were thus opened to his eyes and perpetuated for
> the first time upon canvas have been seen heretofore
> only by divers. A series of these paintings, installed in
> this Museum, would bring the beauties of these sub-
> marine vistas of coral architecture vividly to the eyes
> of thousands of visitors.[20]

The Merman's star was in ascent. He toured Latin America in 1922, and three years later, during his second Paris exhibit, the French government bought a number of his paintings for the Luxembourg Museum. They were followed by the Cleveland Museum of Natural History which obtained nine of his pictures. Then the Carnegie Museum in Pittsburgh and the Boston Museum of Fine Arts each acquired one for their permanent collections.

Terrestrial society was finally starting to recognize Zarh Pritchard – an artist committed to paint his undersea part of the world regardless of the art forms that prevailed on land.

In the early twenties, as Pritchard's art was gaining world-wide recognition, another related personality emerged into the public eye. He was a scientist – originally a student of birdlife and jungle environments – who had gravitated to the sea and was fast becoming its great popularizer. His name was William Beebe.

More than a decade before his famous bathysphere dives with Otis Barton, Beebe was already well-known through his lectures, films, and articles. But when he published *Galapagos, World's End* in 1924, the book started to popularize the image of a marine scientist, and for him, it launched an entire series of best sellers. Following Pritchard's second Paris exhibit, Beebe came out with *The Arcturus Adventure* (1926) wherein he devoted a whole chapter to his experience beneath the surface in a bucket helmet and that, in turn, refined his image into Beebe the undersea explorer. That undersea image was then fully solidified two years later with *Beneath Tropic Seas*, for the entire book was based on bucket helmet adventures in the waters off Haiti.

It was a fortuitous – and fortunate – year for the book to come out since 1928 also saw the publication of Edward Ellsberg's epic documentary of his salvage of the "S-51," *On The Bottom*, a best seller which launched Ellsberg's own series of books about diving – from the viewpoint of a Navy salvor rather than a biologist. That disparity wasn't important, however. The fires of undersea awareness were once again being fanned for the benefit of those who needed them. That included both Beebe and Ellsberg the writers, Pritchard the painter, and all the scholars trying to wrangle funds for research projects and museum exhibits.

In that sense, Pritchard and Beebe were kindred souls. As Pritchard had made an art of tapping the social register for his exhibits, so likewise did Beebe habitually and successfully romance the wealthy into sponsoring his expeditions. The New York Zoological Society was both his calling card and his sanctuary; it was for Charles Townsend as well, and through the good aquarium director, Beebe and Pritchard became close friends. Before long, there was a donation by the Merman hanging in Beebe's office and likewise an adulatory paragraph on Pritchard in *Beneath Tropic Seas* – and in the deluxe edition, a questionable reproduction of one of Pritchard's pictures.

Naturally, this subaqueous back scratching helped everybody make a living. Symbiosis promoted the field of endeavor

– as well as personal goals. But though it was eminently practical, it also represented a very genuine love and respect for each other's work. Writing of the sensations he experienced in Pritchard's paintings, Beebe wrote him in August of 1923:

> A number of things in this world are remarkable for some one character, such as rarity or beauty, but almost never is any one thing noted for two superlatives. Your pictures are one of these very unusual things; their inception and execution being carried out in such an astounding place and method, and the abstract beauty, wholly apart from the submarine idea, puts them, in my estimation, in the realm of things which come to one only once in a lifetime.
>
> The picture which I own is redemanding appreciation each day for new reasons, and although I have been trained throughout my life to see and observe quickly, yet time after time I detect new subtle forms, tints, and qualities which had evaded me heretofore.
>
> I hope that no opportunity will pass for your pictures to be given permanent public exhibition in museums or wherever people may be made happier by seeing them.[21]

The admiration was a case of two men who shared a lifetime love for the undersea, and who, at the time, were among a select few humans on earth who had enjoyed the privilege of seeing its mystery and beauty firsthand. Beebe was so captivated by the submarine world that, in one book, he urged his readers not to leave this earthly existence without having begged, stolen or crafted some kind of diving device to see what he regarded as the most wondrous place on earth.

As the only suitable alternative, he asked them to seek out the paintings of Zarh Pritchard.

In the spring of 1926, Pritchard got a sort of returning hero's welcome in Pasadena. It was in the form of a large exhibit at the prestigious Grace Nicholson Galleries – founded in 1901, a date, by California standards, that made it fairly old and venerable. The following year, he trekked back to the Florida Keys to dive and paint his way through the winter months and prepare for a new European tour. As he was riding the wave of undersea interest, however, some unsettling adaptations of his work emerged. It wasn't in the world of fine or naturalist painting, but in his old province of decorative arts, and the stuff was terrible.

One of the more garish contributions to interior design emerged – the subaqueous bathroom. The room assaulted the occupant with intense, creamy enamel as huge conch shells and sea fans patterned the walls and angel fish swam across the shower curtain. To this day, the residue of that period still haunts the far corners of curio stores around the world. Shamefully, its origins were even inspired by Zarh Pritchard's work.

The basic idea, of course, was as old as the Greeks. They, too, put their ocean motifs in places that utilized the most water. Then, centuries later, when the filigree and varnished woods of Victoriana started to go out of fashion, designers decided that Poseidon's realm should recapture the lavatory. It may have quickly evolved into proletariat junk, but the ideas were actually developed for some of the more affluent apartment settings of New York City in the mid-twenties.

A similar movement had started in France around 1910, but the French had a more refined approach. The first to popularize the new use of ocean motifs was an artist-designer team named Méheut and Verneuil. Méheut was an absolute master at sketching individual sea plants, invertebrates, and shellfish – from all angles and with quite a loving flourish instead of in a static, encyclopedic fashion. Verneuil would then translate those sketches into intricate and multiple patterns – extracting every design quality the sea life offered. His patterns were as studiously worked out as a Renaissance tapestry, and by 1914, their work was being applied to screens, fabrics, wallpaper and issued in catalogs by Robillot of Paris. Following the lead were relief sculptors Jallot and Benedictus and ceramicists Groendahl and Galle. These people were even more delicate in their approach. Their creations were fine extensions of deco-age thinking and could be comfortably placed anywhere in the home.

More than a decade later, however, American decorators took the ocean consciousness and headed straight for the bathroom where they presumed to make their statements as large and loud as possible. The hack muralists, especially, took what they saw in Pritchard's paintings (and Beebe's and Longley's photographs) and splashed it on the wall without any forethought for modest adaptation. The poetic underseascape acquired the subtleties of a circus wagon.

By 1927, Beebe was lecturing everywhere from flower clubs to dental conventions, and the theme of the undersea world was starting to permeate many avenues of domestic life. As an example, Dr. Beebe authored an article in *House and Garden Magazine* dealing with current decorator inspirations taken from the ocean's floor. Pritchard's work was prominently displayed as were some of the tasteful screen and wallpaper creations from France. But it was necessary for Beebe to be all-inclusive and the tacky interpreters were also featured, including new arrivals Harry Hoffman and Katherine Van Cortlandt, who painted the undersea in the style of grade school children. Beebe was condescending but quick to point out that, although some of the colors and delineations were "accurate," they were "unsoftened by the pastel film of aquatic perspective."[22] It was as firm a statement as he could afford and still sound enthusiastic about the "movement." Frederick Church was mentioned, as was C.C. Holden, whose work had graphic impact, but needed a ceramic ship and a bed of marbles to make it complete.

For his own particular purposes, Beebe might have accepted the value of anything that extended ocean awareness. Pritchard, on the other hand, rather wished the whole craze hadn't occurred. For him, it cheapened the imagery of a world he had worked so hard to convey.

One evening in July of 1928, Zarh Pritchard slipped aboard a trans-Atlantic liner to commence a long stay in Europe. The schedule included some helmet diving around his old haunts in Scotland as well as arranging gallery exhibits in London. Somewhere along the way, a reporter cornered him with a question about his art to which Pritchard snapped, "I am not an artist at all. I am a naturalist who happens to be a painter."[23]

In his own mind, the Merman had evidently made a firm commitment to that label. Perhaps it was by choice, but more than likely he was forced into it by obvious necessity – and perhaps with a degree of resentment. Regardless of all the poor practitioners who were loose on the public, the popularizing of undersea art forms continued. Inevitably, it then made inroads into the exclusiveness of Pritchard's painting and, in the eyes of some, his work had bordered on being fine art only as long as it was a novelty. That attitude wasn't well founded because, unless he was detailing fishes, Pritchard's broader panoramas were delicately elusive and haunting compositions that reflected as much mood as any impressionist landscape.

Nevertheless, a lot of those qualities were being overlooked in the shuffle and it's possible that Pritchard felt he could counter the shabbiness of his imitators by, reluctantly, adhering even more to biological details. In a feature magazine article, this paragraph seemed much too bitterly emphatic not to have come straight from the artist's mouth:

> Exactitude is what Mr. Pritchard has sought. He has not attempted to produce art, but to reproduce nature. If people want to think his paintings artistic, they need not tell him about it. Once, when he was young, he aspired to be an artist but the critics condemned his efforts and he changed his vocation. He has never since dreamed of art. He has remained a painter, but he has become a scientific naturalist.[23]

In fact, this was really quite a turnabout from the image Pritchard had sought more than two decades before. It certainly sounded as though the title of naturalist was resentfully, rather than joyfully, accepted. Nevertheless, he continued to paint, exhibit, and sell his work while in Europe, and he had a significant showing at London's Arlington Gallery in 1930.

There were modest exhibits after that, but the next one of any size was at the Arthur Newton Galleries in New York some five years later. Whether the show was successful or not, for Pritchard there was something both significant and foreboding about that particular winter in the big city. More events had occurred to further intensify undersea interest. Beebe and Otis Barton had descended in their bathysphere while Pritchard was in London and they went on to exceed two thousand feet just two years after that. True to form, Beebe wrote a book about it and as a consequence, new scholars were drawn to the ocean sciences. New artists were drawn as well and this time they were significantly better than the hack decorators who had preceded them – some may have said, "better," even, than Zarh Pritchard.

Interestingly enough, just a month after Pritchard's December showing in Manhattan, there had been a landmark exhibit of natural history artists at the Brooklyn Museum and it gave special emphasis to ocean life. Curators and department heads from all over had lent pieces from their own museums and Charles Townsend was one of them. In addition to other sea related pictures, there were beautifully detailed fish studies by Charles Knight, Olive Earle, and Hashime Murayama. To top it off, there were also some undersea scenes that were quite good – so convincing, in fact, that viewers assumed that the artist had descended in a diving suit for both his information and his inspiration. But the painter wasn't an Irishman – he was Norwegian – a former illustrator of Norwegian literature named Chris Olsen. Either by personal choice or someone else's, Zarh Pritchard, the Impressionist, the originator of undersea painting, was not represented in the show.

After that, his last recorded exhibit was back in Pasadena in 1937 – once again, at the Nicholson gallery. Whether or not the newspaper or its source of information was to be believed, the *Los Angeles Times* had the old Merman still going down below the waves to paint the works that were on exhibit. It was a wonderful image to entertain because, by then, Pritchard was seventy-one years old. Not until he was middle-aged had he rediscovered his boyhood love of the undersea world and yet he had lived to paint that world for at least thirty more years.

Even if Zarh Pritchard had put away his helmet and easel ten years earlier, the number of his paintings and their dispersal over the world would have been impressive. By 1926, more than 150 of his underseascapes graced homes in London, Paris, Tokyo, Honolulu, and Rio de Janeiro alone. Moreover, along with dukes, barons, marquises, and comtesses – and other lesser royalty – he claimed as patrons Queen Mary (of Great Britain), Prince Albert of Monaco and the royal heirs of Japan and Great Britain. In the United States, he had enjoyed as clients almost every name in the social register including the Mellons of Pittsburgh, the Vanderbilts of New York, Armours and Swifts in Chicago, and Crockers and Sutros of San Francisco. Museums in New York, Boston, Cleveland, Pittsburgh, Paris, and Monaco had at one time or another acquired Pritchard's work for their permanent collections. If all that wasn't enough to give him some notoriety, he was the subject of feature articles in dozens of magazines such as *The Literary Digest*, *Scientific American*, and *London Illustrated*, and he lectured at institutions around the world. His work was praised by authors, dramatists, academicians and even a few men of art.

Of course, patronage of neither royalty nor the wealthy is a barometer of merit. Taken by themselves, neither is geographic dispersal, quantities sold, museum purchases, or journalistic recognition. But all of these facts combined must, at the very least, say that the man occupied a place in the world of art. Whether he is to be considered a decorative painter, or a naturalist painter, or an Impressionist, historically speaking, Pritchard had to be one of the most unusual artists to have ever lived – if for no other reason than because he was the first of his kind, and because, rather than resting on that novelty, he produced conscientious work. His paintings recreated the moods of the undersea – not just the forms borrowed from it.

This point is emphasized because almost no mention is made of Pritchard in most modern art reference works. One of his London exhibits in 1930 is noted in a British directory. And in an old volume of *Mallet's Index* (and a corresponding cross reference in *Art Digest*'s INDEX of the same year) there is a listing of his 1935 gallery show in Manhattan. There is also a capsule description of him in Nancy Moure's herculean project, the *Dictionary of Art and Artists in Southern California*.

Excepting these three directories, as of 1993 there is not one mention of Zarh Pritchard in any of the dozens of art reference works in the United States – not even in the voluminous *Index to Artistic Biography*, *American Art Annual*, or *Who's Who in American Art*; nor in the Spooner's, Strickland's, Fielding's, or Benezit Dictionaries.

This dearth of information is due to the reliance of these reference works on abstracts of articles in art journals. For the most part, Pritchard was ignored by the art community, and except for a handful of smaller art magazines, he was rarely written about by art editors, either during his lifetime or afterwards. They simply couldn't identify with his world, and most likely, since it was so inaccessible to the average person, they assumed no one else should try identifying with it either. Even if this was a prudent decision, it raises questions about the value of art and how it should relate to the familiar.

Pritchard wasn't a visionary. He was simply an artist who gained access to a certain visual and physical experience in advance of most others and tried to communicate his feelings about it. He made a living because he didn't have to sell either a familiar world or the human condition to his patrons. They bought his art because they thought it was pretty. Had aqualungers and mass air travel existed at that time, the art establishment might have realized something in his pictures that did, in fact, relate to human experience – man's long-suppressed aquatic temperament. Technique or æsthetics aside, they might then have validated his work as fine painting.

Regardless of the art community, as a naturalist painter, Pritchard was a pioneer. He genuinely, and with some expertise, calculated to increase the normal level of identification with the sea and the world beneath it. He selected imagery from a particular place and manipulated it to enhance a feeling for life there. If nothing else, his ichthyological studies alone might rank him as the submarine counterpart to Audubon – he was the first artist in western culture to paint undersea life as suspended in, and interacting with, its own environment.

When he wasn't being a nature painter – when he broke away from studied executions and painted the broad underseascape that he loved so much – then Zarh Pritchard was nothing short of an impressionist. His pictures then comprised the very elements that make, for instance, a Monet: the image as immediately perceived through values instead of details. And the translations were true. They were soft and misty and constructed from a collective gathering of light rather than from sharp delineations. More importantly, they spoke of man's affinity for interiors and secret places, the psychic restfulness of life in immersion, and the long ignored vestigial attachments to our watery place of origin.

These were the elements of the undersea that Pritchard loved most. But long ago – before scuba gear or sea-scooters or habitats – Pritchard had his own words for it.

> It is a dream world in which everything is enveloped
> in soft sheen. On reaching bottom, it is as if one were
> temporarily resting on a dissolving fragment of some
> far planet. Nowhere does substance appear beyond the
> middle distance and material forms insensibly vanish
> into the veils of surrounding color. There is no visible
> flowing of water, no rushing of streams, tides or waves;
> there is audible no babbling of brooks, no pounding of
> the mighty sea – [which is] all a part of one's ordinary
> conception of water. Here one glides rather than jerks
> oneself about as on earth; here every motion is gentle
> and perfectly poised; here the shoals of fishes move
> with lightning speed in a medium as smooth as oil.[8]

Pritchard painted the undersea exactly the way he spoke of it – with total reverence. Once, long ago, Eugene Delacroix said, "I must think about getting a palette that could be put into water." He never got around to it but a hundred years later, Phillip Diole stated that the world would need a Delacroix to determine whether the undersea could give birth to new revelations in art.

Diole is a thoughtful writer; but, in this case, he could have struck a more correlative reference. We may not have had a *Delacroix* of the undersea; we most certainly, however, had a *Monet* – and his name was Zarh Pritchard.

It appears likely that Zarh Pritchard remained a bachelor all of his life and left no family, either in the United States or in Great Britain. The place where his home stood in Pasadena is now occupied by a parking lot. The State of California has no record of his death and this author has been unsuccessful in locating anyone who ever knew him. Late in his life, Pritchard built a cabin near Bishop, California, which was later sold to photographer Curtis Phillips and, later still, destroyed in a fire. Phillips' brother once recalled that Pritchard – despite his ailments – returned to England just prior to World War II. Other reports have him spending his last days in the American Southwest.

The locations of his paintings and sketches are difficult to trace. Within twenty years of the American Museum of Natural History opening its Hall of Ocean Life, the exhibition's approach was outdated and it was then restructured to more contemporary standards. For decades, thirteen of Pritchard's works lay in the memorabilia storage room of that great romanesque building. They can be viewed today through prior arrangement with the museum's library. Through similar arrangements, twelve paintings can be seen at the Cleveland Museum of Natural History. The art in Cleveland suggests the immediacy of pictures painted underwater, while in New York, it has the studied quality of studio work.

Pritchard's paintings are strange phenomena in whatever category art historians may place them. He descended to a land engulfed in monotones; yet, once there, he transposed the bright prismatics of the surface world and he often fearlessly redesigned the shapes and forms to suit his fancy. Often, he used the environment to satisfy his decorative impulse; a trait not unlike some Impressionists who abstracted color and form expressively and not representatively. Contrary to the journalists, Zarh Pritchard, in later years, most likely fed from his memories and sketches; imaging on land far more often than in the ocean. By then, paintings depicting Tahiti were signed and dated in Rio de Janeiro. Others depicting Scotland were signed in Bishop.

Just as his clientele were amazing, so were the prices they paid: in some cases between two and three thousand dollars. It was impressive remuneration for *any* artist at that time and it's possible that Pritchard's travels, lectures, socializing, and charisma were as much the guide of his worth as was his art. But then, how different might that be from the protocol and the patronage of our own time?

Whatever promotional dynamics are in place in the art world today, one has the feeling "The Merman" would heartily approve of all of them.

The Brothers Who Made Undersea Films

(1913–1932)

JOHN ERNEST AND GEORGE MAURICE WILLIAMSON WERE children of the maritimes as much as children could ever be. Short of having stowed away on a spice schooner, both grew up with more nautical stereotypes than one finds in a mariner's songbook.

They were born in Liverpool in the late nineteenth century. The progeny of a clipper ship captain, they could easily date their respective conceptions by using his log books. The Captain was never in port long enough to make the matter confusing.

When they were still young fellows, the Captain relocated the family to Norfolk, Virginia, where he capitalized on the boom in grain and cattle shipping outbound for Europe. Williamson's new yard partitioned the holds of vessels and equipped the grain ships with wing feeders, which channeled the grain to lower compartments as the ship labored at sea. This balanced the load and kept the ship from turning over in a storm.

Ernie and George worked after school in the Captain's yard and spent summer days playing water tag around the moorings, using the anchor chains as home base. After dinner they were usually found in the dining room listening to some half-crocked shipmaster romanticize his travails at sea. If the evening's guest happened to be "standing out," little George got the dubious privilege of rowing the old croaker back to his command – and, no doubt, listening to the rest of his half-truths along the way.

When they each got out of school at sixteen, they were off to a prearranged apprenticeship at the Newport News Shipyards – not by the Captain's request, but by his order. Between the two of them, this translated into many years of pattern shops, moulding lofts, foundries, and drafting rooms. To be sure, there was a robust quality to working in the yards, but the romance of the sea was hard to contemplate – especially if, all about you, men were throwing rivets or hammering steel plates into places they didn't want to go.

Victoria's influence was gone. People were riding around in trains and planes and cars and, generally speaking, there was an enticing society on the horizon. George and Ernie knew they weren't going to see the benefits of that society working in shipyards.

In reality, George had always been intrigued with the more grandiose forms of free enterprise. He fancied himself becoming a financier or a promoter. Ernie had a good pair of hands at the drafting board, but after years of penciling every piece of metal required to build a ship, he dearly wanted to follow the siren call of the printing arts and become a commercial artist.

As it happened later, they both were able to make an exodus from the shipyards, and land, of all places, in Denver, Colorado – a significant distance from the great Atlantic Ocean. George's liberation came in the form of a family task, having shuttled his little sister and her tuberculate husband out for the recuperative climate. Ernie then threw down his protractor, came out as well, and entered Reed's night school for aspiring artists. In the daytime, both of them turned a buck at the Colorado Iron Works, which was instinctive for two experienced pattern makers.

Later on, when Ernie had drawn quite enough apples, nudes, and pyramids, his recollections of the seaboard lured him back to Norfolk. George, on the other hand, had developed a boarding house romance. He wasn't as quick to think of coastal icons – except one of the shipyards, which wasn't at all appealing. They parted with Ernie promising he'd give a yell if any grand schemes arose and George promised that he'd respond by hopping the next train east.

A few seasons passed, and when the spring of 1913 came around, George was still domiciled in Denver, selling sheet music, and taking life on a day to day basis. Ernie was five years into his transition, having landed jobs as a cartoonist and photographer for the *Philadelphia Record*, and later, Norfolk's daily paper, *The Virginian Pilot*.

Time and tide just might have allowed the brothers to pass comfortably through life at three knots – having some vague and unresolved identity with the sea – had it not been for two inventions. Neither one was their creation, but when combined, they gave the Williamsons worldwide notoriety for a brief moment in the history of undersea quests – and the history of cinema.

During all the water-logged years of rounding Capes Good Hope, Hatteras, or Saint Vincent, Captain Charles Williamson was never content to pour over charts or suck on his pipe.

The fact was that in good weather, running his ships was a second nature involvement, and it left him large pockets of time to be a compulsive, machine-age tinkerer. Whenever his lines landed at Norfolk, the family stood waiting to see the Captain's newest gadget for tapping a buck out of the industrial revolution.

Over the years, the results of all that shipboard inventiveness had come forth in the form of a folding baby carriage, an automated picture projector and an electric ship's signalling device. There was once even an inverted golf game that was played on the ceiling with balloons.

Around 1908, the Captain built an underwater repair and observation chamber to be used in conjunction with his shipfitting operation. The chamber itself wasn't anything new. Like many previous chambers, it was a cylindrical, cast iron affair weighing about four tons and having a set of view ports. But, in this case, the ports were incorporated into a protrusion on the side of the bell that took the shape of an oversized diving helmet. Accordingly, the chamber had no hatchway leading to the water outside. Instead it had armholes which, in turn, accommodated a pair of sealed hands and sleeves of flexible material and were attached to the chamber by a gasket.

Since the chamber air wasn't pressurized, the worker

inside got a good healthy squeeze on his arms and hands because of the water pressure on the outside. Even though he shoved his appendages into the sleeves before being lowered, the squeeze would start forcing them inward after so many feet. This idea, and its attendant discomfort, preceded Captain Williamson by about two hundred years and like those earlier efforts, it fell to the superiority of the pressurized diving *suit*.

What was workable, however – and genuinely unique in man's never ending quest to get himself drowned – was a vertical, collapsible "hole in the sea" that led to the chamber. It looked like the result of a standpipe having mated with an accordion, and being open-ended at the surface, it permitted free access of men and surface air to the other end below. Ironically, unlike the chamber sleeves, the design of this vertical tunnel reflected much forethought regarding the laws of water pressure. It was strong enough to hold back the tremendous pressure, yet flexible enough to bend like a serpent with the currents. It was as long as it needed to be for observation, up to 60 feet, yet as short as they wanted when hauled topside and stored. Nothing like it had been built before and nothing like it has existed since, and, as is always the case with the brainchildren of earlier mechanical engineers, the most unimaginative thing about it was its name. It was formally and simply denominated "The Williamson Submarine Tube."

The tube, three feet in diameter, was not a telescoping contrivance or even a fully collapsible one in the strict sense. Rather, it was a marvelous annulated arrangement that was quickly assembled or disassembled in sections of varying length. Each tubular section was made up of overlapping steel scales or plates hinged together all the way around and terminating in flanged iron rims top and bottom. The plates opened along radial lines to the axis of the tube and closed under the pressure of the water. Then, permanently fitted to the outside of each section was a vulcanized canvas sleeve that insured watertightness. A gasket and a handful of bolts secured one section to another and so it was repeated down the line.

The barge that played host to this contraption had a well through which the top of the tube extended and the raising and lowering of the workers was controlled. A chain was attached to the chamber and run up to a chain hoist on deck, which, in turn, altered the elevation of the chamber according to the instructions of the men below. A second chain was attached to the topmost flange of the topmost section. The apparatus could, at the end of an observation job, be lifted to the surface, exposing the vertical shaft and permitting it to rise through a housing that was built around the well. As the tube came up, each section was secured by the second chain and the preceding section unbolted and stored away; nothing could have been simpler.

Once it was out of the water, one can understand why the Captain wanted to minimize the tube's displacement. But there was also his meticulous engineering to achieve more flexibility, and if it seems excessive, one must keep in mind that moving around was a big part of the concept. A rigid and heavy tube dragged through the sea by its supporting ship would have inevitably been torn away from the vessel by leverage and resistance in the opposing mass of water.

Records indicate that Charles Williamson worked on perfecting his "hole in the sea" for possibly a decade or more. Surely much of his spare-time-genius was thrown into it, because it had still another impressive design property to consider: because of the unique system of hinged steel plates, its sections would stretch apart or flatten together with the relative depth and pressure; some sections compressing from eight feet to three feet. As the tube got longer and deeper, it became compressed and heavier at its lower end. With the displacement of its sections growing ever less, it not only forced the tube downward, but it automatically straightened and balanced the bell even though the upper end was being flexed by the motion of the barge.

Captain Williamson had created an easy passageway to the bottom of the harbor, but, since his chamber didn't work the way he intended, he could do nothing but look around once he was down there. For a man who viewed the sea as a dollars and cents proposition, the rig wasn't of much use except to direct an occasional grapnel job. Williamson's "hole in the sea" would ultimately fall into younger hands for its practical deliverance – one that had nothing to do with salving junk from Norfolk's sea bed.

Although the government had tested the tube and a friend of Williamson had wrangled a cover story in the April, 1908, *Scientific American*, nobody jumped to duplicate the thing. Salvage and ship repair firms didn't need such a cumbersome arrangement just to see under the water.

Five years later, the Captain's iron and canvas monster was lying around the yards developing a nice patina and being a dockside curiosity. It would have stayed that way had it not been for a drama that was unfolding some three hundred miles to the north in New York City. There, a dirty little business was becoming both mammoth and respectable overnight.

Thomas A. Edison, the wholesome backyard scientist and national hero, had transformed into a vengeful old man with respect to his motion picture patents. In the twenty years since he had invented the medium, the proliferation of his competitors made him increasingly resentful, and so, in 1909, he had formed a trust called the Motion Picture Patents Company. It enabled him to enforce a monopoly over movie production in America. He had even created a subsidiary called the General Film Company to extend his monopoly to the distribution of films. This left the country's other producers and distributors the choice of either joining Edison or closing shop.

A good many firms took the peaceful route and signed up with the trust. Literally hundreds of others moved to the relative safety of a farming community called Los Angeles. There they could have more frequent sunshine and the Mexican border in case Edison should sick the cops on them.

But the industry had attracted many clever and ambitious immigrants like Adolph Zukor and William Fox who had no intention of being closed out of this goldmine. They continued in their buccaneer productions and the Patents Company countered by cutting off shipments to any movie house that accepted bootlegged reels. Then equipment became unavailable and had to be smuggled in from Europe. Mysterious accidents occurred, films were destroyed by arson, and thugs appeared to send independent crews and actors to the emergency wards.

The whole thing was getting very rough, but with the help of exhibitors who resented Edison's tactics, the independents succeeded in circumventing the traps he laid. Ultimately, they launched an aggressive attack in the courts in Manhattan.

By January of 1913, they had enlisted the aid of government lawyers and initiated the case of *United States* v. *the Patents Company*. Although the trial was to drag on for some time, its very existence was a de facto declaration that the trust had been busted by the sheer growth of the industry. Hundreds of new firms were being incorporated in anticipation of a decision favorable to the independents.

As a declaration of their forthcoming liberty – and as a way to show the community how expansive and diversified they were, a first Annual Exposition of Motion Picture inventors, manufacturers and producers was organized for July.

As news of these events came filtering down to Norfolk via *The Virginian Pilot*, something must have started incubating in Ernie's head. He didn't quite know how to relate motion pictures to his present station in life, but he did know that this business would grow to become one of the largest in the country within just a few years and it was all going to happen right under his nose. He and many other future entrepreneurs would do some radical and imaginative thinking over the next few weeks as publicity mounted out of New York.

Before it hit the courts, the raucous and precarious film business was something no clean-cut, Southern gentleman of seafaring stock would think of pursuing, and no conservative, Southern businessman would think of backing. But with a legal victory over Edison that seemed imminent and a bonafide public exposition about to begin, a new and respectable movie industry was opening its doors to the enterprising of the world – and John Ernest and George Maurice Williamson would not be left out.

One day as the summer was descending, Ernie went into a barbershop and prepared for the heat by getting his blond locks removed. He passed this boring ritual with a copy of the

London Illustrated News – the same sensationalist publication that had featured so many sea serpent and submarine stories in the last century.

As it happened, there was an article about Zarh Pritchard. There was still another about a gentleman in England who had constructed a subterranean room with a window abutting the steep bank of a pond. The Englishman could indulge in the quietude of his view and ultimately he began to photograph some of the underwater images. Ernie cautiously pinched the magazine and then, not so cautiously, sent a wire off to Denver. There was an idea here and it was getting considerably warmer by the minute.

We can imagine the animated discussions that must have transpired in the Williamson house after George arrived – especially on summer nights when a man's capacity for dreams and enterprises is usually at its most robust. They talked about the article, they talked about the undersea, and, likely as not, they talked about their present state – which was *not* rich and famous. Most of the conversations, though, dealt with making movies and the upcoming exposition. If there was enough light for a still camera to register an image underwater, they reasoned that possibly motion picture stock, with its even slower film speed, stood a chance if the conditions were right. But first, they had to try their hand at stills and their father's contraption was what they needed.

Whether the boys infected the Captain with their enthusiasms or tired him out by begging, their persistence resulted in a fully rigged trip down the Elizabeth River and out into Hampton Roads. There, the barge was anchored and the great submarine tube set into position. The "expedition" carried an inventory of Ada Williamson's sandwiches, a camera appropriated from the *Pilot*, and a frame containing a reflector and a battery of tungsten lamps. It aggregated a thousand candle power and could be lowered down slightly above the chamber. Ernie scampered down the tube and looked out the ports into a field of pale greenish brown. With the camera pressed against the glass, he sat and waited for something besides silt and mud to make its appearance.

At first they experimented with natural light at a depth of

ten to fifteen feet and exposures that ranged from 1/50 to 1/10 of a second – which was as much visibility as the Chesapeake Bay could offer. After that, the bank of lights was used, and during the weekend, they lowered the bell and frame as far down as 30 feet.

They took pictures of seaweed. They took pictures of pilings. They took pictures of fish and when the fish lost their curiosity, bait was dropped on a line to get them back. When they ran out of natural elements to shoot, they took pictures of junk. George, always the promoter, even swam down and held a *Scientific American* in front of the port; after all, the family might entice another front page article out of them after five years (which *did* come to pass in July).

Considering all the effort expended, it was probably just as well that neither Ernie nor George had ever seen a copy of *La Photographie Sous Marin* or heard of its author, Louis Boutan, whose undersea snapshots dated back to 1893 – or of Simon Lake's photos from inside his submarine, the *Argonaut* – or of Etienne Peau in 1906 or of H. Hartman, who that very summer of 1913, was obtaining a patent in England for an underwater still camera. Even the *National Geographic* had scooped them by four years using a glass-bottom boat off Catalina.

Back in their darkroom, however, all those predecessors were of no consequence. Still photography was a genesis. The Williamson boys wanted into movies, and when every negative came out of the soup looking beautiful, they had their first tangible promotional tools for getting there.

That night they left the lab and knocked about the dockside alleys in an imaginary trip below the ocean. The reality may have been Norfolk harbor, but Ernie and George were moving through the submerged ruins of Atlantis and Port Royal. Long shadows and half-light turned every mundane article of merchant transport into a treasure galleon or a sleeping submarine beast. "Motion pictures from the bottom of the sea!" No intricate metaphors were needed to help sell a line like that. Captain Williamson had provided the hardware to make it real, and short of owning a dirigible or a locomotive, few fathers have ever been in such a good position to indulge their sons' wild notions.

Ernie and George knew full well that the possession of a noble idea, a handful of pictures, and the use of papa's marvelous machine wouldn't bring them within a mile of the film business – much less transport them to the tropical waters they needed. The only plan that even touched reality was the American standard equation of bravado times backers.

Understandably hesitant to ask the Norfolk businessmen, Ernie decided to first try an easier route: to lay out a proposal before his editor and see if the chief would respond with a bankroll. So one day, Ernie walked into the lion's den with a handful of pictures and a data sheet.

The man behind the desk, Keville Glennan, fanned everything out, stared for a few seconds, smacked his fist down, and declared it to be the kind of investment any editor would jump at. However, Glennan didn't mean that the *Pilot* would sponsor an expedition. What he meant was that the prospect of it would sell a lot of newspapers.

And so the story was set up to be thrown on the press for a Sunday special, barring a massive Model-T collision or someone getting a shot of Eva Tanguay's knickers. When it finally broke, it was an outrageous feature that covered the whole page. It was evident that when the ink kissed the paper, Glennan had given the brothers the audacity they needed to tout a theoretical cinematic business and a presumptive expeditionary force.

The feature was headed: "Submarine Movies to Reveal the Wonders of the Deep" and it was resplendent with photographs, diagrams, and a romantic illustration of Spanish galleons being recorded on film – the entire layout designed and executed by Ernie except for a sketch by Pritchard. The body copy was a monument to publicity tactics:

> To take the camera into the deep, bringing to the surface
> and flash upon the canvas its hidden secrets; to pictorially
> display, for the knowledge and entertainment of the
> world, its marvelous beauties, its plant and animal life
> and unfold the enormity of buried wealth, to which

172

nature and commerce have so liberally contributed,
would be an event for which the world has been waiting.[1]

It is doubtful that the world was, in fact, waiting for under-sea movies, but one thing is certain: with the publication of the *Pilot* on June 22, 1913, two Scottish-American shipwrights who had never turned a movie crank were suddenly in the business – or so they hoped.

The minute that movies broke away from stage-sets, it became evident that future cameramen were going to ride trains, fly planes, or go through burning buildings to get attention.

The Williamsons were going to go under the sea.

The motion picture exposition was opening in New York in two weeks and the Williamsons wanted to parlay the home-town article into some trade exposure as quickly as possible. They figured on begging for space at the affair, using the news-paper story as a wedge. But before they could plant their story in the mails, someone in New York spotted it and they received a last minute invitation instead.

It was a hot Saturday afternoon when George and Ernie arrived at the Grand Central Palace. They were instantly intimi-dated by all of the expertly crafted displays – especially when they looked at their empty booth and tried to relate it to a hand-ful of four by five pictures. Ernie assured the manager that they would fill the booth up and then he started running up and down Forty Sixth Street and Herald Square – trying to find a studio that was still open and would make enlargements for them. It was a working weekend, but on Monday morning Ernie and George were at their stations. Behind them hung their sponge-dyed enlargements of Chesapeake Bay's underside.

Almost seven thousand people appeared on opening night, and for a solid week, the exposition ran at full throttle. There were exhibits of new equipment, a tourbus to the Fort Lee studios, and iced Pilsner "capsules" for delegates who had discovered that, in the summertime, New York bears a certain resemblance to Bombay. The whole affair was meshed with the

Convention of Motion Picture Exhibitors and, necessarily, had to accommodate members of Edison's trust as well as the independents. Four theatres were kept in constant operation.

Exhibitions ranged from the most prosaic to the most dazzling. Compared to the people hawking new coin counters or exit gates, the submarine pictures turned out to be a magnet. But compared to A.H. Wood's "moving picture target" game or a concession that staged a three minute sketch, "photographing it while you wait," the brothers had trouble holding an audience.[2] Even against such high-powered rivals, however, the exposition week would prove that their little patches of sea bottom could do the job that was intended.

As the hoopla of the exposition died away, Ernie and George dismantled their booth and trained back down to Norfolk, armed with letters of interest and a visitors book they had used to tally the traffic. There had been outright money offers from the north, but the brothers only wanted to use the endorsements as a way to coax coins out of their Southern neighbors.

Ernie drew up a proposal for their expedition to the tropics and George went out into the oaken offices of downtown Norfolk and started shaking hands. Just how they ever convinced business veterans that undersea films would be a limitless financial waterfall, we'll never know. But in the autumn of 1913, the Submarine Film Corporation was spawned with Thomas S. Southgate, a Norfolk broker, as president. As it did with so many ventures of that era, Coca-Cola money flowed to the Williamsons as well. It was invested by Alonzo F. Cathey, a regional bottler, who appointed himself executive vice-president. C.R. Capps of the Seaboard Railway and Nathaniel Beaman, the power behind Norfolk's First National Bank, also took a gamble on some stock. Ernie and George walked away with the titles of general manager and secretary-treasurer, respectively. It was the best they could expect since they were well-heeled with ideas and little else. Captain Williamson simply, and wisely, capitalized the value of his tube for a piece of the company.

Within weeks, office space was acquired back in New

York. The Williamson boys then moved up to be in the midst of the movie industry and start laying out plans for their conquest of the deep. One morning Ernie was drafting blueprints for the construction of a new chamber and George was figuring how to get the rest of the $100,000 of company stock subscribed. Even with the generous support of the founding members in Norfolk, more than half the stock was still outstanding.

Suddenly, one of those very backers dropped in and announced that for himself and some of the others, the whole thing might be a little too crazy. At that moment, the brothers could see their undersea adventure going straight down the drain. However, George and Ernie had met a few contacts at the exposition and some very fast footwork ensued. Before the day was over, George produced a man named C.J. Hite who was president of the Thanhouser Film Corporation, an extensive film distribution service. Hite was ready to spring for the outstanding capital or its equivalent in needed materials, if his company could have exclusive distribution rights.

This unexpected show of confidence from a man who knew the marketplace sent the Southern gentleman home feeling comfortable and still committed. It also instantly made Hite the majority stockholder of the Submarine Film Corporation. George and Ernie hadn't wanted ownership to be that concentrated, but, given the immediate situation, it was the only way to save their venture. Thanhouser Films ultimately furnished the camera equipment, all the film stock and all marketing services. This freed the Williamson's bank balance for travel, provisions, and the manufacturing of a new chamber that would better conform to the needs of movie-making.

The Williamson brothers would act only as producers on this first film expedition. As a way of insuring his investment against their inexperience, Hite furnished a crack cameraman named Carl L. Gregory, a Thanhouser employee who, in reality, became the world's first undersea cinematographer.

Seven months later the Williamson Submarine Expedition was ready to depart for tropical waters and make history's first movies of the world below the brine. The Bahamas were the location of choice, and having been elected to do the advance reconnaissance, Ernie sailed for Nassau on February 21, 1914.

George departed a month later, husbanding the precious cargo of bell, tube, and camera. Sailing with him were Carl Gregory and, of all people, the erstwhile editor of *The Virginian Pilot*, Keville Glennan, who had chucked his desk job to be in on the adventure.

The new diving chamber that was hoisted aboard weighed four tons and had been cast and machined in Pennsylvania. Its glass ports had come from Germany, and, with its radically new design for making movies, it was appropriately christened the "Photosphere." As the name implied, it was a globe instead of a cylinder, and projecting out from one side was a long conical chamber.

The globe section that would house the cameraman and his camera was simple enough, but the projecting funnel was an involved piece of engineering that had to solve many problems. It was intended to shield the camera lens from unwanted reflections, while broadening the circumference rapidly enough to maintain a wide field of vision. The large end, facing outward, was five feet in diameter and was fitted with a glass disc or "window" two inches thick. The smaller end, which terminated inside the sphere, was only eighteen inches across and had a glass port as well, but one only large enough to accommodate the camera lens – about three inches in diameter. (Five inches away, the cameraman had a separate view port in order to gauge his framing. Early cameras had no reflex viewing.)

The outside glass, as thick as it was, still needed some help in defending itself against the water pressure. This problem was solved by making the funnel air tight and connecting to it a pipe that led from a hand pump operated by the cameraman. This way, the air space between the large window and the little lens port could be pressurized (or bled) at will according to the depth at which they were shooting.

The large window would have air pressure on the inside equal to the water pressure outside. Because it was so small, the little window could withstand the pressure difference between the air inside the funnel and the surface air inside the photo chamber. An air pressure gauge for the funnel's interior and a water pressure gauge for its exterior registered the information to keep things balanced.

Among the dozens of other things loaded aboard, was a twelve foot reflector and a new battery of nine Cooper-Hewitt mercury vapor floods arranged in a gridiron, each light having twenty-four hundred candlepower. In the end, these lights served mainly as an insurance policy.

However, generous as they were to approve funds for equipment, the backers in Norfolk knew better than give the crew everything they wanted. They ultimately economized in the classic corporate tradition – few personnel. A portion of their departing news release, filled out here with the parenthetical realities, read:

> Simultaneous with the shipping of the equipment, a staff of expert mechanics [George] and a corps of photographers [Carl and Keville] will sail from New York to join the Submarine Film Corporation forces [Ernie]."[3]

The much heralded Williamson Expedition was four men and a lot of moxie.

With March winds hammering the pier, an expedition seemed rather insane. In New York harbor, a world of transparent seas was dream stuff. Nevertheless, five days later, equipment was being unloaded in the shadows of palm trees and the Union Jack. The brothers were reunited as tropical sunshine pushed its way through the surface of the water to the white marl bottom surrounding New Providence. Ernie, already a veteran of thirty days, watched smugly as George and the others stared over the side of the pier. A lifetime in the waters of the north was no preparation for the experience of seeing this crystal clear element that wrapped itself around the pilings of Nassau harbor.

Ernie presented the new arrivals with a work vessel much like the Captain's barge, but better trimmed and a little more accommodating. Their initial venture to the reef was delayed by a 12-day storm, but the first calm morning saw them off to play in the mottled pockets of blue ocean.

The Photosphere was craned into position over the well and the tube segments were connected one by one. Then the chain hoists lowered away until thirty feet was paid out. Ernie slowly, and almost reverently, descended the "hole in the sea," and when he reached the chamber, he stood spellbound at his first view of the incredible undersea world that only tropical waters can provide to the fullest.

It wasn't a diffused collection of greens or browns that he saw, but a realm of real space; space created by clarity. It had planes and distances just like the earth above, but all immersed in a beautiful liquid that could host a parade of buoyant creatures. The solid shapes he saw were fairy tale forms dyed shades of blue and looking every bit like a thousand years of undisturbed growth.

Everyone took his turn looking out the ports spellbound, and understandably, the work was forgotten for a while. With ice castles and aerial kingdoms, still, no nursery legend could top this world for imagery. As George and Ernie were envisioning little phantasmal dramas, they slowly became aware of the presence of sunlight. They studied the luminous shafts refracting from the surface and streaming to the bottom. They were reminded that the sun was moving, time was passing, and they should get on with the business at hand.

The precious camera was lowered down the tube, still in its case – and it was indeed precious. The industry wars with Edison had, even in their aftermath, made equipment scarce. As a result, professional gear was still being custom built, machined, and tooled in people's garages, and then combined with bootlegged parts from Europe. Naturally, there was a price tag for all this work.

The Williamsons were lucky. They had inherited a genuine French-manufactured Eclair – 40 to 50 pounds of iron, steel, and brass that, by today's standards, more closely resembled a strong box than it did a camera. It was a nuisance to winch up and down the tube, but back then, manufacturers did not think in terms of light-weight construction: they thought in terms of precision and, in that day, precision meant plenty of brass. It was symbolic of quality, and besides that, brass was one of the few available metals that wouldn't rust. This was meaningful for George and Ernie considering their moisture-laden environment.

Although many cameras had intermittent movements where the sprocket itself turned in quarters, the Eclair had a pull-down claw. It also had a variable shutter which, at the time, was a very innovative feature. Regarding cameras, C.J. Hite was evidently not going to risk cutting corners on the Williamsons, considering the remoteness of their location.

Down in the Photosphere – after much squirming and adjusting – Carl Gregory and Ernie Williamson were ready to make a movie. Ernie passed Carl the magazines: two square wooden boxes which fit inside the camera body. One was the feed and one the take-up. Their movements linked by a tandem shaft, they sat one on top of the other, each with its own door. The load was 400 feet, so with hand-cranking at sixteen frames per second, it contained about five or six minutes of film.

Once the camera was threaded, Carl looked out one of the ports and into a great blue field of water. He must have thought to himself: "what in God's name could the reading be on *this*?" Except for the "actinometers" that worked off heat and radiation, there were no real photo-electric light meters back then. There were, however, a few factors to make his problem still worse.

In the first place, almost all lenses were f4.5 or f3.5. These had sufficient depth of field to compensate for mistakes in gauging distance, but they were meant to be used in sunlight. Secondly, the orthochromatic film was slow – extremely slow. It was actually sharper than modern day film, but its filmspeed was only 24 compared to today's average of 200. Finally, to make matters as bad as possible, Kodak always sent test stock with each individual order. It wasn't a courtesy – it was a necessity. This gave the cameraman a clue as to the state of the emulsion: manufacturing was such that the filmstock varied a stop or two from one batch to the next.

When Carl was finally ready to take a chance on all his guesswork, George positioned the barge in a narrow strait between Hog and Athol Islands, where the depth varied from

15 to 25 feet. Crewmen then pulled the barge across submarine gardens with a previously set anchor line and Carl cranked his camera in the hope that his judgments were sound. As was later evident, even in the deeper recesses of coral, it was not difficult to obtain good exposures at 1/75 of a second with a lens opening of f6.3.

Ernie then lined up a sequence with young Bahamian boys diving for coins. After having been drugged by all the natural beauty under the sea, it must have seemed strange to break the quietude with such frenetic scenes, but everyone in the group agreed it would be a good test of what they could or could not accomplish relative to photographing action. Once they began, the images turned out to be a ballet of muscular, black bodies against a field of silver bubbles and yellow sand clouds – all dancing around on a light-blue stage. One wonders if, at that moment, any of the four crewmen thought of a future day when, in addition to the shapes, *colors* could be committed to film.

Carl left his lens wide open and, for a while, cranked away at a standard 16 frames per second; then to be safe, he gradually slowed down with each descent of the native divers. It was a common practice for silent-era cameramen to crank slower to emit more light onto the film. Confronted with a marginal light situation, they would actually "undercrank" as far down as 8 frames per second, getting twice the normal exposure. The picture would speed up when projected, but back then, getting an image was more challenging than trying to match normal motion. As concerned as Carl was about the light level, he probably filmed the divers at 8 frames per second.

After all the variables in coin-fetching were exhausted, the quartet remained out on the barge past sundown in order to resolve the artificial light matter. After setting up the grid and lowering it over the side, Ernie pressed a switch and gave the group their first glimpse of the ocean bottom's night shift – a disarrayed little army of legs and feelers that stirred about like a slow-motion display of surgical instruments. Gregory rolled some more film and the exposure for their artificial lights was more or less what they had used in daytime. If the islanders watching from shore were in any way cautious about this new form of white man's tomfoolery, their feelings just may have turned into down-and-out fear as they saw a great circular arc of undersea light moving slowly along the black field of night water.

Ultimately, the crew all hobbled ashore at some ridiculous hour of the morning and into a little stone house that was the darkroom. Ice was used to cool the place, the water was hauled from a well, and everything considered, the arrangements were primitive. Gregory fumbled in the dark for a contraption called a Steinman Reel. It was a huge circular plate with a high lip that spiraled continuously from the outside edge all the way to the center. Carl held the disc flat on a table, and as one of the others held the camera's take-up magazine, he twisted the un-wieldy thing around and around, gradually feeding film off the magazine and onto the disc. Tightly coiled, 400 feet wasn't an unreasonable amount of film stock to handle unless it was being processed a thousand miles from the nearest laboratory. What made the Steinman Reel so large was the quarter inch of space between spirals for solutions to circulate.

A Caribbean island was a remote place to make a movie in 1914, but, even as they began to manhandle the disc through a bathtub full of chemicals, Carl, Ernie, Kevin and George all agreed that the adventure overrode the inconvenience. What came out of the bath before sunrise was what the last ten months of their lives had been about. Ultimately, there would be 20,000 feet of it.

The images were in black and white negative and no larger than a postage stamp, but Gregory could tell they were all there. Oddly enough, his best exposures were his first, and, from that point on, he had greatly underestimated the amount of light available at a 25-foot depth. The four of them stood around the lantern like medieval alchemists squinting at their handiwork – the world's first undersea motion pictures.

The boys wrote a report to the financiers, enclosed a strip of the developed film and sent it off *On His Majesty's Service*.

In the weeks that followed, the submarine four bobbed around the coral banks and filmed every configuration and creature they could find. Anchored near a drop-off, they could wait for anything that was mobile to come and play before the window. Under modest power, the Photosphere could take advantage of the "trucking" effect that occurred while moving in and out of coral beds and grottoes.

Carl Gregory, as moved by the sensation as anyone, was to later write: "To your inventive genius, Mister Williamson, I owe the most solemn and wonderstruck moments of my life – I am thankful to be the instrument whereby a glimpse of this arabesque fantasy may be given to the world."[4]

The camera was locked in position and moved only when the chamber moved. Gregory wasn't able to tilt up or down, so many exposure problems were circumvented. If the weather picked up on the surface, the chamber only swayed gently through the jungles of gorgonias and sea fans.

George occasionally dressed in a diving rig and went over the side to act in some contrived little "discovery" scene or to just be a prop in the overall panorama. On one occasion, they came across a presentable wooden hulk, and while Gregory cranked footage on "the treasure-laden galleon," George pulled a brass bell out of the wreck. On another dive, George became "salvor" on a Confederate Blockade Runner – one of hundreds that had made the 500-mile run from Nassau to Charleston.

News was getting around, and sometime during the island sojourn, both His Excellency, the Governor, and the U.S. Consul paid visits to the dive sites and wriggled themselves down the tube for a look. The Governor loved it so much that he brought his wife back and they both wriggled down the tube to gaze in wonder at a submerged piece of the British Empire.

And if all of that weren't flattering enough for the troupe, a marine science team from the Carnegie Institute and another from the Brooklyn Museum dropped in, and, after their first exposure to reality, spent the rest of the day lamenting the pickle-jar and glass case life they led back at the office.

Ernie and George were already starting to collect friends in their deep-sea enterprise and it felt good to be on more peaceful terms with the ocean instead of being in a shipyard. Three thousand miles across the same water, however, Europe was being thrown into a massive conflict. Though it seemed far enough from the peace of Nassau's coral gardens, World War I would ultimately have its effect on the Williamsons and their film work – as it would on the entire industry.

By the end of May, the four men had spent almost two months around New Providence and its satellite islands. The barge with its well-housing and roof that kept light from traveling down the tube, looked like a kid's backyard version of the *Merrimack*. It had been christened the *"Jules Verne"* and was usually seen being towed by a little skiff appropriately named the *"Nautilus."*

Tucking their toes into the inner rings, the camera operator and his companion would descend the tube with ropes fastened around their waists to brake them in case of a slip. George would often share the chamber duty with Carl, scanning the terrain through one of the ports and leaving Carl to operate the camera. In that case, Ernie would then assume the deck watch, leaning over the open tube, listening for directions and relaying them to Joe Bethel, the captain of the skiff. Later they would rig a telephone system from the Photosphere to the deck, but initially it was all lung power aboard the *Jules Verne*. In addition to all the forward and lateral commands, a voice from the tube would occasionally bark "raise her" or "lower her" and with that, a couple of strapping young gentlemen at the hoists would throw some muscle into the gear. Carl and his partner would rise over the coral forests and descend back down into the sand meadows, craning up and down through the sea gardens like two of Verne's characters in a hot air balloon.

Through all of this optical tranquility, time was drawing to a close and there remained one particular drama that had not been committed to celluloid. Back in the United States when the whole idea was in its crackpot infancy, there had been two sorts of enthusiasts involved. One sort wanted the dream of floating under equatorial waters and cranking film. The other wanted to make an investment. At some critical point when it looked like the money tree wasn't going to sprout, Ernie had jumped up and said something about a man fighting a shark to the death.

Of course, some time had passed since that vaporing outburst, and although the film cans were full of wondrous creatures, intrepid divers, and even a galleon, the men back in Norfolk just couldn't get that sharkfight out of their minds. And they didn't want Ernie to get it out of his mind either. And so, understandably put off until the last, the Williamson Submarine Expedition set up to film a man and shark showdown. There was one encouraging factor built into the shoot day; the sharks were ready and plentiful.

Ernie promised a healthy bonus to a pair of Bahamian free divers for this cameo role and the very generous offer of a whole dead horse was extended to the sharks. There were a few interesting factors that prevailed. The sharks were quick, the horse was heavy, and the black divers had never seen a movie, so couldn't fully appreciate the camera's field of vision; especially while being underwater and trying to kill some gray devil that was trying to kill them. These all combined to make the kind of shooting session that's wrapped with abundant rum drinks.

Straightaway, two big grays charged and tore pieces off old dobbin before he could be yanked out of the water. The action was captured anyway and resulted in the world's most unsavory footage for years to come. The sharks then became too frenzied and took off out of camera range. Worst of all, the first diver took off, knife in hand and made a successful thrust. All the quick shifting of the barge anchors, however, couldn't swing the chamber around fast enough and Ernie paid the diver off with a sigh. The second man dove in and began evasive action, keeping the horse between himself and the shark. Ernie was, of course, trying to keep the horse out of the picture, but it made good comedy if you happened *not* to be an investor in the film.

The upshot became a story that Ernie would recall all the way to his octogenarian days. He cut off his pants, took a ten minute course in theory and dove in as only a movie hero could do – a knife in this teeth. His original idea was to first do some practicing. But, as it happened, a new candidate lined-up to charge him and Ernie noticed that he was dead ahead of the chamber window and that Carl was feverishly cranking away. In the midst of this insanity, Ernie's ego suddenly took command. He veered off properly, grabbed the right fin and swung himself straight into the shark's belly. Through all the flashing, jerking, blood, and swallowed water, the knife somehow struck home and Ernest Williamson became a leading man in his own undersea vignette.

After filming the great shark spectacle, the gear was put away. A week later the crew was on a steamer heading back to New York. From the time they arrived there, and for five weeks hence, some red-eyed member of the group slept either in the lab or on the cutting-room floor. The reason was celluloid film stock: a compression of guncotton and camphor. With a nitrate base added, it meant that movies, back then, were printed on long strips of sheer destruction. Since fires in the business were all too prevalent, someone had to be on watch with a large bag to scoop up the elements and run if necessary – that is, if they got the chance. When contained, as in a small editing room, the film might not just burn. It could literally explode.

George and Ernie had brought back 20,000 feet of the volatile stuff and the editing went slowly. Although some as-sorted machinery was available for the process, most people "cut in the hand" using a ground glass with a light underneath. The splices were also made by hand – an ordinary razor blade doing the surgery. But with the undersea footage, method wasn't the problem. Any good editor of the day could judge pace and rhythm without a machine. The problem was that the subject matter, being so unfamiliar, was hard to build into any sequence or continuity.

However, when the last splice was made, they had com-pressed two months' worth of dailies into six respectable reels of a thousand feet each; a kind of standard feature length that had evolved over the last two years. One morning, with their precious cargo in hand, they boarded a train for the Washing-ton of Woodrow Wilson and arrived that afternoon – the city and the scientific community waiting for them. Also waiting for them was the old captain, T.S. Southgate, and the other three backers who all came up from Norfolk for the event.

The following day, July 16, 1914 was a banner one for the

Williamson family and a landmark for motion pictures. The public had been thoroughly primed with news releases announcing the film's premiere at the Smithsonian Institution. Not only was the four o'clock screening committed to capacity, but a second show was arranged to precede it at noon and that one also filled to overflowing. In the evening, the National Press Club hosted the film and crowds were there as well.

An eminent scientist at the Smithsonian said to the audience: "You are about to view the most remarkable photographs ever made." The Washington papers cried: "Films that pierced the sea – each picture an absolute revelation."[5] And in a scientific sense, they were. Although the production utilized certain contrivances here and there, it was not only one of the first feature-length nature films ever put together, but the first nature documentary to later become an international hit.

To fully appreciate the audience reaction that day, one would have to go back in time and think of the undersea world as something depicted only in encyclopedic engravings. With the exception of some esoteric foreign journals and the Williamson publicity, few others had made even a *still* photographic image available to the general public. W.H. Longley and William Beebe were not yet on the scene to popularize the subject, and prior to this moment, the undersea had been as visually unattainable as a far-off planet.

Suddenly people were being transported below the surface and moving with the chamber across the ocean's floor like one of its creatures. Many marine scientists were looking at sea life in its natural habitat for the first time in their careers and Charles Townsend of the New York Aquarium was even finding species he had never before recorded. A year before, Townsend had curated an exhibit of Zarh Pritchard's work and he was now seeing Pritchard's images come alive, although opinion differed on the faithfulness of paintings. As the *Boston Independent* put it: "These ocean meadows and forests look very different from the pictures we have seen in books and the specimens we have seen in museums, for we realize that it is life we are looking at."[6]

Regardless of the praise, Ernie and George took the film back to New York for more work. After talking to a few distributors who were pessimistic about its market value, they began a new edit to include more footage of tropical landscapes, Bahamian life, and some other assorted items that started the thing on its way to becoming a travelogue. There was even a photo-essay on the sponge industry.

While changes were still in progress, the film's first New York screening was held at the American Museum of Natural History on August 11th and the audience response equalled that of the Washington premiere. Albert I of Monaco, "Prince of Oceanographers," was there and presented the brothers each with a Malacca cane in honor of their absolute triumph.

After all the endorsements from the scientific community were gathered up and publicized, the process of making money had to get under way. The final cost of the expedition had come to a modest $30,000, but Hite, Southgate, and the others were anxious to see how the film performed in the marketplace. The first commercial premiere was arranged to coincide with the grand opening of the host theatre – the spanking new Broadway Rose Gardens.

Sometime before the big day, either Hite or another Thanhouser executive became bothered by the academic ring of "The Williamson Submarine Expedition." So with or without the Williamsons' agreement, the film was ultimately introduced to the public as *Terrors of the Deep*. Ironically, it would play under that name for only a few months until it acquired still another title, but, at the outset, whether "Expedition" or "Terrors," it definitely started making money for the little corporation. After a critic barked: "Something never before viewed by mankind,"[5] the cash receipts doubled. It hit the distribution circuits, played Chicago alone for seven months and also played London.

For some unknown reason, although the film was doing well – or because of it – Hite, Thanhouser, and The Submarine Film Corporation would later sell the distribution rights to mammoth Universal; a commonplace transaction, but one that would lead to bigger involvements for the Williamsons.

After the film was generating revenues, George, Ernie and the other officers sat down and looked at each other with one question in mind: Now that a precedent has been set, what do they do with a thing called the "Submarine Film Corporation"?

The answer to that question was a few blocks up Broadway at 1600 where Carl Laemmle sat behind the biggest desk at Universal Studios; then known as the Universal Film Manufacturing Company. He pondered a particular problem. His company was cash rich from the assembly line production of small features and those films had remained a standard for some time. The industry was reluctant to tamper with an already prosperous market. One year in particular, Edison's Biograph Studios had earned a seventeen hundred percent profit using the same formula.

But there was a profound and more profitable change on the motion picture horizon. It was, quite simply, a change to greater size and scope and expenditure; the kind of film that assented to America's love of bigness – the movie spectacular – the "big" film.

Adolph Zukor was releasing Charles Pathe's "films d'art" that featured dramatic figures like Sarah Bernhardt as Queen Elizabeth and his profits from the cinema imports were enormous. Italian period spectaculars, already world famous for their lavish sets and casts of thousands, were starting to land in New York. *Quo Vadis* had arrived the previous year and its profits overshadowed even those of Zukor's films.

Laemmle also knew that D.W. Griffith had left Biograph more than a year ago to start work on what was being rumored to be the greatest movie yet produced; an epic film history of the America Civil War. Griffith was working with a $100,000 budget and industry gossip had it that the picture was going to run a spectacular three hours.

Universal needed its own spectacular, but nobody in management was jumping to produce stage or biblical dramas. If they looked to current events for an answer, it invariably was the emerging war in Europe. But it was 1914 and, up to now, the war had been too short and too distant to extract stories that would captivate the American audience.

Laemmle was certainly aware of the Williamsons. His firm would soon acquire distribution of the expedition film for a two year period. But the Universal president might have never related the brothers to the making of an epic had it not been for an incident that occurred on September 3rd.

On that day, in the waters of the North Sea, Captain Otto Hersing of the German U-21 fired a single torpedo and sank the British light cruiser *Pathfinder* off May Island. Three thousand tons of metal went to the deep in four minutes' time and it was the first incident in the twentieth century where a submarine had sunk a warship. Captain Hersing had given the world a dramatic example: the capability of undersea vessels to contest a stronger navy. He had also given Carl Laemmle an idea for his spectacular film story.

After more than forty years of distribution in English, Jules Verne's novel of submarine exploration was still enjoying immense success as the nonpareil of science fiction. Laemmle lost no time in realizing the profitable correlation between World War I, Jules Verne, and the Williamson brothers. A partnership was formed between Universal and The Submarine Film Corporation to produce a film version of *Twenty Thousand Leagues Under the Seas*. The talks between Laemmle and Hite explored a 55 percent share for Universal, 45 percent for the Norfolk group, and a $150 per week salary for Ernie.

Stuart Patton, a budding, young captive-director of Carl's, was appointed to write a screen adaptation. Patton had cut his teeth directing adventure serials and since Verne's book was originally serialized for young people, Laemmle saw him as the logical choice for this project. Ernie and George were assigned to co-directorial and production responsibility for the underwater sequences while Patton was to command all the topside filming and assume executive directorship of the entire film.

So, as it turned out, within months of having completed their first experiment in undersea cinematography, the Williamson brothers were now going to begin co-production on a major motion picture, and, through it, carve another small niche for themselves in the history of moviemaking. Overnight, with the whole of America already in line to see their expedition film, George and Ernie were in the limelight as pictorial messengers from another world – the world beneath the sea.

On the northeast corner of Forty Second Street and Broadway stands a red brick tribute to both Victoria and Art Nouveau called the Longacre Building. Today, the street level is a battery of trinket shops and its architectural beauty is overshadowed by the indecorous shapes and colors of the Times Square circus.

Back in 1914, however, the Longacre Building was practically a corporate center for the movie industry in America and the Williamson brothers were able to grab a new office on the ninth floor. Although men like Thomas Ince and Mack Sennett had transferred a lot of production facilities to California, their management had to remain in New York. As a result, the little Submarine Film Corporation was sharing space with sizeable neighbors like the Keystone and the Metro Film companies.

In the weeks that followed, as production planning for *Twenty Thousand Leagues* started to gain momentum, George and Ernie found themselves working and aggregating with the practitioners of a golden craft, in the golden age of movie making. The medium may have been black and white, but the people and their involvements were far more colorful than they ever again would be. Timing was on the side of the Williamsons as well. They were introducing the world to undersea movies at a time when so many incubating movie formulas were being hatched and delivered to the public for their lifetime adoption.

In November, Mack Sennett came out with *Tillie's Punctured Romance* which made an overnight success of Charlie Chaplin. Then December saw the premiere of a two-fisted horse-opera called *The Bargain*, starring William S. Hart. It was the first full-length Western written expressly for the screen instead of being adapted from a novel or play.

A few weeks after that, as 1915 came around, both comedy and westerns stepped aside in mute arrest for the introduction of another competitive formula. On January 12, a devastating package of limbs and breasts hit the silver screen in the form of Theda Bara and the sex theme in film was immediately solidified. In *A Fool There Was*, this first of the cinematic vamps was launched into a five-year siege against happy marriages. But her victims weren't even cold in the ground when Griffith's *Birth of a Nation* opened at the Liberty Theatre and Carl Laemmle had to rush down to see the cornerstone epic that he had so long expected – and feared.

It was in this atmosphere of rapid-fire launchings: the comedy of Chaplin, the western screenplay, the prototype sex film and the first epic of America, that George and Ernie Williamson now rushed to begin production on the first full-length undersea drama.

This was a frightening prospect. The brothers were not only fresh from their first effort in movie-making, but *Twenty Thousand Leagues* was a story of outrageous logistics – especially for the year 1915. Submarine warfare, combat with sea beasts, and the geographic conquests of a band of men who were mobilized and living beneath the ocean – all were a far cry from the singular quietude of a cowfish feeding on coral. Universal's sanction aside, Ernie and George were two young mermen with their hands quite full.

The movie-going public would ultimately stare in wonder as Verne's grotesque imagery plodded across the theatre screen, but not until almost two years of pre-production, location shoots and editorial agony took place. Nevertheless, George felt so confident that he ran back to Colorado to marry his girlfriend, Ruth, and indulge in an abbreviated honeymoon. Ernie, by March 26, was at the Century Club lecturing on submarine photography to promote the forthcoming epic.

In the propping department, many films were already upscaling the work of their stage-drama predecessors. What with outer space fantasies of George Méliès coming from France and biblical dramas like *Quo Vadis* coming from Italy, the acquisition of extraordinary props was not an unfair demand on production budgets even in 1915.

But in the case of *Twenty Thousand Leagues*, the extraordinary props had to be genuinely life-supporting and functional. Unlike the illusory snowstorms and housefires of other productions, the background element of this film was indeed real and the undersea wouldn't accommodate a paper-maché diving operation. With their new and healthier budget, the Williamsons wanted diving suits that would enable the crew of the *Nautilus* to wander over the sea floor in film just as they had in literature – without the customary life lines and air hoses. The Rouquayrol-Denayrouze apparatus described by Verne was already part of mechanical history.

One day the brothers wandered over to A. Schrader's Sons in Brooklyn, at that time an important contractor of diving gear for the U.S. Navy. Their timing could not have been better. A chief petty officer had been using Schrader's pressure pot in the absence of suitable equipment at the Navy Yard, and, through the chief, Schrader had learned about a demonstration of self-contained suits at the Yard. Ernie lost no time in setting up a dinner engagement for four.

The next evening could not have found George and Ernie in more advantageous company. Demonstrating the suits was Mr. H.N. Elmer, Chicago representative of the venerable Siebe-Gorman Company of England and the particular gear he was peddling consisted of a helmet-jacket combination fitted with chemical canisters for breathing. The outfit was not really intended for a working dive but for submarine escape.

The Navy chief was none other than George D. Stillson, who just two years before, had plowed through sluggish bureaucracies to form our Navy's first experimental diving unit. Having located in the Brooklyn Navy Yard, he and an English medical officer were determinedly working to establish U.S. standards for deep diving, and, following the British lead, his five man team had broken the 200-foot barrier for compressed air in Schrader's chamber. Stillson himself had just returned from setting a new world's record of 274 feet in the open sea.

It must have been an evening of cordials, cigars, and agitated conversation. Here sat not only a representative of the world's largest diving equipment firm, but also the redoubtable Chief Stillson, who would soon become the father of the U.S. Navy Diving School, and two brothers who were producing a film version of Verne's undersea classic. The end result was a gluttonous order for fifteen of the submarine escape suits from England, the cooperation of the Navy Department, and the use of some of the best divers in the United States to star in the production.

As it happened, the order for the suits was timely. A few months later, with Europe already at war, the British government would requisition Siebe-Gorman. After that, their output could not be purchased. The German submarine campaign would be decimating and, if England couldn't build a vast fleet of her own subs, she could at least keep the escape suits out of foreign hands.

Timely also was the diving contract with the U.S. government. Just how Stillson obtained permission for his military divers to engage in a commercial movie production is not known, but the Navy had an active public relations office even then and Stillson needed the exposure.

In March, however, the U.S. submarine F-4 mysteriously went to the bottom off Hawaii. On April 1, Stillson's unit was notified that they would soon have to disengage themselves from the film production and by the 29th, the Williamsons had lost three of their best divers. The job turned out to be a 300-foot-plus situation; the greatest depth in the history of salvage for the raising of a complete vessel. Needless to say, it also led to new depth records for three men.

Ernie and George would have to depart New York with only two civilian divers: the renowned Jack Gardner and a fellow named Chin Chin, and the promise of a third from the Gulf Coast. As it happened, though, Navy crews would salvage the tragic F-4 in a little over three months and Stillson's men would later be released for the Nassau location before too many ambitious undersea shots had been started. Stillson himself even went to the shoot for the novelty and involvement.

Another potential problem was Nemo's undersea guns. After experimenting with everything but the obvious, Ernie and Universal realized one day that ordinary firearms could be used underwater just as they were on the surface. They knew about the density of water, but there were no really wide shots planned and as long as whatever the gun discharged went out of frame, it would be convincing. Springfield army rifles were finally decided upon and wax plugs were used with the charges instead of regular bullets. When a diver fired one underwater, black gas would belch from the muzzle and a fine stream of bubbles marked the path of the projectile. Now the crew of the *Nautilus* was ready to hunt for food on the ocean's floor.

The submarine *Nautilus* was a propping job that wasn't resolved quite that easily. Granted, there was no longer any mechanical mystery about either the construction or the operation of subs. Considering the number of them that had been launched, Ernie and George figured there would be no problem in acquiring one for scrap steel rates.

But the war was taking shape in Europe and although, for the record, America was maintaining an isolationist policy, her military men were starting to stockpile materiel for action. In February, Southgate and the Williamsons had actually met with Franklin Roosevelt – then Secretary of the Navy – about using an Otis Type-A sub, but, by March, Ernie was working on his own designs. From those drawings ultimately two boats would be built; a large sub by shipwrights in Nassau and a smaller, more submersible "double" by a prop man named O'Neil at the I.M.P. Studios in New York.

The large boat would be more than 100 feet long with a beam of 15 feet and a draft of four. Topside, she was practically clear except for a small conning tower and a hatchway. Below decks, compressed air tanks and inlet ports allowed the vessel to be submerged or brought to the surface. However, Ernie's Nassau submarine was not conceived to meet pressure-hull standards. She was largely constructed of wood, canvas, and metal paint with patches of lead on her underside. Consequently, her dives were limited to just below the surface – and with no power of her own, a towline was used for momentum. Ernie's engineering was clever but flawed. The Williamsons were yet to learn that the big boat would sink far too slowly for the cameras. As it would later occur, the cinematographer, instead of cranking at 16 frames, had to go down to a frame-a-second and, in extreme cases, expose single frames every 2 to 3 seconds in order to record the descent within any tolerable time period. The action would obviously be too eratic for practical editing.

However, at least one advantage was that the entire sub could be controlled by one man at one station, so neither Universal nor the Williamsons had to worry about ever drowning a whole shipful of mariners. But Jack Gardner, who had been selected to handle the craft, was no fool. As it was being towed back from a maiden voyage, he emerged in full diving dress with a compressed air bottle attached.

As for the smaller, "stand-in" sub, she would be just 32 feet but made to perform underwater and accommodate two divers. One man was to operate the rudder, diving planes, and air control; the other to operate a manual propeller mechanism. However, as it happened, the hand-cranked screw would prove to be near-powerless and secondary divers would have to push the small boat into the camera's field. As a result, the "location reality" had little advantage. In the movie, framing of the submerged boat was usually too tight to encourage belief in the action. The few wide shots that were filmed depicted an air lock arrangement or the semblance of one, and through this, Nemo and his men made either real or simulated exits and re-entries when submerged. The scenes were convincing enough, although the sub was suspiciously stable – and, most likely surfaced and secured when filmed from underneath. Finally, although Verne never described one, this cinematic *Nautilus* had a torpedo tube that fired a wooden torpedo.

Of course, the magic *Nautilus* had its interior back at Universal's eastern studios. There, Patton would shoot his players in all the comfort that Leonia, New Jersey could provide. Verne had been an unbridled romantic and when he described habitations, he spared neither romance nor expense; it was all just ink and paper anyway. Accordingly, he gave his undersea ship a twelve-thousand volume library, an oaken dining room and a parlor resplendent with paintings and tapestries. Universal would be damned if their Victorian submarine turned out any less florid than Verne's, so the prop men were given carte blanche. The accoutrements ranged from oriental rugs to hassocks to mother-of-pearl taborets and Nemo's undersea abode finally emerged something short of a Turkish brothel.

On May 14, 1915, the Williamsons left New York on a Ward Line steamer with the first wave of production people. To be sure, they were still in loving awe of the monster they had created, but some inconvenient realities of a large production and their marriage to a major studio were already becoming apparent. Of the first forty souls bound for Nassau, many were wives or girl friends; some were cousins or nephews of Carl Laemmle. A man of traditional family ties, Laemmle had become the butt of industry humor due to the number of relatives he employed. "Most of them were unable to do anything," Erich von Stroheim was to later recall; "You took them whether you liked them or not."[7] So George and Ernie were getting their first exposure to the kind of budget manipulation already in common usage. Ernie, especially, lamented the lost privacies of their first production effort.

Nor was the community of Nassau ready to accommodate what was happening. Hotels overflowed, banks were perturbed, and older Bahamians experienced the disquieting effects of having a film crew domiciled on their island for six months of waterborne filming and what turned out to be a year and a half of other projects. Moreover, if the movie makers weren't enough, the apparent manifestations of their work looked too otherworldly, what with divers, Civil War-era people, and other assorted characters walking around loose; the harbor hosting an odd assortment of vessels for them to play upon.

In the shipyards stood an old steam frigate brought down from New York to serve as the armed reconnaissance vessel of Verne's story, the *Abraham Lincoln*. Beside it was a huge sacrificial yacht destined to receive Nemo's torpedos broadside. While both frigate and yacht were being rebuilt to look their antiquated best for the cameras, they were joined by two grotesque, steel-plated *Nautilus* and the Williamson barge with its undersea tube. It was all a bit overwhelming for either the Sunday sailors or the working seamen of Nassau harbor. People who had never seen a motion picture could not easily understand the insanity inherent in making one. Mercifully, the islanders were spared witnessing a colonialist Indian uprising and sundry scenes borrowed from another Verne story. The studio chose to shoot these elsewhere.

Luckily for George and Ernie, *their* particular form of insanity was most often isolated from shore and removed to the gin-clear waters. But there were harbingers of a long and taxing production on the horizon. Without rolling one foot of film, their first yacht was wrecked off the Florida coast. Having gone back to the United States for a replacement, George piloted the second yacht through a two-day storm to reach Nassau, almost loosing it as well.

All of the Siebe-Gorman chemical suits arrived for Nemo's crew. However, the production was temporarily robbed of all but three of its professional divers due to the F-4 tragedy. As a consequence, Ernie recruited among the fine swimmers and free divers of the West Indies, and he found enthusiasm plentiful. After a dozen gentlemen had been enlisted, he, Jack Gardner, and Tuck, the new diver from the Gulf, organized a little waterfront classroom. There, they began to instruct the recruits in using the new diving gear – which, in reality, was intended for submarine escape.

The rig had a thin brass hood with a single viewport; much simpler and lighter than regular diving helmets. It was sealed at the shoulders to a vulcanized rubber jacket – one with the usual sleeves and tight cuffs, but ending just below the waist and having a belt and crotch strap. Fitted to the inside of the jacket were two small cylinders of compressed air; one to keep water to a safe level when submerged and one to inflate a buoyancy chamber when the wearer reached the surface. With the latter, he could safely open the face plate on his helmet and breathe fresh air without sinking. Needless to say, body motions underwater were limited for fear of spilling air out of the bottom of the jacket. Weights were as necessary for the outfit as for a fully enclosed suit.

The element that would allow George and Ernie's divers to stay submerged for almost an hour and consequently make

the filming of Nemo's undersea activities possible, was a preparation called Oxylithe; a form of sodium peroxide in a canister.
When breathed upon, it gave off oxygen, and, at the same time,
absorbed the carbon dioxide in the expired air. The stuff had
been around since 1904, and at the time was popular because it
was the best alternative to compressed oxygen and its particular hazards.

But, used for air regeneration, Oxylithe had terrible properties as well. Although the canister compound could withstand the moisture in a person's breath, if allowed to actually
get wet, it suddenly turned on the diver, throwing off a lethal
gas. Many times due to tilted motion, water would creep up the
jacket and slosh around as high as the diver's chin, so the
Oxylithe was drawn from a breathing tube which had to be
kept between the diver's teeth to prevent water from reaching
the dangerous compound.

The native students listened attentively as Tuck and Gardner went through an assortment of demonstrations and dry
runs. They were at home under the water when breath-holding.
They were also resigned to blurred vision, but the prospect of
leisurely walking around with air to breathe and a clear view of
the scenery was an exciting one.

On the morning of the first ocean trials, the lads gathered
on deck to watch Tuck and Gardner stage an undersea fight
scene for the camera; Tuck in one of the escape suits and Gardner in a fully enclosed diving rig that had been modified to use
the Oxylithe and compressed air system. They held mock combat on deck so that Tuck could get used to tumbling about
while keeping the breathing tube still firmly in his mouth. Tuck
then went over the side as Jack and Ernie were making some
final adjustments. The lesson seemed to be going normally
until someone suddenly spotted Tuck on the surface flounder-
ing about like a crazy man. At that point, Ernie and the company doctor leaped into a skiff and started rowing frantically
for the distressed diver. As they pulled Tuck up into the boat
and opened his viewport, blue smoke poured out of the opening. They yanked the helmet off and found him unconscious
with his face turning an ebony black. The doctor had a *pulmo-
tor*, and, with help from the crew, worked for twenty minutes

before Tuck regained consciousness. As he lay propped up on the deck of the barge, the story was pieced together.

It seemed that Tuck forgot to clean the mouthpiece on his breathing tube or, for that matter, check his suit over in any way. A tiny granule of Oxylithe had lodged on the tube right under his lip and once wet, burned through his flesh in seconds. The pain made him spit the tube out of his mouth and with his reeling about, water rushed into the tube and into the Oxylithe canister. Pouring back out the tube, deadly gas then filled the helmet. Instinctively, Tuck grabbed the valves for both bottles of compressed air to flush his helmet and fill up the jacket, but neither valve would budge. Nevertheless, his diver's logic prevailed. Before blacking out completely, he ditched his weightbelt and shoes and it was just enough to start him rising to the surface.

It appeared that Tuck would be around to do more diving and acting, but Ernie's short-lived school was over. The entire student body decided they didn't like the outcome of being an educated diver and politely told the three faculty members to look somewhere else.

As a point of interest, had they accepted the work, it might have created a humorous precedent; that being the first time in cinema history – and maybe the last – where not one but twelve black men stood in for twelve white men throughout an entire feature. Certainly, in the general history of man's labors, it had happened uncountable times.

At any rate, on June 14, George Stillson's crew returned from Hawaii and the filming regained its intended pace. It was an all-star cast that included Gardner and Frank Crilley, who along with Stillson would be immortalized in the annals of navy salvage. However, as expert as these men were on straight-air or helium dives, they were still vexed by the problems of Oxylithe. Additional to its moisture intolerance, the exhaust from the compound had the effect of alcohol. Even though filming sequences were religiously interrupted every hour to change the canisters, it didn't help the cumulative effect over many hours of breathing. Working overtime to a get a particular scene finished, the actors would become thoroughly intoxicated. Quite often, after playing out their parts, they would, instead of coming to the surface, just start wandering away.

When the director shouted "that's a keeper," everyone topside and in the tube would prepare for the next scene. But the mighty crew of the *Nautilus* – hardened veterans all – had waddled off the set and into the blue void to pick sea anemones. The unit manager finally had to keep a couple of men out of camera range in regular, hose-tether gear to start rounding up the submarine thespians after each scene was finished.

Sometimes the situation wasn't that benign. Once, while preparing to rise from the sea floor into the air lock, the crew suddenly started knocking each other about. One man, totally besotted, hit the air valves and thrashed his way to the surface. Ernie and the doctor had a repeat performance of the Tuck incident on their hands plus a number of undersea drunks who had to be yanked up through the air lock and quieted down.

Ultimately, due either to the actors' demands or just their personal preference, some additional equipment was brought into use. Scenes that "made the edit," employ not only the submarine escape suits but also two similar to Jack Gardner's – regulation diving outfits converted to a rebreathing function.

With the hard lessons of chemical diving accrued, the brothers passed most of July creating their subaqueous marvels in black and white celluloid. George took over the interaction between their own company and Universal; moving materials and paperwork to their destinations. Ernie stayed on location with Stuart Patton and photographer Eugene Gaudio to help solve shooting problems.

After a time, the camera crew became sensitized to a certain graphic interplay between actors and the elements underwater. As a filmmaker's awareness grew, so did the efforts to utilize all the eeriness surrounding the chamber. The undersea, however, is a prime example of beauty being a relative thing. Maurice Tourneur, as director in a later film employing the Williamson tube, was to be quoted as saying: "The bottom of the ocean isn't all it's cracked up to be."[8]

Patton, on the other hand, always had an affinity for the

dream-sequence and the incongruous. As a complement to his thinking, photographer Gaudio had the inclinations of a surrealist, so Ernie was in good company. None of his enthusiasms about the undersea fell on deaf ears. Patton and Gaudio, in fact, were pre-sold on the mysterious visuals that loomed in front of the viewport.

In Verne's story, some of the more poetic passages have to do with man's excursions into the sea as much as with the beauty of the sea. Likewise, neither Ernie, Patton, nor Gaudio regarded the presence of Nemo's grotesque crewmen as an intrusion into the seascape. Rather they were treated as otherworldly creatures acting in concert with an otherworldly place. The brass domed, one-eyed spirits would plod along the sand floor in a kind of somber resignation to being a part of sea life. Moreover, whether hunting in the coral forests of the Caribbean or salvaging gold bars from Vigo Bay, time would prove that these eerie scenes would be the favored among everything else in the film.

The best product of their artistry turned out to be the burial of a crewman. Due to editorial and scripting decisions, this drama would ultimately represent Captain Nemo's funeral. Later additions to the story included the death of the captain. The two directors had determined to yield æsthetics out of the ceremony, but one major alteration was necessary. When Verne spoke of an area on the ocean's floor ". . . raised in certain places by slight excrescences with lime deposits and disposed with a regularity that betrayed the hand of man," he was talking about a vast underwater cemetery. The prop men could build coral mounds or even fabricate crosses of coral that are mentioned in the story, but then a crewmember of the *Nautilus* "began to dig a hole with a pickaxe," and that the moviemakers could not do. Ooze and marl would cloud the whole scene in seconds, and besides that, the hole would fill in as fast as it was dug. It was decided to have the divers inter the body of their comrade in a coral grotto.

One day Patton gave a sign from the bell and Gaudio started cranking. The procession moved slowly and rhythmically into a vast glade; "this resting place at the bottom of the inaccessible ocean," and thence toward the undersea tomb.

Five men carried a shrouded figure "enveloped in a tissue of white byssus," and after the remains were placed within the grotto, limestone was rolled over the entranceway. Their leader crossed his arms upon his breast and all the crewmen – like silent blue ghosts – knelt to pray in the shafts of light that streamed from the surface.

Cut to coral cross with fish swimming about. It was an editorial option.

By August of 1915, most undersea episodes had been staged, but the work – although distilled to only fourteen days of actual filming – was halted. Only in October was it resumed and then much of it restaged and reshot. Though framed in phantasmal settings, Universal felt the action was too serene and often plodding. Also, the men in Gotham still didn't have a much-wanted "hype shot" – a thrilling and terrifying spectacle that could be blown out of all proportion on the theatre facades.

The material was there, of course. In his book, Verne had provided all the promoters could want – the battle with giant squid. The problem was, when Verne told a story, he didn't restrain himself. The *Nautilus* of literature was actually attacked by no less than a dozen of the things. Driving to the surface, Nemo's crew emerged with axes and staged the most nightmarish combat since Hercules slew the Hydra. However, ink being cheaper than film, producers of the silent age were masters of compromise. Patton and the Williamsons settled for one demon. Forty years later there would be another, more ambitious, film version, but it would still limit the fight to a single cephalopod. Not even Walt Disney would spring for twelve of them.

Understandably then, in 1915, the state of film art made for even worse logistics. Once Gaudio and his prop men were through conferring, not even the magnificent Universal submarine or its gallant crew would qualify for the scene. Ernie, George and Patton agonized over their options and finally narrowed it down to one man – Nemo himself – and they changed the creature to an octopus. An octopus was more in the public's frame of reference. In their script, Nemo battled the creature to save a native who was diving for pearls. The unfortunate fellow was really Patton's transplant from an earlier segment of the book where Nemo performs his rescue by battling a shark off Ceylon.

It isn't known how long this scene was in preparation. Nevertheless, one day, the one man–one octopus showdown was near readiness and the crew paused to roll film on man versus demon of the deep. Ernie had found a cavernous area – enclosed by coral embankments and full of moving shadows and sinister formations. Although the light level was marginal, the yawning black caverns made the place too dramatic to pass up. This was definitely loathsome octopus territory.

Soon, camera gears were whirring and the native diver plunged into view. He swam around the seafloor – intent on tossing his oysters into a sack, totally oblivious to the green eyes that had opened in the shadows. Then, as a horrific image slowly glided into the light, the native turned around, but it was all too late. A tentacle shot out and wrapped itself around him. As he struggled, belching bubbles and screams, the octopus began to draw him back into its lair. The cameraman cranked on with a cold detachment.

Enter the helmeted figure of Captain Nemo. With resolute moves, he comes abreast of the freediver, and, with a single swing of his axe, the tentacle falls and the native shoots upward. A cloud of ink billows out into the water and through the midst we can see that the hideous monster is attacking Nemo with all seven. There is more ink, more flailing, writhing tentacles, flashes of the axe and the glint of a helmet. The creature abandons the fight and withdraws into the shadows. Nemo emerges from the cloud and the scene is over.

There were moviegoers in America who didn't stick their toes in the ocean again for years. John Barrymore was to tell the brothers that he'd never been so frozen to his chair as when he saw the footage. Actually, Barrymore wished for the role of Nemo. As a twist of fate, his older brother Lionel would get the lead role in a later Williamson feature and wind up fighting that same tired old octopus.

However, this was the creature's debut and the *Philadelphia*

Ledger would say: "There can be no question of fake or deception. It is all there and our vision tells us that it is true." With respect to the *Ledger*, what was "true" lay basking in the sun every day between takes. Every writhing, slimy inch of it was Ernie Williamson's U.S. Patent No. 1,378,641; a contraption of rubber, springs, and compressed air, with a head that accommodated one of Stillson's divers to man the controls.

For his model, Ernie had used a facsimile at the Brooklyn museum. For tentacles, the mechanical cues were less academic. They came from the party favor that straightens out when blown into and coils back when the air is released. Refinements included an inner rubber sleeve, fine coil springs for shape and stability, and high pressure hook-ups that worked to manipulate everything. The sucking disks were a tribute to backyard engineering. They turned out to be rubber balls of graduated diameter, cut in halves and attached to a fabric that served for skin. When inflated, each of the tentacles required around a hundred pounds of metal to neutralize itself, and with weights also needed for the head, it meant the even distribution of a thousand pounds over the entire device. Despite its heaviness, however, Ernie's creation was both flexible and fragile, so it took a veritable army of men to coax her anywhere on land.

The creature had actually had its beginnings in April. Its birthplace, a basement in the Brooklyn home of Chin Chin, the hardest drinking but most creative of Ernie's divers. Later, the construction was upgraded to A.E. Neilson's Machine Shop in Manhattan and, in fact, Neilson soon became a regular advisor on Williamson's "octopus team." Advice was sorely needed because the beast sank like a stone, was often unmanageable, and consistently leaked fine, cloudy bubbles out of hundred places.

One of the Bahamians came up with a black organic sludge from the local swamp and when diluted with water, it made grade-A octopus ink. Ernie had storage bladders built into the creature and the goo was force-pumped out through its arms. The lonely diver sat amidst valves and gaskets in the dark, water-filled interior of the monster's head. Listening to Ernie or Patton over his earphones, he would direct his beast with compressed air and pursue his victim by looking through a hole. A man encased in a diving suit, sitting inside a mechanical creature, and both of them on the floor of the ocean – the job was not for claustrophobics.

With the octopus battle over, so was most of the undersea filming. The *Nautilus* had been through most of her paces but had yet to ram the *Abraham Lincoln* as in Verne's description. Ernie piloted the sub and accidentally knocked the frigate's rudder to pieces. The final act for the *Nautilus* was to then torpedo the yacht. It was a one-take situation since the playtoy was really going to be destroyed. But that ominous fact didn't render the shoot immune from miscalculations. Two men were on the pleasure craft to set the charge, jump in a power boat, and go. An assistant who was given the job of firing a signal shot, decided to first test his pistol, not remembering that tests also make noises.

When the shot was heard, the unit manager had not yet cleared the area. The charges were lit, and, cruising up within camera range was Governor Haddon-Smith on another of his royal inspections. His launch party lost more than their sherry, but no one was seriously hurt. Starlet Jane Gail was filmed by the photosphere crew as she fell from the deck of the exploding yacht (as per the editor's craft) – swimming down a few yards for a sub-surface rescue by the *Nautilus*. On the strength of that one dip beneath the waves, she thereafter padded all her interviews with a story from "the first woman to go down among the tropical creatures."[9]

Working into late summer, this kind of insanity was aggravated by requests for still more shots that didn't relate to the original story. By October, there was 100,000 feet of negative in the can and the trade had been told to expect a completed feature by January. It was evident that the production was a year behind schedule. Executives in New York still felt there was insufficient drawing power to the undersea classic as it was written, and they had long ago talked Patton into altering his script to incorporate elements from another Verne story, *The Mysterious Island*. By itself, the tale had such extravagant scenes as a hot air balloon ascent from Richmond, Virginia – all staged, with a great deal of chaos, in downtown Nassau.

To this blend of two stories was added material to furnish a love theme – something the literarily asexual Verne would never have done. The romance came complete with a sort of native girl who dwelled in the trees and ran around in a costume of animal skins – again at the behest of Universal's front office. This was the reason for Jane Gail.

To top it off, the studio still felt it did not have a "lot" scene of great magnitude. The truth was, that for more than a year, they had covetously eyed Griffith's unparalleled receipts for *Birth of a Nation*. As far as Universal was concerned, the factor that made box office magic for the three hour film was Griffith's muralist approach to things; vast panoramas of Atlanta burning, Sherman's march to the sea, and all the rest. Predictably, the studio writers went back to Verne to see if they could find themselves a panorama.

Like many Frenchmen of the day, Jules Verne believed that everyone else's colonialism was bad – largely because it wasn't French. Nemo was, in origin, an East Indian prince and the culmination of his anti-British sentiments occurred in the Sepoy Rebellion which destroyed his home some nine years before he encountered Professor Aronnax. On the strength of that story, somebody in Gotham blew a cloud of cigar smoke into the air and suggested they destroy the walled city where Nemo once ruled and therein would be the spectacular shot they needed. At least it would help them compete with an ancient Babylon that Griffith had recreated in Hollywood and would unleash on the public in September; *Intolerance*.

So incredible funds were allocated to film an uprising in India. In resignation, Ernie left the Bahamas November 18 and, four days later, presented his remaining bills to Laemmle. It was the genesis of a lawsuit he would file against Universal the following year.

By late June of 1916, every ship that pulled into New York from the Caribbean carried more reels of undeveloped film from Bahamian waters. A man from Universal's laboratories would be on the docks to sign for the cargo and within hours, the work prints would emerge from behind lab doors, spooled into manageable amounts for the editorial staff.

On the twenty-third of that month, another dockside occurrence some four thousand miles to the east, would help Universal transform all that undersea celluloid into the fantastic monetary return for which they had gambled. In the city of Kiel, Germany, a long steel machine slipped from the docks and proceeded to the open waters of the Baltic, and, in the most destructive of ocean wars yet, it would seem that another raider was off to do her deadly business in the North Sea. But this U-boat was twice the normal width and she sported no deck guns or torpedo tubes. Below she was festooned with the customary array of valves and tubing, but there were no metal fish for the British merchantmen nor war instruments of any kind. Instead, the holds were loaded with high grade inks and dyes for the textile trade and she was headed not for a sortie in England's shipping lanes, but for George and Ernie's old playground, the Chesapeake Bay.

Her name was *The Deutschland* and she was the world's first merchant submarine. With a 700 ton freight capacity she was running the British blockades to trade her wares for a return cargo of zinc, copper, and other much needed metals. Some weeks later in Baltimore, the sub was given a kind of capitalist-hero's welcome. American industry had been making quite a few bucks on the European war and was selling its goods to belligerents on both sides. Even though the U.S. was only eight months away from joining the conflict, commercial interests were prevailing to the very last.

The Deutschland's treatment was also indicative of how romanticized the German U-boats and their crews had become in this country – this despite the *Lusitania* disaster and the resultant anti-German sentiment. Over the next few months, awareness of submarine escapades and the mysterious science of undersea warfare would accelerate. The front office at Universal could not have asked for better advance publicity on a motion picture about submarine navigation.

Before this epochal voyage, the sub was, to Americans, part of a far away drama that existed only in newspapers. With the arrival of *The Deutschland*, however, people realized that her huge displacement and long range capabilities announced the end of America's geographic isolation should Germany decide to wage war in our waters.

Later that year, in Rhode Island, the point would be further emphasized when a fully armed German U-boat, the U-53, pulled into Newport Harbor – ostensibly to deliver a message to the German ambassador. Seventeen days out from Wilhelmshaven, she would further indicate her self-sufficiency by mooring only three hours. Then, before slipping quietly back under the surface, her captain would state: "We require nothing, thank you."[10] His mission would supposedly be a far cry from warfare, but this country was due for a surprise; a well-timed surprise for Universal's stockholders and the Williamson brothers.

For a long time, work prints of *Twenty Thousand Leagues* decorated a Universal editing room in bits and pieces. Ernie thought the Indian rebellion and other extraneous items were commonplace when spliced with the undersea shots. The front office liked any scene that was spectacular. Many insiders worried about the amalgamation of so much story material and some thought the photoplay had become an outright cryptogram. Patton had to defend his ideas about scripting and sequence. Depicting events past and present, the story was also structured so that Patton could cut back and forth between simultaneous events that occurred in different places. Later to be termed "parallel action," the technique got Carl Laemmle's support because he saw it employed in Griffith's *Intolerance* which had just opened September 5th. Laemmle determined that if Griffith could do it, so could Patton and Universal.

The upshot resulted in a new continuity, whole segments discarded, and new scenes filmed. By the time a release print was in its shipping carton, the cost of the picture came to rest at a half million dollars. Although this was only a fourth the price tag for *Intolerance*, it was five times the cost for *Birth of a Nation*, and, in those days, sufficient to have Universal's name on a healthy pile of bank notes. With all of this money and effort,

Twenty Thousand Leagues still emerged as a cinematic puzzle. The final edit was packed with embellishments and extra characters: five Union Army scouts, the native girl, a daughter for Professor Aronnax, and an ocean trader named Charles Denver who had his own entourage of characters.

The overall plot began as a reasonably faithful translation. Our Navy dispatches an expedition to exterminate a sea serpent who feeds on our merchantmen. Of course, their hunted serpent is the *Nautilus*. Nemo sinks their ship and takes Professor Aronnax (with daughter), his man-servant Conseil, and harpooner Ned Land as prisoners-passengers. Their journey under the sea, fascinating for the professor, frustrating for the others, is marked by Nemo's vengeful fits that are directed toward some unknown person.

At this point, the plot quits aligning itself with the book and goes slightly awry. Union soldiers, having crashed their balloon, are stranded on a tropical island. They come across the native girl, and their leader, Lieutenant Bond, falls in love straight away. Then, this Mister Denver arrives on his yacht. Years ago, in India, he had assaulted a maharani and kidnapped her eight year old daughter, leaving her to die on this island. Now, plagued by phantoms, he has come back to see if he can find her alive.

Meanwhile, divers from the *Nautilus* discover the yacht and establish the owner. Charles Denver, it turns out, is the man against whom Nemo has sworn undying vengeance. Denver and his crew have, by now, captured the girl and Bond is pursuing them to the yacht for the old fight and rescue. Nemo torpedos the yacht, but pulls Bond and his girl from the drink alive.

There is a dramatic twist that was supposed to rationalize all of this nonsense. Nemo was an Indian prince and the girl turns out to be his long-lost daughter. There's the flashback to India and then Nemo dies so that the undersea funeral can wrap the picture. It was a far cry from the great novel of undersea engineering and geography that helped spark the era of science fiction literature.

One reviewer for *Moving Picture World* was so concerned about the integrity of the thing, he timed the sequences and found that the original story supplied only a third of the picture.

Photoplay Magazine said: "In truth, the thing is a masterpiece spoiled . . . in story and acting it is a childish story-paper belonging to the moving picture infant class."[11]

It was decided to premiere the film at Chicago's Studebaker Theatre on October 9, 1916. The midwest location was probably booked to determine how much money should be spent for East Coast promotion based on the picture's success in Chicago. Their concern, as it turned out, was unnecessary.

Not only was *Twenty Thousand Leagues* destined to make a bundle by virtue of its undersea imagery, but the distributors unknowingly tied the opening to a very noteworthy event – and probably the most fortuitous promotion device a motion picture ever inherited.

In the late afternoon of the seventh, the German U-53 left Newport, Rhode Island, with everyone assuming her to be on the way home. The British had previously posted warships off our shores – mostly in an effort to trap *The Deutschland*. However, the United States viewed them as an infringement on commerce, so Washington protested the patrols and they dispersed.

The following morning, the U-53 suddenly showed up near the Nantucket Lightship, and in full accordance with international law and America's neutrality, began ravaging the sea lanes into New York harbor. In the span of one day, she sank three British freighters, a British passenger liner, and a Dutch and a Norwegian ship. Fortunately, it was during the somewhat humane period of submarine warfare and few lives were lost. The German sub surfaced and ordered passengers and crew to take to their lifeboats before blowing the ship up or opening its sea valves – these practices saved torpedoes as well as lives.

News of the attack hit the papers on premiere day. America stood dumbfounded for a minute, pressed Wilson to chastise the German ambassador, and then ran down to stand in line for the movie. As a Chicago paper put it: "If the Kaiser had been its press agent, *Twenty Thousand Leagues Under the Sea* could not have been timed to better advantage."

In the East, Universal held off until it could arrange the

premiere to coincide with the Christmas holidays. The film opened at the Broadway Theatre in Manhattan on December 24th. Premiering that same week was Douglas Fairbanks in *The Americano*, and still another story which preceded Disney's adaptation by many years, *Snow White* – a live action film in which Marguerite Clark recreated her stage version of the Grimm Brothers fairy tale.

But *Twenty Thousand Leagues* easily eclipsed its competition, and went on to enjoy a two and a half month booking; the second longest run of any picture ever shown in New York up to that time. It also smashed every record for cash receipts in a given period: over $22,000 in two weeks. In that time alone, over 60,000 people saw the eight-reeler and it then played into early March and always with a live orchestra.

During the evenings of 1917, almost every crossroads' hamlet across the country had a chance to run the epic movie. Except for short comedies, no feature film had ever possessed such all-inclusive marketing potential. People wanted to see a submarine boat. They wanted to see the undersea world the way citizens of the sixties would want to see the moon's terrain. In New York, teachers had already been motivated by Zarh Pritchard's undersea paintings at the aquarium, and based on the shots of marine life, Universal had obtained an endorsement from scientists and educators, so that the studio could encourage parents to send their children to the matinees.

One distributor paid a whopping $50,000 for the exclusive state rights in his territory and still made a personal fortune renting prints at $30 per day. In the heartland, those who had never seen the ocean above or below, sat down in darkened shoe-box theatres and anxiously looked back at the operator's box – waiting for the flickering, sword-like beam to transport them into a mysterious dream-world that lay on the ocean floor.

In spite of its scrambled plot and the bastardization of Verne's classic, theatre houses were packed month after month. Moreover, almost all of the public's enthusiasm was for the undersea photography, made possible by Ernest and George Williamson and their crew, and not for any of the contrivances thrown in by Universal.

Even in a conservative review, Edward Weitzel said: "it is

when the action is transferred to the bottom of the ocean that the picture makes its strongest impression. Here the opportunity for new and startling effects, the almost incredible views of the strange life in the depths of the sea . . . brings a novel phase to motion picture making."[12] It is on record that the premiere night audiences offered generous rounds of applause on seeing the undersea segments of the film. *Motion Picture News* wrote: "Whole gardens of undersea life hold and fascinate and seem like a dream. . . . Some will say, 'impossible,' 'ridiculous,' but the majority will say 'marvelous,' 'how did they do it?' And those whose fancy and imagination will not carry them into the spirit of the drama, will see enough sensation in the undersea scenes alone to bountifully satisfy them."[13]

And finally, a remark from one critic that surely must have given the Williamsons smug satisfaction after all their agonies with Universal: "If the rest of the picture were discarded, the undersea scenes alone would be worth three times the price of admission."[5]

In spite of itself, Universal had a hit on its hands. In eight weeks' time, the Williamson-Universal production had completely paid for itself. Universal claimed $75,000 as their portion of the Broadway Theatre's ticket receipts during that period alone. Oddly, in late 1916, with gross receipts already at $445,000 and net profits at $42,000, the Norfolk consortium suddenly wanted to cash-out and they sold most of their interest to Universal for only $51,000. Although a percentage deal was made for the unsold state rights, divestiture was an extraordinary concession given the film's potential. Also, at that point, Canada was the only foreign country sold. That income, however, the Williamsons might never have seen anyway.

A frequent reason were agreements that excluded certain subcontractors from the revenues in foreign distribution; a market infinitely larger at that time than it was in later years. Silent film titles could be changed much easier than the ones burned out of live action and certainly with less effort than it would later take to dub a sound track. The message was contained in a convenient black field and isolated from the rest of the visuals. More than once, when a distributor was short of prints, some hack editor with a copy stand, a pair of scissors, and a bilingual dictionary could transform an English-language film into more or less a French or Italian film overnight. Captain Nemo was to speak in many tongues, but the Williamson brothers weren't around to collect the lecture fee.

The United States was on the verge of entering World War I, and in a year the war would be over. As soon as peace came to Europe, so would new American films and *Twenty Thousand Leagues* was prepared to cross the Atlantic for an enviable distribution – especially in Jules Verne's native France. As an interesting sidebar, the news of its profits prompted another Verne to jump headfirst into the movie business. Michel Verne, entrepreneur and only son of Jules, was holding the rights to all his father's works, and, with over 100 titles at his disposal, he possessed an endless supply of screenplay material. He put together a company called Les Films Jules-Verne and commenced to crank out "cinematograph" versions of his father's "Les Voyages Extraordinaires." Although four stories were completed – each less ambitious in scope than *Twenty Thousand Leagues* – Michel tried to do too much on his own and the family ultimately sold the film rights.

Just before the Christmas Eve premiere of *Twenty Thousand Leagues* in New York, one chance for untapped revenues did present itself. George and Ernie had gained a premonition of the film's incredible success right after the Chicago opening in October, so when Universal's distribution contract on the *Williamson Submarine Expedition* film ran out on December 10, George seized the opportunity to pick up their option under a new corporate structure. He then placed the film on the state rights market. Possibly, they could realize as much revenue from *total* ownership of a modest film as they would *partial* ownership of an epic.

Back when Universal had acquired distribution rights from Thanhouser, they possibly sat on the circulation of the film to keep interest in *Twenty Thousand Leagues* from being pre-empted. Twenty-four states were still virgin territory and had not seen the first film.

It was now Williamson brothers property, and to enhance the correlation between the two features, Ernie opted for a third name change on the original picture. As it had gone from *The Williamson Submarine Expedition* to *Terrors of the Deep*, it was now to become *Thirty Leagues Under the Sea*; an obvious and homonymous alignment to the larger epic that had opened in Chicago and would soon hit New York. Considering recent events, George was uncomfortable about losing the word "submarine" in the title, but the similarities gained made it worth the sacrifice.

The distribution of *Thirty Leagues* did manage to bring in a few extra dollars for George and Ernie. It was all filtered through a separate entity with the unwieldy name of Thirty Thousand Leagues Under the Sea Incorporated. Despite this arrangement, the brothers knew they would never realize the kind of plunderous profits coming to Universal unless they produced and distributed their very own photoplay. Their first undersea epic had been little more than a sub-contracting job and that fact was all too apparent once the revenues were divided.

Ernie and George sat back and contemplated their situation. They had a small studio in the Bahamas, an office in New York, and some stockholders in Virginia who were wondering what was next on the agenda. Did they still have a sellable commodity or had it all been expended in one grand production? George was concerned about how to evolve. Ernie saw no end to undersea drama, providing they could keep the big studios from compromising their work.

Another way to phrase the question was: Could the undersea photoplay sustain itself as an art form or would it quickly be relegated to the special effects category, just a segment of some larger production? It was possible they hadn't been given the chance to find out. The first production was a demonstration and a travelogue. The second was a classic spoiled by Universal's dictates.

Admittedly, the Williamsons were peddling rather placid subjects. There was also some doubt as to whether they had enough variables once they had staged the shark and octopus fights. The documentary was easy but feature films were a different matter and the applause of marine biologists wasn't enough to sustain them. And subject matter was only half the problem. Undersea cinematography, taken by itself, had some limiting characteristics as well. At least they were limiting relative to the trade formulas for success at that time.

In the first place, when Griffith had utilized the "close-up" back in 1908, he created more than an editing device. He freed the actors from stage techniques and allowed them to project real human emotion to the audience. The trade picked it up and cranked out every emotionally charged scenario they could think of from Hart's frontier morality to the seductions of Theda Bara. The undersea, however, was an environment that limited human expression at a time when every director in the trade and every audience in the country was crying for more.

In the second place, undersea activity was a slowly paced thing. Men like Mack Sennett had linked the elements of automobile speed with driving ineptitude to create thrills for the white-knuckled moviegoer. His vehicles operated on the studio's rule of thumb: always miss the moving targets and always hit the stationary ones. Other movie makers placed cameras on the tops of trains, and, currently at theatres, was an airborne production called *Flying With The Marines*, where the camera was mounted right in the cockpit. This had been preceded years before by shots from a roller coaster.

All these vehicular devices were compounded by the camera's increasing mobility on lot scenes where booming and tracking were already in use. With *Intolerance*, Griffith had even panned his ancient Babylon from a balloon. However, even with their barge in motion, George and Ernie Williamson could not match the studios in that kind of mobility – and they certainly had no speed to offer the audience. America was soon going to be in a war, and when the public wasn't working and sacrificing to whip Kaiser Bill, they would want escape. That might mean a preference for Pearl White being flung from a cliff rather than for a diver plodding through a languid undersea environment.

But Ernie Williamson didn't see it that way. Considering a wealth of divers' tales – creatures real and mythological and shipwrecks with lost gold – movies on the ocean floor would never want for fresh and exciting material. As far as Ernie was concerned, there was only one difference between his form of theatre and that of the others: his stage was full of water. George, on the other hand, was in favor of diversifying the stories as much as possible; giving moviegoers at least as many – if not more – topside involvements as deep-sea scenes.

Joining in the debate was their newly acquired business manager, Ernest Shipman. Described as an advertising expert and "motion picture exploiter," Shipman had been Universal's booking agent and was responsible for getting the brothers and Laemmle together. Now hopefully, he was going to lead George and Ernie down the path to fully independent production.

They all argued a bit about goals and directions, but the decision was made to crank out a third film containing (as even Verne had wisely done) an amalgam of settings. They would write it, produce it, and distribute it – with nobody hovering over their shoulders and no one but their own journeymen directing or cranking the camera. For the first time since they had started, the Williamson brothers were completely on their own.

They threw themselves into the picture straight away. George stayed in New York to juggle logistics and paperwork – managing the income from *Twenty Thousand Leagues* and feeding it into their new production. But, as if these involvements weren't enough, by January he had started laying the groundwork for still another project. It was designed to prove to Ernie that there was more story material for them than just divers and sunken treasure. In the meantime, however, Ernie was back in the Bahamas setting up the third undersea production – about divers and sunken treasure.

At the Library of Congress in Washington, D.C., there is a sort of cardboard mausoleum for the paper remains of a lot of early film efforts in the United States: photos, clippings, handbills, and so forth. Their entombment is in little makeshift containers; and, in just such a box, marked "SL110," there lies the disintegrating production stills – every cut in every scene – of the first undersea story written expressly for the film medium. They are the oddments of a time when producers submitted paper prints, in lieu of the motion picture film, for copyrighting. Whoever assembled them into two small booklets did it with meticulous, loving care, but today they are so brittle that they can barely be touched without falling apart.

Ernie Williamson wrote the story and it was called *The Submarine Eye* – the opportune word "submarine" finally put back to work. The "eye" in the title was really born out of a need and that *need* was a rationale for cutting to undersea landscapes in the middle of a topside story. Accordingly, in the movie, the "eye" was an invention: a long, extendible periscope affair that looked from the surface into the deep rather than vice versa. Anytime the story dictated someone's visual contact with the sea floor, an actor or actress would simply walk over to the periscope, look in, and – *cut* – the audience then saw footage taken from the Photosphere. Scenes from the Photosphere became scenes as seen from the periscope or "submarine eye."

For his photography, Ernie hired Arthur A.C. Sintzenich, whom he had met through Universal when working on *Twenty Thousand Leagues*. As well as being a veteran of the *Kinemacolor* company and Universal's movie news division, *The Animated Weekly*, "Hal" Sintzenich had been cameraman for Lady Grace Mackenzie, the grand dame of filmed safari expeditions, and was credited with the earliest motion picture record of a charging lion.

In addition to *Submarine Eye*, the swarthy Briton would ultimately go on to film the next two Williamson productions, but despite his diverse background, this first assignment in Nassau was a somewhat modest one. Given Ernie's ambitious attitudes about the undersea, his story was an exercise in economic practicality. Not only did it circumvent the need for vast diving armies, monsters of the deep, or submarine boats; it also did away with any complex problems in matching action: surfacings, descents, and the like, shot at different times and in different conditions.

The screenplay ran something like this, as translated from the almost two hundred perfectly sequential stills:

The young inventor of the "eye" has acquired information on the whereabouts of a long lost safe that sank in a storm. It seems the contents may either be a treasure or may somehow relate to the modern-day destinies of his girl friend. The couple have flashbacks to a bygone day and images of a scuttled boat, pirates, a man and a woman, and a distant island that holds a fateful secret.

The girl persuades her well-heeled father to sponsor an expedition to the possible site using her boyfriend's new invention for a search. He agrees, but only after a healthy amount of screenplay "cooing" on her part. Later, tagging along in the seabound entourage, is a rival for the girl's affections who wobbles about in a Brighton Beach commodore's uniform, arching his eyebrows. There is also an equally questionable first mate and both he and the rival are covetous of the treasure and allied against the young inventor.

The denouement occurs when the scanning "submarine eye" finally picks up an image of the safe. The inventor–boyfriend goes over the side in full diving dress – Ernie was the double – and proceeds to get both his hands pinned down when the open door of the safe suddenly falls on them. Of course, he has plenty of air as long as someone is willing to crank the manual compressor, but there suddenly appears a shark who starts circling around and deliberating on how to get that fresh meat taste with a minimum of canvas suit.

Witnessing his situation through the "eye," the girlfriend is helpless. There's not another diving rig on board and nobody else can even swim. Obviously, the ship can't move with a diver tethered to it, so the decision is made that someone row to the nearby island for help – once again, the filming is in Nassau. When the rescue party returns with a native free diver, the girl does much pleading and the native is persuaded to plunge beneath the waves and to try saving her boyfriend from the safe's clutches and the shark's appetite. In the interim, the sinister commodore has tried to cut the airhose, but is thwarted when the first mate has a change of conscience.

The free diver then pulls off his heroic feat; the shark is killed, the boyfriend is saved and the safe's contents – a diary and locket – are salvaged to the satisfaction of the girl and the disgust of the sinister rival.

The Williamsons were both enterprising and enticing. Their starlet was Jane Gail, the "nature girl" of *Twenty Thousand*

Leagues – a smart bit of what advertising hucksters call "borrowed interest." The Bahamian diver was "Angel" (in film, he was dubbed "Buller, the Human Fish"). He was Ernie's favorite subaqueous stuntman and had participated in every project since the "expedition" days when he first dived for coins.

Interestingly, Angel was cast neither as a subordinate nor as a roustabout. Quite the contrary, for the film contained a landmark beyond its undersea connections. The free-diving, shark-slaying Angel was probably the first black man scripted as a hero in an American commercial film; though we don't know how his remuneration compared with the salaries of the other stars. While doing nothing more than embellish a screenplay, the Williamsons may have unwittingly struck a first for equal rights in the movie business – at least as far as screen image is concerned.

Ernie and George released *The Submarine Eye* in May of 1917. By releasing it themselves, The Submarine Film Corporation should have reaped all possible profits instead of handing the better part over to a large studio. It probably did make money for the company because this time the brothers covered the foreign markets they had earlier forfeited. In addition to state rights distribution, prints went out to London, South Africa, and South America. Even had the distribution been limited, *The Submarine Eye* was an adequate barometer of interest in undersea themes because the trade embraced it. Certainly it can't be said that the Williamsons skimped on promotion, for there is on record the purchase of $16,000 for posters and billboards; in those days, a monumental order for a two-man film company. Also, Sintzenich prepared all the film's undersea scenes for blue tinting which was, most surely, a promotable enhancement.

Not so promotable, however, was Ernie's ongoing feud with Universal and the *Twenty Thousand Leagues* project. It finally culminated in a New York State trial which began on November 12th of 1917 and lasted until the 23rd. Having filed claims early in 1916, Ernie's initial charges were over what he viewed as unpaid expenses. His displeasure, though, was further aggravated both by The Submarine Film Corporation's decision to sell their interest and his subsequent witness to Universal's immediate and astonishing profits. George was either resigned to their allotment or felt he was adequately paid or possibly even a target of – though not a defendant to – Ernie's suit.

In court, Laemmle brought his minions, Ernie brought his friends, and the transcript reads like the ultimate satire of Hollywood business squabbles. Among other things, Ernie claimed: he tended sick and injured divers, worked on non-underwater projects, never possessed a script, and was forced to take over accounts that studio intermediaries and his brother had managed. Universal countered with numerous charges including: an octopus not functioning as promised, a naval architect having to rework the big submarine, a small sub that was never self-propelled, and a torpedo that had to be designed elsewhere.

All of this nonsense included nearly two years of pre-trial fighting. The curtain descended with a jury that was reading of lost doughboys in France and Ernie walked out of Gotham with the grand total of $3,175.

All of this aside, it still left the brothers with their separate philosophies unresolved. Ernie wanting to go deeper into the sea and George wanting to grow by creating dramas of the sea – either above or below. After their experiences with Universal, Ernie really did not care much about growth – if growth meant answering to hundreds of other opinions, he would gladly stay small. At least he could be under the ocean filming his own photoplays.

George, on the other hand, felt they would either expand their involvements or they would quickly phase into the category of cinematic oddities, sitting by the phone to get their once a year assignment. Also, in contrast to Ernie, he had been somewhat intrigued by the big studios. They argued the point often and it became an ever-present source of irritation.

George had also been exposed to an interesting concept that he couldn't get off his mind; the creations of a man named Thomas Ince. Basically, Ince was the master architect of the great studio-lot concept. His facility, Inceville, had back lot "colonies," each with a different geographic and architectural theme, and Ince scattered them throughout the hills, all with access roads to the others. His major commitment at the time was to William S. Hart and the production of western movies.

Ince had just built a pirate's cove complete with two brigantines and he was promoting the actor Douglas Fairbanks, who would soon be climbing all over those ships for moviegoers. It was this kind of formula that interested George Williamson. There was literally thirty centuries of sea literature to draw upon compared to a few decades of western lore. If westerns were to play a large role in the movie industry, then surely there would be a correspondingly large market for sea-themed stories. The wellspring ran from the ancient Greeks to the buccaneers to Uncle Sam's Navy.

With a new corporation and new funding, George figured that a studio could be built in Bermuda along the idea of Inceville, but dedicated exclusively to producing dramas of the sea. This arrangement would keep both Williamsons not necessarily *under* the ocean, but close to the ocean and involved with the ocean, yet generate enough diversity to satisfy the distributors and maybe build an enterprise. Ernie had some reservations, but long before *The Submarine Eye* was finished, he agreed to the formation of a new company, The Williamson Brothers Incorporated; still retaining The Submarine Film Corporation as a separate entity and continuing to finish their third production.

In no time, money was being subscribed, when The Williamson Brothers Incorporated decided to prematurely flex its production muscle – this time, of all places, in the arena of escape artistry and prestidigitation.

Back at the beginning of the year, when *The Submarine Eye* was still in its infancy, George had made friends with a brilliant escape artist in Brooklyn named Ehrich Weiss, better known as *The Great Houdini*. Harry Houdini had remained a pre-eminent attraction in American vaudeville for twelve straight years since his return from Europe. But it wasn't just the mystery of his shows that kept him in the spotlight. Time after time, he had confronted any possible challenges to his supremacy; not only by creating new escapes, but by milking them for every conceivable dramatic twist.

Whenever he wanted to enhance the drama of a particular escape, he just made his own situation more precarious, and to do this, he would invariably introduce the element of water. It always caused the audience to hold their breaths along with the performer.

Germany was the first to see his manacled body thrown in a river, then Detroit six years later. If the Williamsons had procured Houdini for their coin-fetching sequence in the first expedition, they could have seen him retrieve the loot with his hands tied, using only his mouth, for he had done exactly that in Fiji a few years earlier. Back home in New York, reporters watched him emerge from the bottom of the harbor after being scuttled in a packing case. If no outdoor stunts were needed, Houdini would still transport the underwater element to his stage as he did with the milk can escape and his famous Chinese Water Torture Cell.

This time, Houdini had more serious competition to worry about than Ziegfield's girls or his cheap imitators. It was the movies. They were starting to take their toll on vaudeville and no escape in the world was going to stop a crowd on its way to the flickers. Besides that, transporting his show around the country was heavy logistics and now the same entertainment could be shipped in a few flat cans for a few dollars.

George Williamson was probably the first to suggest to Houdini that he meet the challenge by getting into movies himself. Since underwater escapes drew more attention than all others, thought George, why not create a scenario around this very theme? He came across a scriptwriter who was an ardent Houdini fan and the end result was a story called *Houdini and the Miracle*, the escapist's first film effort, to be filmed under the water by the pioneers of undersea cinematography, The Williamson Brothers Incorporated.

Houdini loved the idea and between himself, George, and Ernie, a production schedule was laid out that would accommodate his stage obligations. However, in the spring, as cameras began to roll, a new impulse grabbed the one and only star. America declared war on Germany in April, and by June,

Houdini decided that the time required to make a movie didn't fit with his emerging patriotism. After trying to enlist, he was turned down because of his age, but at that point, he simply volunteered for camp shows and bond rallies. Before the conflict was over, he would sell a million dollars worth of Liberty Bonds.

Predictably, the halt in production aggravated the feud between George and Ernie. Besides the aborted project with Houdini, it was now going to be a rough haul acquiring capital for the Bermuda studio, especially with most investors focused on war industries. Yet, had the war not been a factor, Ernie and George would still have been in total disagreement over what to do with their share of the movie business. Yet to be bared in a trial were their differences from the Universal project.

Whatever form the arguments took in those final days together, they were severe to the point that, a year later Ernie was sitting back in the Bahamas and George back in Colorado. From that period on, the brothers neither saw each other nor communicated again.

Interestingly enough, not only was the war over in eighteen months, but Houdini wound up in the movie business after all. Among other industry friends, he sought-out Hal Sintzenich – the Williamson's cameraman on *The Submarine Eye* – and in less than a year after the armistice, Houdini co-authored and starred in a thirteen part serial entitled *The Master Mystery*. It was replete with underwater escapes which were shot in a Hollywood tank. One installment employed a diving suit of Houdini's design.

He went on to make two features for the Lasky Company; one, *Terror Island*, having still more underwater rescues and escapes. However, the films barely paid for themselves, so he formed his own Houdini Picture Corporation, but the new company didn't generate any overwhelming productions either. The trouble was that Harry Houdini couldn't act. At least with George and Ernie, he would have had his first stellar moments under the ocean.

As for the Williamson feud, time would prove both correct. As it turned out, Ernie would make more undersea pictures as a small independent, and George's idea of sea literature for the screen became one of early Hollywood's successful formulas.

That kind of success would escape the Williamsons. On top of the war, Houdini's ambivalence had been too much for the new investors. The Williamson Brothers Incorporated was scrapped, and with it, George's hopes for large-scale production.

After the breakup, Ernie sat in Nassau beside his beloved tropical waters. He still paid rent in New York and he had possession of the Captain's submarine tube. However, neither he nor his undersea machine sat idle for long. After a few months, he was contacted by Maurice Tourneur, former producer/director for the French Eclair Company, who was later to film the 1920 version of *Treasure Island*, and a year after that, *Last of the Mohicans*. Exotic, often fantastic, atmospheres prevailed in his work.

Under his arm, Tourneur had an English melodrama about the tribulations of a poor commoner named Marion Hume. The heroine had been secretly married to a certain Lord Angus Cameron many years before and had borne him a child. Financial crisis opens the story when Lord Angus finds that he has made some unfortunate moves on the stock exchange. He's refused a loan by his brother because he will not contract marriage with a member of his own class.

If these story elements sound far removed from the mysterious deep, they certainly were – until Tourneur and Ernie Williamson worked the story over. Ruin staring him in the face, Cameron goes to work with high-bred selfishness to rid himself of the marriage. When Marion finds out that he "accidentally" nicked their child during a hunt, she blows the whistle on her marital status to keep any more "accidents" from happening. In court, Cameron denies everything, and, as class prejudice goes, Marion's case is almost collapsed for lack of evidence.

At this point, Ernie Williamson was put to work. In the story, the marriage took place on Cameron's old yacht which later sank in a storm. The marriage contract was enclosed in water-proof wrappings and went down in the ship's safe. Ernie was back in business filming the salvage attempts and an undersea fight between the villainous Angus Cameron and a young admirer of Marion's, both of whom donned diving suits for a competitive assault on the yacht's safe and then on each other.

This was Tourneur's first assignment in California and he wanted to keep the entire production there. As a result, Ernie traveled west with the Photosphere in tow. The underwater scenes were then shot in San Pedro Harbor with Tourneur being the first director, besides Ernie, to actually dress and descend in a diving suit in order to supervise a filming.

The film was released through Paramount in May of 1919 under the title "The White Heather." Ernie's contribution was small, but the experience with Tourneur gave him the confidence to get off his hammock and start writing and producing his own material again.

Girl of the Sea was his first offering to the roaring twenties. The "girl" was most literally what the title implied – having washed ashore on an island with her father's gold mine deed tied around her neck. She grows up swimming amidst the coral gardens of the Caribbean and the screenplay created for her was an entangled, convoluted charmer:

Her steam ship had been scuttled by a villain who got her gold mine.

Her lifeboat was then scuttled by a giant octopus, who, presumably, got her mother.

The captain, undeservedly, got the blame.

Years later, the captain's son, searching for the truth, gets both the truth and the girl.

The two of them get the gold mine back.

The villain gets eaten by a shark.

By way of his undersea scenarios and no small amount of charisma, Ernie Williamson was adding some rather lovely water maidens to his life. The starlet of *Girl* was Betty Hilburn, and through her choreographic talents underwater, she became a mobile work of art among the sea fans and gorgoneias. From the records available, one gets the idea that the film may have contained some poetic interaction between the human form and the submarine environment, but the press wasn't of a mood to appreciate the images.

Photoplay had this caustic review:

> *Girl of the Sea* reminds us of a Coney Island shore dinner.
> If it weren't for the fish, there would be no point to the
> thing. The best thing to do is to forget the plot and make
> up your mind to take a trip through the aquarium. The
> leading man is an octopus and the leading woman is a
> shark. Human actors lend them good support and the
> Girl of the Sea is attractively played by Betty Hilburn.
> The spirit of the bounding main is here – so if you like
> water stuff, swim to it.[14]

The movie was released in the spring of 1920 by Republic
and whatever was the limited success of *Girl*, it seemed that
Ernie's faith in undersea scenarios was well founded – at least
for the time being. He was working steadily when he was
noticed by Sam Goldwyn. Goldwyn met him in New York and
offered some distribution help if Ernie would continue the kind
of screenplays he had fashioned for *Girl*. Anxious to keep his
momentum, Ernie went to work on a new script and the result
of their understanding was a prosaic six reeler called *Wet Gold*.
Foot for foot, and much like *Girl*, it was exactly the kind of
scripting formula that his brother George had proposed for the
Bermuda studio: the undersea portions were held to a minimum and the buccaneering took precedence.

The story was a testament to the simplicity of silent films.
A man named Cromwell, who has escaped pirates, meets a
plucky old Southern colonel and his wispy daughter, Grace, in
Havana. Always getting mileage out of the sub-oceanic junk-
yard he had created, Ernie has the Havana threesome set out
to find – predictably – a *sunken treasure ship* belonging to the
pirates. As Cromwell is diving the wreck, his Southern comrades man the pump, then the pirates show up. They go after
Cromwell underwater and maroon the colonel and Grace.
Intrepid Cromwell escapes the attack and boards – it's true – the
pirate's *submarine*. The villains are then dispatched with – true,
again – *explosions* and Cromwell rescues the old man and his
lovely daughter. The End.

Although Ernie had known a taste of independence, both
in *Girl* and in *Submarine Eye*, he was still dealing with the collective participation inherent in the movie business – and his con-

sequent job description. Producer-writer was his title in *Wet Gold*, but Goldwyn's offer of help carried a stipulation in the form of Ralph Ince, who served not only as director, but played lead role in the flicker which was released in June of 1921. The directorial task was aided by the camerawork of Jay Rescher, who would ultimately have three Williamson films to his credit.

After *Wet Gold* was released, Ernie was referred to – in the trade journals – as "a writer and director of submarine stories and life beneath the briny deep,"[15] an identity he wanted above all others. Especially he like the last part of that label; it inferred that he held domain over deep sea creatures, as well as the intruding humans. That's where his identity gave him trouble. The nature aspects of undersea filming were what Ernie loved. He enjoyed a response from scientific communities more than he ever did from a movie audience. In reality, he was a shipwright turned commercial artist turned filmmaker. He now was having a mid-life crisis contemplating marine research.

Some of the hokum he had cranked out for adventure's sake was starting to bother him, so after *Wet Gold*, Ernie returned to plying his trade without any contingencies from distributors. The result was a modest four-reeler called *Wonders of the Sea*; written, produced, and directed by John Ernest Williamson. It took on the scientific mantle of the first expedition film, but with little vignettes about a party of undersea enthusiasts. Secretly, the story played to Ernie's aspirations, because he found a way to compound his vision of himself. Following Ralph Ince's example, he starred in the movie as well. He played an oceanographer.

Wonders of the Sea had no real plot or moral. It was basically an exploration "documentary" that retained a few extravagances to help it sell. There was the ever-popular shipwreck and a couple of hard-hat divers who walked about poking and spearing things like a "killer" moray. Then, the film's credibility was stretched a bit when the old rubber octopus was dusted off and thrown in for its third movie role.

Normally, bathing beauties would not have correlated to such a film, but Ernie was still single and he met another lovely named Lulu McGrath who was a veritable underwater ballerina. Like Betty Hilburn in *Girl of the Sea*, Lulu free-dived to caress the fish, touch the coral, and generally complement the rest of the scenery. In later years, Esther Williams would display emotions for the underwater camera as well as swim for it. Yet the name of Lulu McGrath shall be forever emblazoned in history as the first girl to do so. Her great contribution to cinema obscura took place in a marvelous shot where she plummeted down twenty feet to kiss a suited diver right on his brass-framed faceplate.

With Ernie controlling his own product, it made a somewhat better film – at least, æsthetically. In the five years since *Submarine Eye*, he had apparently done some homework. *Wonders of the Sea* opened at the Rialto in New York City in October of 1922, and the usually caustic *New York Times* declared it an improvement over his previous work. In mentioning the beautiful scenes, they did however say that "the attempt to work them into the story adds nothing but length to the film."[16] Ernie's undersea æsthetics could often override his movie salesmanship. Despite his obvious love for the oceans and his love of women, the extended undersea scenes were, for some critics, becoming tiresome.

The modern-day movie business is a sprint for the public's dollar, but, all things being relative, there was as much fierce competition in earlier times, if not more.

When *Wonders of the Sea* opened at the immense Rialto Theatre, it had a successful run – one week. That was common policy for anything but the most spectacular productions. In addition to the mortgage on all those gilded columns and plush seats, the Rialto had an army of uniformed ushers, a 25-piece orchestra, and a hundred other running expenses. If your flicker didn't fill every seat in the house, you were off to the one-piano theatres straight away. This was not always a detrimental event. It was, in fact, inevitable; but the sooner it occurred, the harder were the promotional tasks and the more self-reliant the theatre owners had to be.

Modern theatres are provided with media tools to entice the public – tapes, posters, or ads; they are all prefabricated and ready to plug into the system. In the silent era, it wasn't that facile. Although the magic of production stills and posters was recognized early on by the industry, the theatres – especially the independents – were left to do some very inventive hustling.

In the first place, if the picture playing didn't come with music suggestions, the management had to either get some appropriate material or have a pianist who could improvise. Many times secondary music would be employed. In *Wet Gold*, for instance, the trade manuals suggested having a quartet to sing sea chanties for a prologue. A live introduction to the film was quite common and an accepted expense for the theatre owner. Sometimes it took the form of a speaker as it did for *Wonders of the Sea* – exhibitors were asked to find someone who could lecture on fish life before the projector started up.

Movie hours were hard to regulate from one picture to the next, because picture length varied immensely. In their trade listings, producers would give the footage of an available movie so the exhibitor would know how many preliminary pictorials had to be created to fill the time. Either with a film strip or an opaque projector, ocean scenes were always a standard suggestion for Ernie's pictures. Lobby displays were also a big involvement. There were some enterprising little theatres around the country that actually took the trouble to get a diving rig and set it up out front to help convert curiosity into nickels and dimes.

In its own small way, however, no gimmick was quite as close to homespun capitalism as the product "tie-up." A precursor of merchandising techniques to come, it was especially colorful in the silent days because it was so makeshift. For an upcoming Williamson film, Ernie had acquired Jean Tolley as his leading lady. Jean was somewhat thin on acting experience, but she had long since put her face to work in advertising photos. The exhibitors were instructed to stock up on a certain *Happiness Candy* and vend it through the audience since it sported a picture of Miss Tolley on the wrapper. To make up for a lack of display material, the theatre owners were also told to hustle their drugstore proprietor for Pepsodent toothpaste stand-ups. Ernie's starlet was flashing her smile on those as well and the theatres simply cut off the Pepsodent and stuck pretty Miss Tolley in a pile of scallop shells.

With all his graphic talents, it is uncertain whether Ernie ever contributed any promotional illustrations for his movies. A good many years had passed since he sat at *The Virginian Pilot* inking cartoons and lapsing into fantasy. Commercial artists were then – and are today – notorious castle-builders. Their capacity for dreaming exceeds that of most tradesmen since their minds are fueled by the things they sketch.

It is most certainly a fact, however, that when Ernie's life was thrust off the drawing board and into reality, it reached extremes. If ever there were two occupations that became the causal agents for adventure, it was movie making and deep-sea diving and Ernie had embraced both trades at once.

Then, if filming and assembling an undersea production weren't enough, Ernie started playing in some of his own scenes, ostensibly to correct a troublesome performance, but also because he just liked to throw on a suit, drop down to the bottom and feel his mobility extended beyond that of the Photosphere.

Along with his helmeted principles, producer Williamson then began to accumulate his own collection of diver's yarns and some of them were reasonably unnerving; especially so when he recalled that his efforts were directed to an amusement industry. Once, while filming *The Submarine Eye*, one scene called for the door of a toppled safe to slam down on a diver's hands, pinning him where he stood until he was rescued. Ernie was the principle and missed his safety marks on the lid when a passing shark accidentally knocked against the door ahead of time. The movie rescue turned out to be a real rescue, and Ernie's hands were a bit mutilated.

Another time, in *Girl of the Sea*, he learned the value of checking a rig out before you jump into it. While playing to an old skeleton on the sea floor, he suddenly felt a scorpion crawling through his hair – a slightly horrifying experience in a helmet rig when your hands can't reach any other part of your body.

Ernie was enjoying the modest success of *Wonders* when Ralph Ince, his director friend from *Wet Gold*, got back to him with a new script by Curtis Benton. It was a reversion back to the same cheap, tropic thrills; undersea scenes sandwiched between fist-fights and kisses. Ernie wanted to work and the Submarine Film Corporation wanted the money.

A young heiress named Olive – Jean Tolley – is ship-wrecked on an island with a couple of professional gamblers, one of them a woman. A ne'er-do-well sponge diver named Paul rescues Olive after the gamblers have taken her credentials and left her to die. There's another diver named Boomer who is both jealous and morally lax, but early on he is dispatched: while diving for pearls, he is caught in the clutches of a *you-know-what*. Olive and Paul make it back to New York where they nail the imposters and then get married.

The Uninvited Guest was its title and as with most William-son fare, critical accolades would elude it. It had, however, one outstanding characteristic which made it another little mile-stone in Ernie's esoteric career. Segments of the film were to be in a marvelous new medium called Technicolor – not all, but many of the undersea portions, naturally. At the outset, color film stock was so expensive to print that producers, gambling on its ability to draw a crowd, only inserted portions of it in an otherwise black and white movie. Release prints were stag-gered so that color reels went on one projector and black and white reels on another; the practice continuing into the thirties.

For *The Uninvited Guest*, a process called "two-color sub-tractive" was used. Like its "additive color" counterpart, it was a way of trying to reproduce many colors by mixing varying densities of primary colors – sometimes three, but in this case, two primaries. There wasn't just one film stock involved, there were two; and the color wasn't in the emulsion, it was in a dye that was later applied to the emulsion.

Up until then, Ernie and his cameraman Jay Rescher had been able to carry the weight of any technical problems by themselves. This time, however, they required the help of

J.O. Taylor, a cinematographer who knew more about the intricacies of the new medium. The only problem Taylor *didn't* have was the kind of incredible exposures that confronted early experimenters in color *still* photography like W.H. Longley. Whereas Longley's undersea work was actual color in the form of autochrome, the Williamson team was still working in two different forms of black and white – at least at the filming stage.

The two rolls of film had to be "bi-packed" into the same camera. The outer roll was *ortho-don* which was filtered with a yellow coating. It was fed through the gate, emulsion to emulsion with a roll of *ortho-chromatic* – meaning that the base side of the *ortho-don* roll faced the lens. All light would penetrate the base, leaving an image for blue on its emulsion. The remaining red and green light would then pass through the yellow coating and the green would register on the second roll of film, the red never being recorded.

As usual, both black and white rolls would be developed and printed positive. But then both positive rolls would also be bleached, which took out the silver and left only emulsion; the emulsion then being dyed its desired color.

Of course, all of this meant that the glorious "color" was really manufactured in the laboratory. With historical respect for the innovators of early Technicolor, the process was quite synthetic and looked it; the black and white film becoming the Frankenstein of a cinematic Easter egg party. The positive roll that represented blue was usually dyed some shade of blue, and it was somewhat representational. But the image on roll number two was up for grabs. Most often, it became red with the yellow being sacrificed, as was the case in *The Uninvited Guest*.

Despite the liberties, one advantageous phenomenon occurred that rarely could be a plus for other movies. Whereas certain portions of the film suffered from lack of color accuracy, the inherent limitations of "two-color subtractive" actually favored Ernie's undersea footage. On the surface, the absence of yellow in scenes of tropical sunshine gave a totally unreal effect, but scenics on the sea floor received any benefits the system had to offer; every value of blue and plenty of red for density and definition.

Metro pictures ultimately became the distributor for the

movie. Although Ernie couldn't know it at the time, between Metro and his former dealings with Sam Goldwyn, a surprise was in store. The project would surpass *Twenty Thousand Leagues* in its frustrations, production time, and budget – all, of course, in an effort to treat the undersea as a backdrop for futuristic excesses – instead of the place of beauty it had remained for millions of years.

Six years had passed since Ernie's parting with his brother George, and during that time, he had written and produced three more feature-length pictures and filmed the undersea segments for two others. For him, this was proof enough that his watery world still had attraction for the post-war public, but he knew also that time was running out. He had managed to keep both himself and the Submarine Film Corporation alive, yet there was no longer the kind of publicity success that attended the first efforts. Even at the modest rate of a picture a year, Ernie could not count on a predictable market for his undersea movies. The novelty was wearing off.

By now, society wanted the film world to help it celebrate the "roaring" decade, and, in fact, to lead a way to the party. Clearly, not even in mood, could undersea scenarios answer to the cinematic worship of silk step-ins or bathtub gin or the saxophone. People had crossed the post-Victorian frontier, fought a bloody war, and they now wanted entertainment that played to their liberation.

When *The Uninvited Guest* opened in February of 1924, it was already surrounded by competition that all but eclipsed it. *Flaming Youth* was a ninety minute marathon of kissing and drinking. Young men and women went to the movies to absorb the social extravagance their wallets would allow them to copy. Harold Lloyd was spreading white knuckle syndrome by climbing up the side of a building in *Safety Last* and what nerve-endings Lloyd missed in his comedy, Douglas Fairbanks would soon stun in *The Thief of Baghdad*. Finally, if sex, comedy, and swashbuckling didn't part the public from it's money, there was DeMille's first production of *The Ten Commandments*, which, even then, came complete with a parting of the Red Sea.

Ernie's plodding images could no longer match the competition, and, in truth, he was getting as tired of the diver-shipwreck scenarios as anyone. Besides, although unwilling or unable to penetrate the sea, Hollywood technicians were, nevertheless, making inroads into his themes. Without a marvelous device like the Photosphere, natural underseascapes were missing but, for the most part, directors utilized models, tanks, and tight framing to obscure their artifice. As to sub-merging a camera, one or two scientific devices were in use, but the motion picture industry would have to wait until the early thirties and E.R. Fenimore Johnson for its first underwater camera housings. In the meantime, the backlots of 1924 created charming *illusions*.

The underwater ballet Ernie had captured in *Girl of the Sea* was now embodied in Louise Fazenda, "the diving Venus," who was appearing with her trained seal in a film opening in March of 1924. Then in October, Buster Keaton would don a diving suit for Metro-Goldwyn in *The Navigator*; he and his girl later boarding a submarine to escape a hostile island. Buster even battled another studio-made octopus while strolling the "sea-floor" – in reality, Lake Tahoe. For this, the cameramen were 20 feet down in a double-timbered crate. It sandwiched a layer of vulcanized canvas and held 300 pounds of ice to keep the camera body and glass from fogging as Buster dived the frigid mountain waters. Divers and Subs had already themed one of Pearl White's serial installments entitled *The Tragic Plunge* and a diver had shown up as hero in *Partners of the Tide* just months before Ernie finished *Wet Gold*.

All these efforts, however, were to present for the audience an *underwater effect* as opposed to an *undersea pictorial*. The ele-ment over which Ernie still held cinematic dominion was the actual ocean floor. It was also the one thing that still excited him. Floating through his spirit land and filming its life forms was something he could spend the rest of his days doing – although, considering the period, documentaries were a path to obscurity.

It was, in fact, William Beebe who would soon become master publicist for the undersea. His interests, however, were akin to Ernie's – the kind that, by themselves, no longer sold movies. Though he had published his first of many books on the subject, it was the beginning of an ocean awareness that could be tailored to less costly mediums than motion pictures – and certainly mediums requiring less "action." People were content to read Beebe's books. They were content to sense the pleasures of a submarine landscape when they viewed Zarh Pritchard's paintings. But in 1924, when people went to the flickers, they went to be thrilled.

To be sure, the naturalists were keen. In the forthcoming spring of 1927, Floyd Crosby of Beebe's Haitian Expedition, would carry a motor-driven De Vry beneath the surface in a brass case; the result being 1200 feet of reef life on film. A year later, Beebe himself would roll movie film from inside his first chamber and later still, his partner Otis Barton, would use the famous bathyscaph to film productions of his own. The projects, however, led to no public demand for undersea films. Excepting the love of scientists, there was yet not enough public interest – and in all candor, not enough cinematic technology – to make nature films a very marketable proposition. Besides that, some 25 years before Jacques Cousteau's emergence, there was no popular conscience for ocean ecology. There was no general affinity for intelligent sea mammals and no sustained interest for a world in which people had yet to build a framework of sensual responses.

Ernie had fallen in love with the moon while most of society had fallen in love with itself.

Ernie was soon to bid farewell to the movie business for a seven year stretch, but, as it turned out, his swan song was destined to be a bang and not a whimper. It appeared that someone in California was still willing to gamble on an undersea theme – providing it was as big and outrageous as it could be.

Early the following year, Metro-Goldwyn, satisfied with their receipts on *Wet Gold* and excited about the progress in color stock since *Uninvited Guest*, contacted Ernie regarding the production of a new Jules Verne classic. By March, he was on a train for Hollywood; presumably as co-director on a million dollar spectacle.

As it turned out, the new Jules Verne classic was exactly that: new. Verne would have never recognized it. It was to be the same amalgamation of *Twenty Thousand Leagues* and *The Mysterious Island* that Ernie had helped Universal put together ten years before. This time, however, it was going to be called *The Mysterious Island* instead of *Twenty Thousand Leagues*, and it was going to be in glorious color. The basic difference was that all the outrageous prostitutions of story line were going to be used right from the beginning, and when Metro-Goldwyn was through with the script, it made the Universal production look like the faithful transcription of a monk.

Ernie's script, set once again in the American Civil War-era, was as faithful to the book as possible. It was the first to be thrown out. Nemo became a twentieth century contemporary and his island was a futuristic stronghold from where he could hold the entire world for ransom. It was abundant with the sort of destructive hardware no sane man would employ, but then, if it wasn't used, the special effects men couldn't make Sam Goldwyn the really big picture he wanted. So it was determined that Nemo should be thoroughly crazy.

Ernie accepted the decisions as final, but he was yet to have his baptism in creation-by-the-numbers, Hollywood style. Civil War America was out, but in less than two weeks, so was America in any period. In its place was Russia. Nemo, now Count Dakkar, and the whole cast were to be Russians.

By the time studio officials were ready to let Ernie take the undersea portion of the script and leave, he had passed close to five months in captivity. Just before he walked out the doors to freedom, however, the lot supervisor cornered him with a final mandate; one which was the essence of quantitative thinking in the twenties. "Now – where you have ten divers," he said, "I want a hundred divers – two hundred if you can get them."[5]

With this piece of inspiration under his hat, Ernie took off for New York to outfit his new expedition, little suspecting that he was in for one of the most adverse meteorological experiences any film director had ever coped with. On the fourth weekend of July, 1925, the entire cast and crew were incarcerated on a freighter when they ran straight into a hurricane. Winds and seas hammered the ship all night and by the time they pulled into Nassau harbor, the storm had devastated New Providence. Amidst uprooted trees and wreckage, the Williamson studio was in splinters and most of his boats were sunk, the equipment an inch thick with mud.

Exactly two months later, the company was at Highbourne Cay, fully repaired and in the middle of shooting, when hurricane number two struck. The boats were able to ride this one out, but the entire camp was blown away, forcing the cast and crew to fight the iguanas for cave space. This storm went on to kill hundreds in Florida and almost level Miami.

Ernie wired Hollywood for the extra funds to rebuild and he got them, but when the next full moon arrived, it brought hurricane number three along with it. This time it drove the company into their one strong building and they later shared it with the passengers and livestock of a ferry that had piled right into their location.

Considering that throughout the problems of human survival, color film stock had to stay ice-boxed and the temperature of gelatin filters controlled with an incubator, it was amazing that one can of exposed footage ever made it to the studios. On top of that, Hollywood had weathered three storms of its own – all of them directorial. Ernie's old associate, Maurice Tourneur had walked off the set and gone back to France over the initiation by Louis Mayer of a new supervisor system. Tourneur's replacement was Benjamin Christiansen, a Dane renowned for his horror and occult films. Christiansen stomped off and returned to Europe after a pitched battle over the scripting. The studio filming was finally completed almost four years later by a third director, Lucien Hubbard, who also contributed large portions of script material.

What with earthly storms and temperamental ones, the whole production finally wrapped at about one and a half million dollars. The studio, however, had just finished pouring six million into a successful *Ben Hur*, so Goldwyn figured that if *Mysterious Island* could do even a fourth as well as the biblical drama, all investments would pay off.

Ernie's end of production was a thing to be remembered. Together with MGM's effects group and art director, Cedric Gibbons, he took his undersea budget and went happily berserk, hurricanes notwithstanding. The story sported not one but two submarines, the old octopus had companionship in the form of a marvelous dragon, and there was even an undersea city complete with "crustacean men."

All of these playthings were germane to a story that went through other transmutations after Ernie started filming and kept right on changing until the day it left the shop. Even Count Dakkar, as played by Lionel Barrymore, turned out to be a good man against evil forces. Devoting his life to probing the ocean's secrets, he is shanghaied in one of his own submersibles by an evil nobleman who wants to use it in overthrowing the government. Dakkar is saved by his followers, but not until the sub has been damaged by the nobleman's men, causing it to sink into unexplored depths – which is where the fun begins. For the Caribbean unit, the most spectacular changes resulted in one submarine getting wrecked, the old octopus having his first victory – over Barrymore – and the dragon being slain with torpedoes.

Despite all these grand undersea fantasies, the movie was destined for immediate obscurity. When *Mysterious Island* was released in a test market in 1928, folks walked right past the undersea scenes, right past the glorious Technicolor, and right down the street to see a man act – and hear his voice. It was Al Jolson in *The Jazz Singer*. Sound movies had arrived in February, burying the silent film forever.

Goldwyn and Mayer pulled the picture at once, and armed with the newly-arrived technology, had Hubbard patch-in sound sequences and music. It was finally premiered in New York in October of 1929, but the four and a half years of disjointed creativity was apparent to moviegoers and the film just disappeared into Hollywood's sea of red ink.

The moment "talkies" came into being, every screenplay produced was overstuffed with conversation and music for a num-

ber of years. Hollywood had a new playtoy and it wasn't about
to waste a minute of film stock on anything that didn't make a
noise. Accordingly, not even the prospect of narration, mood
music, or a looped "bubble track" could persuade anyone to
invest in movies about, what Cousteau was to later term, "the
silent world."

For awhile then, feature films were removed from Ernie's
life; although the equatorial undersea would never be. He
parked the *Jules Verne* with its Photosphere and dug into Bahamian soil to make a home for the rest of his days. A girl named
Lilah broke his bachelor's resistance of 46 years and they had
children shortly thereafter. Ernie lectured and wrote a little hop-
ing that someone, somewhere, would put him back to work in
the water, and ultimately someone did.

Being more familiar with Bahamian reefs than probably
anyone in the colonial community, Ernie helped The American
Museum of Natural History in its acquisitions for a new hall of
ocean life some six years before; the project that was now using
Zarh Pritchard's works as backdrops. It was probably on the
strength of this gesture that the Field Museum now searched
Ernie out and offered him the same type of requisition job. Not
to be outdone by New York, Chicago had decided it wanted an
ocean exhibit as well.

Ernie was probably happier than at any time since his first
filming trip in 1913. The transition from drawing board to
undersea explorer had occurred a little late in life for him to
then switch to academia, but he had always wanted to play in
the scientists' realm. Now, he had his very own scientific expedition and he could poke, prod, and dissect just like the biologists. For a good part of 1929, Ernie shot both stills and motion
pictures to match fishes with their proper neighbors and territo-
ries. He then worked with a museum artist and a taxidermist to
sketch and plaster cast more than two hundred species, and,
finally, he took on the awesome job of collecting close to 25 tons
of coral that, once packed, translated into three train-car loads.
That much pirated coral seemed respectable back then since,
other than books, there was no home media to teach millions of
city kids about the beauty of the ocean floor.

After about three years of exhibition arts, Ernie decided to break out of cinematic exile and produce one last feature. *With Williamson Beneath The Sea* was its name, and if ever there was a pasticcio of all his life's labors, this was it. It had the sharks, the divers, and the shipwrecks. "Old springs and rubber" was even trotted out for one last menacing performance. Conveniently lining the ocean floor was an assortment of metal boxes and, here and there, a human skeleton popped into frame. The format was documentary, but the narration was pure misproportioned oratory. The tired old octopus was "the most dreaded of the sea" and the playful Bahamian divers became "hardened desperate men who will stop at nothing." It was a questionable trait of Ernie Williamson that he never felt hesitation about juggling documentary elements with outrageous melodrama to fill-out a movie.

After this picture, he odd-jobbed through the undersea for the rest of his days – which actually turned out to be quite a few. He once made the Movietone News and in 1934 set out for a lecture series in Great Britain. By the time he returned, the following year, a somewhat self-serving autobiography was in the stores and it gave him the exposure that prompted still more lectures on marine life.

If nothing else, John Ernest Williamson remained colorful in later years. Through his self-styled experiments, he became an authority on sharks and around 1940, he wrangled an expedition sponsorship out of Bahamian Government under Explorers Club Flag Number 97. During that same year, post office status was acquired for the Photosphere and with this neat little promotional device, Ernie started posting outgoing mail with cancellations that read: "Sea Floor-Bahamas" and "Posted in Williamson Photosphere at Bottom of Sea."

Ernie loved sharing the Photosphere and playing emissary from Neptune's court. When his post office first opened, he had letter writers come down the tube and commit their first impressions of the sea floor to paper before sealing their envelopes. Years before, his "hole in the sea" had even hosted Alexander Graham Bell who, although he was past seventy, insisted on seeing, first hand, the undersea world before he died. Ernie lowered him down in a boatswain's chair and Bell declared it to be the most wonderful experience of his life.

Paramount gave Ernie one last little Technicolor chore for a 1941 film called *Bahama Passage* with Sterling Hayden and Madeleine Carroll. In 1955, at the peppery age of seventy-three, he was still plugging his underwater world for television on Julian and Sol Lesser's grand old landmark show, *I Search for Adventure*, and as the show's title indicated, Ernie Williamson certainly did just that.

When George Williamson returned to Colorado in 1918, he was still a young, though tired, man. The ocean, he felt, had extracted quite enough of his energies, and if he was to ever return, it would be on his terms and with his plan; not his father's and not Ernie's. His fatigue, though, was short-lived – through dozens of ambitious schemes, he spent the rest of his life trying to accomplish that return. Some grand ideas emerged over the years, and he courted some important people to try pulling them off.

At one point, George almost had Max Fleischman's gin money building him a bathysphere like Beebe's. Still another who indulged George was R.G. Dunn Douglas of the Dun and Bradstreet empire. In the late twenties, George even went to Hollywood trying to drum up interest in a sound remake of *Twenty Thousand Leagues*.

Every time he could escape from subsistence deals in Denver, he would fashion some maritime proposal, spinning new ideas off anyone who would listen. He corresponded vigorously with naval officials and even talked with Franklin Roosevelt when F.D.R. was Undersecretary of the Navy. For reasons known only to Providence, not one of his grand plans would ever pan out. He wasn't unique in that sense. The ocean has a way of romancing people with its riches and then presenting incredible resistance to their efforts. In addition to dead sailors and ships, its floor is strewn with the bodies of promoters, their ideas, and a lot of people's money.

Sometime in the early thirties, George developed a relationship with Simon Lake, the submarine pioneer. Lake was then in his twilight years, and still sore as hell with the government for snubbing his early boat designs in preference to those of John Holland. With George's enthusiasms and Lake's engineering ideas, they resurrected the concept of building an industrial research sub. Time was on their side, for the Electric Boat Company was between wars and sitting on the Thames River like an abandoned saw mill. G.Y. Spear, the company's vice president, was praying for a new idea to come through the door and put him back to work. Eventually, George Williamson came through the door and contracted to build a 100-foot exploration submarine, design number 174-A, to be called the *Atlantis*. The final blueprints included air locks for divers and built-in scanning cameras with external flood lights. There was a darkroom with printing machines, sound recording instruments, X-ray equipment and a laboratory. The year was 1932 and like the other visionary schemes that preceded it, the project broke down somewhere between the engineering plans and reality.

Finally, one day in 1941, George Williamson Junior decided he'd seen enough of that faraway look in his dad's eyes. He dragged out the file folders and waded through twenty years worth of undersea proposals to try and help his father find a project that could be brought to fruition. Between the two of them, a touring submarine was exhumed and declared worthy of an all-out effort. George Junior quit his job and dived in.

Our Navy still had a few S-type boats that hadn't been scrapped and the father-son team went to Washington to negotiate a purchase. They then took off for San Francisco to make presentations. The plan was to tow the sub from Connecticut to the Mare Island yards, and there, they would tear out all the military hardware and build a comfortable observation salon. Proper trim could give them enough underwater hull for windows. The deck would be awash, the boat still running on diesel, and, in the true sense, it would never have to submerge. Many years later, of course, Walt Disney would utilize that concept for his theme park in Anaheim, California.

The sea gardens off Honolulu were to be the cruising ground for the sub. Both Matson Ship Lines and Dole Pineapple were tempted by the proposal, but it was Matson that finally started committing. On a Sunday morning, three days before the decisive meeting with Matson, George Junior was eating a late breakfast when the announcement of another marine matter came over the radio. It was the Japanese raid on Pearl Harbor.

Admiral Nagumo ruined a lot of people's plans that day and along with them, George Williamson's last attempt to return to the undersea world.

George Williamson died in Denver, Colorado, on May 23, 1956. John Ernest Williamson died in Nassau, Bahama Islands, ten years later on July 15, 1966. They never saw each other or communicated at anytime in the thirty-eight years between their parting in New York in 1918 and George's death.

Carl Gregory, the first undersea cinematographer, became chief instructor of photography for the Signal Corps during World War I. Later, he was Dean of the New York Institute of Photography, and, later still, a film preservation specialist for the National Archives. Ironically, the National Archives does not hold a copy of his pioneering undersea film. Gregory died in 1951.

The period between 1910 and 1920 was the most prolific in American motion picture history, and yet the most obscure since literally hundreds of companies emerged and died in that one decade. Although negative materials for some of the early Williamson films were destroyed in a hurricane, it is quite possible that certain film study centers, currently in the process of documenting and salvaging materials from that era, may yet unearth heretofore lost prints. The George Eastman House, the Museum of Modern Art in New York City, the U.C.L.A. Film and Televison Archives, and the Library of Congress are the main institutional repositories for early films and are especially active in restoration projects.

Despite the losses, the Williamsons' magnum opus, *Twenty Thousand Leagues Under the Sea*, can be viewed at the Museum of Modern Art in New York by special arrangement with the museum's Film Study Center. Film Preservation Associates, a private firm and successor to the Blackhawk Library, also owns a print and it has been transferred to video. A

VHS cassette is available from Kino International, which markets the restored and tinted version, and a laser disc of the same version is available from Image Entertainment.

The disposition of Ernie's films following 1918 is unknown to the author, except for *With Williamson Beneath the Sea*. U.C.L.A. holds a print and it can be viewed by arrangement with their Film Research and Study Center. As with so many films of the period, I have failed to locate anyone possessing either original negatives or original interpositives for any of the Williamson productions.

This absence of materials includes even a print of MGM's 1929 production of *The Mysterious Island*. The project bears special mention because the American Film Institute does not have a record of the Williamson involvement and this is at variance with Ernie's autobiography and other related writings. Both sources may be correct, however. The movie went through years of alterations and, in the final compositing of elements, it is conceivable that film footage taken under the sea was supplanted by stage effects.

With respect to motion picture adaptations of *Twenty Thousand Leagues*, the 1916 Williamson-Universal production was, in fact, preceded by two modest screenplays; a 1905 Biograph production and a 1907 version of George Méliès. According to Phil Hardy's *The Encyclopedia of Science Fiction Movies*, the black-and-white Biograph version ran 18-minutes and that of Méliès employed hand-coloring. Although replete with special effects, neither film utilized any underwater cinematography since no appropriate methods existed at the time.

In their own right, however, these two stage-bound treasures would be as grand to see as any Williamson photoplay.

Seeking realism under the sea is our intrepid nature.

Contriving that image is our fanciful—and more wonderous—nature.

Footnotes & Additional Reference Materials

The Men Who Wrote an Undersea Novel

FOOTNOTES

1. "A diver of Oman's coral sea," Canto Seventh, stanzas IX–XIII, *The Revolt of Islam*, 1817.

2. Actually, there had been a few applications of the undersea theme in Elizabethan times. Shakespeare (in *Richard III* and *The Tempest*) and John Donne (in letters) both used the theme sparingly. A generation before them, the Portuguese poet Camoens had employed it in the *Lusiads* (1572) and more than a century after them, John Hughes wrote *The Court of Neptune* (1735). John Leyden also contributed *The Mermaid* (1802) and around the same general time, J.C.F. Schiller authored *The Diver*. However, none of these individual contributions was the start of a literary movement using the undersea theme on a broader scale.

3. The majority of which are contained in the following:
   – *The Revolt of Islam* (1817)
   – *Prometheus Unbound* (1820)
   – *Ode to the West Wind* (III) (1820)
   – *A Vision of the Sea* (1820)
   – *Arethusa* (IV) (Posthumous 1824*)
   – *Ode to Naples* (Epode IIa) *
   – *Stanzas* (II) *

4. *He Saw in the Concave Green of the Sea*, 1820.

5. *Macphail of Colonsay and the Mermaid of Corrivrekin*.

6. Much later, in 1852, Bayard Taylor also employed this theme in *Sunken Treasures*.

7. Oddly enough, Wordsworth had as much reason to fear the sea as Whittier or Miller. Although he was raised near the coast (Cockermouth), he was early on absorbed with the news of storms and shipwrecks. Later, in 1805, his much loved brother, John, a merchant officer, went down with his ship off Portsmouth.

8. As far as *France* is concerned, her writers had long romanticized the sea – at least its surface. In a scientific and mechanical sense, France was also destined to be a leader in exploration *under* the sea. However, it was not until later in the nineteenth century that her literature reflected any sub-ocean thought. Even then, there were very few poems

on this theme. In chapter eight of his book, *The Undersea Adventure* (Julian Messner, New York, 1953), Phillip Diole, a Frenchman and Cousteau companion, relates this point. He goes on to discuss the strange absence of words in the French language which could be used in undersea description.

9. *Telliamed*, Beniot de Maillet, 1748.

10. *Gazette de France*, May 6, 1774.

11. There were some crude predecessors, two in Holland and one in Italy that date from the mid-seventeenth century.

12. There is evidence that Americans perpetrated a number of submersible attacks against the British in the War of 1812, but documentation was poor. There are no drawings or written descriptions of the boats' configurations, nor the names of their builders/designers. There is also no record of a *successful* attack.

13. Then known as the Corps of Royal Sappers and Miners.

14. The single predecessor was a British fresh-water project in India. A Dr. O'Shaughnessy put one across the river Hugli for the East Indian Company in 1838.

15. Le Capitaine Merobert, *Voyage au Fond de la Mer*, Comptoir des Imprimeurs – Unis, Paris, 1845. The Bibliotheque Nationale has a copy.

16. *Voyage au Fond de la Mer*, Chapter II, pages 34–35.

17. *The Times* of London, 13 October, 1848.

18. *Moby Dick*, LXXXVII.

19. *ibid*, CXIV.

20. Published under the pseudonym of Salvator R. Tarnmoor in 1854.

21. Written for the unpublished *Voyage en Ecosse* (1859–1860); but later applied, in parts, to *The Green Ray* (1883).

22. Hartwig, Dr. G., *The Sea and its Wonders*, 1860. Two other notable books of that year were *A History of British Zoophytes* by Dr. William Johnstone and Alexander Croal, and *A History of The British Sea Anemones and Corals* by Phillip Henry Gosse.

23. Hetzel's granddaughter, Mme C. Hetzel Bonnier de la Chapelle, and A. Parmenie published, in 1953, the interesting correspondence between Hetzel and his authors: *Histoire d'un éditeur et de ses auteurs: P.J. Hetzel* (Michel-Paris). Naturally, Jules Verne is featured in this volume.

24. The *aérophore* was actually conceived and built far from the ocean. Rouquayrol was employed in the mountain town of Espalion and his invention was initially utilized for mining operations there. After Denayrouse arrived, the two technicians converted the device for underwater use, and it was first tested in the nearby River Lot. Some records state that the canister could have been pressurized to between a low of 25 atmospheres to a high of 40 atmospheres. (Verne raised it to 50.) Considering the pneumatic and metallurgical expertise of the

day, one suspects the tank rating might have been lower. Modern reconstructions of the device have the tank displacing two gallons and charged to 250 (p.s.i.) of air pressure. Chronicles of the time state that the divers were not inclined to detach the air host past about 20 feet down, and, at that depth, they were able to walk about 50 yards before either ascending or reconnecting the hose.

25. Early in the twentieth century, a rumor circulated that, indeed, the whole concept of *Twenty Thousand Leagues* originated with still another woman, French poet Louise Michel. Like Hetzel, Mme Michel was a political figure during the Commune, and, because of this, she was later exiled to New Caledonia. Politics were of great interest to Michel, but so also was biology, and, in fact, later in life, she wrote two or three science-fantasies. However, the Michel-Verne rumor went so far as to state that, in 1900, Michel sold Verne a near complete manuscript that ultimately became *Twenty Thousand Leagues*.

Although the alleged incident was obviously placed more than thirty years after Verne's well established authorship, the literary gossip was perpetuated by at least four French authors: Ferdinand Planche, Hélen Gosset, Gerard de Lacaze-Duthiers, and Françoise Mozer. These writers had, in turn, received their anecdote from a single source: *La bonne Louise*, a biography of Louise Michel which came out shortly after her death in 1905. (Verne also died in 1905.) The book was written by Ernest Girault, and just how M Girault published with such blatant error is as unknown as it is astounding. This was in the face of Michel's own memoirs which mention nothing about her having ever met Verne.

In an exhaustive document, *Louise Michel–Jules Verne: De Qui est 20,000 Lieues Sous Les Mers?* (Paris, 1959), one author devoted 61 pages to discrediting the Girault theory. However, he then fell into his own knowledge gap when he tried to establish dates for the publication of *Twenty Thousand Leagues* in book form. In his explanation, the Girault theory survived so well because the book, *Twenty Thousand Leagues*, was not published until after Verne's death – the serialized version being its only manifestation for some 30 years. After its appearance in the *Magasin d'Education et de Recreation*, it is claimed that the manuscript was placed in a trunk, lost for some time, and then later discovered by Verne's grandson. This bit of information is as completely at odds with established fact as the Girault story that the author so painstakingly worked to disprove.

26. Titles listed in English are for convenience only. The English language versions of these books generally followed a few years after the original publication date.

27. An interesting similarity between Melville and Verne is that they both had successful sea captain brothers. It's probably of psychic importance. Equally prolific in sea imagery was Wordsworth, who also had a sea captain brother.

28. Not to be confused with the previously mentioned children's novel *Voyage au Fond de la Mer* (1845).

29. This passage, as others to follow, is extracted from the first American edition of *Twenty Thousand Leagues Under the Seas* published by George M. Smith & Company of Boston (1873) – an edition of James R. Osgood & Company. As a reprint of British text, it is the translation of Mercier Lewis (Louis Page Mercier). Newer and more accurate translations of the book are available, but, this passage and others utilized herein, are generally unaffected by contemporary refinements – if consideration is made for earlier English form.

30. Roger, Aristide: *Voyage Sous Les Flots*, P. Brunet, Editeur, 31, Rue Bonaparte, Paris, 1868. The Bibliotheque Nationale has a copy.

31. Other contributors to undersea literature had such backgrounds. John Leyden held a diploma in medicine and John Keats was a practicing surgeon when he started writing. In general sea literature, there was Joseph Marie Sue, who was also a surgeon.

32. *Voyage Sous Les Flots*, Chapter XVII, "La Mer de Corail," p. 156–162.

33. *Twenty Thousand Leagues Under the Seas*, Chapter XXIV, p. 139–140.

34. *ibid*, Chapter XV, p. 86–87.

35. *ibid*, Chapter XVI, p. 93.

36. *ibid*, Chapter XV, p. 86 and 88 (remarks in brackets are mine).

37. *ibid*, Chapter XIII, p. 76.

38. *ibid*, Chapter XIII, p. 75. However, for some reason, Verne was far more accurate when dealing with light absorption and the transformation of color in varying depths. See also: Walter James Miller, *The Annotated Twenty Thousand Leagues*, New American Library, 1976.

39. *Voyage Sous Les Flots*, Chapter XVII, p. 162.

40. Known in English today as *The Toilers of the Sea* (1866).

41. The first being the *Magasin Pittoresque* in 1833. It was, however, preceded by numerous illustrated journals in England.

42. This medium was originally used by the Armenians, then revived and perfected by an Englishman, Thomas Bewick (1753–1828). "Standing wood" meant wood cut against the grain. In this way, the whole surface had equal resistance. The engraving tools turned easily in any direction to make thin, exacting lines and it yielded all the later effects of copper.

43. As well as having illustrated textbooks to work from, de Neuville could have received a little inspiration from the publicity drawings of Durand-Brager. Working from a diving bell, Durand-Brager had recently been Hippolyte Magen's expeditionary artist at the Vigo Bay salvage site.

44. De Neuville's most durable painting is *The Last Cartridges* (1873).

45. As an indication of Verne's popularity, the Société Jules Verne was founded in Paris by Jean H. Guermonprez and from 1935 to 1938, the society published an illustrated bulletin. It was, in fact, an international collaboration, and later, in 1955, a world-wide audience attended a Jules Verne exposition in Paris, Nantes, and Amiens.

For the poems of Keats, Shelley, and Taylor; as well as those of Tennyson, Whittier, and Wordsworth, I would like to acknowledge the wonderful poetical series published by Houghton, Mifflin and Company – in these cases, between 1895 and 1907. The piece by Matthew Arnold is from a collection of selected poems published in London in 1878 without publisher's indicia; and the excerpts from both Hugo's *Toilers of the Sea* and the writings of Mrs. Hemans are from editions of T.Y. Crowell and Company, 1888 and 1890, respectively. For Kipling, a 1907 edition of his collected verse from Doubleday was referenced – for Melville, a 1923 edition of *The Piazza Tales* from Constable and Company of London. The poem by Percival was taken from *The Poetical Works of James Gates Percival*, Ticknor and Fields, Boston, 1859; and excerpts from Scott's *The Cruise of the Midge* from the edition of Gibbings of London, 1894. Selections from Whitman's *Leaves of Grass* are from the 1935 edition of E.P. Dutton. The autobiographical piece, *Diving With and Without Armor, Containing the Submarine Exploits of J.B. Green, The Celebrated Submarine Diver*, was published by Faxon's Steam Power Press of Buffalo, New York, in 1859. *Letter from a Passenger on Board the Submarine Steamer* from the *Comic Almanac*, 1843, was extracted from *The Conquest of the Sea* by Henry Siebe, George Routledge and Sons, London, 1873. The article on *The Corps of Royal Sappers and Miners*, 1855, by Charles Dickens, is extracted from *Deep Diving and Submarine Operations*, by Robert Henry Davis, St. Catherine Press, London.

ADDITIONAL REFERENCES

Aldiss, Brian W., *Billion Year Spree: The True History of Science Fiction*, Doubleday & Company, New York, 1973.

Allen, Gay Wilson, *The Walt Whitman Handbook*, Hendricks House, New York, 1962.

Allott, Kenneth, *Jules Verne*, The Macmillan Company, New York, 1941.

Allotte de la Fuÿe, Marguerite, *Jules Verne*, (translated from the French by Erik de Mauny), Coward-McCann, New York, 1956.

Arvin, Newton, *Herman Melville*, William Sloane Associates, U.S.A., 1950.

Auden, W.H., *The Enchafed Flood or The Romantic Iconography of the Sea*, Vintage Books, New York, 1950.

Barlow, Nora, editor, *Charles Darwin's Diary of the Voyage of H.M.S. "Beagle"*, Cambridge at the University Press, 1934.

Barnhart, Clarence L. and William D. Halsey, editors, *The New Century Handbook of English Literature*, Appleton/Century/Crofts, New York, 1967.

Bright, Charles, *The Story of the Atlantic Cable*, D. Appleton & Company, New York, 1903.

Brinnin, John Malcolm, *The Sway of the Grand Saloon: A Social History of the North Atlantic*, Delacorte Press, New York, 1971.

Brodie, Bernard, *Sea Power in the Machine Age*, Princeton University Press, 1941.

Chorley, Henry F., *Memorials of Mrs. Hemans – Illustrations of her Literary Character from her Private Correspondence*, Saunders and Otley, London, 1837.

Clarke, Arthur C., *Voice Across the Sea*, Harper & Brothers, New York, 1958.

Darwin, Charles, *Journal of Researches into the Natural History and Geology of the Countries Visited During the Voyage Round the World of H.M.S. "Beagle" under Command of Captain Fitz Roy, R.N.* (second edition), John Murray, London, 1912.

Davis, Robert Henry, *Deep Diving and Submarine Operations* (fourth edition), The Saint Catherine Press, London, 1935.

Day, Hem (pseudonym for Marcel Dieu), *Louise Michel–Jules Verne: De Qui est 20,000 Lieues Sous Les Mers?*, Pensee et Action, Bruxelles/Paris, 1959, The University of Michigan Library has a copy in the Labadie Collection – Rare Books Department.

Deacon, Margaret, *Scientists and the Sea 1650–1900*, Academic Press, London/New York, 1971.

Doukan, Gilbert, *The World Beneath the Waves*, (translated by A. & R.M. Case), John De Graff, Inc., New York, 1957.

Dugan, James, *The Great Iron Ship*, Harper & Brothers, New York, 1953.

————, *Man Under the Sea*, Harper & Brothers, New York, 1956.

Dunham, Arthur Louis, *The Industrial Revolution in France 1815–1848*, Exposition Press, New York, 1955.

Evans, I.O., *Jules Verne: Master of Science Fiction*, Sidgwick and Jackson, London, 1956.

————, *Jules Verne and his Work*, Twayne Publishers, U.S.A., 1966.

Ford, Newell F., editor, *The Poetical Works of Shelley*, Houghton Mifflin Company, Boston, 1975.

Furtado, R. de Loyola, *Shelley: Concept of Nature*, Firma K.L. Mukhopadhyay, Calcutta, 1958.

George, Albert Joseph, *The Development of French Romanticism: The Impact of the Industrial Revolution on Literature*, Syracuse University Press, 1955.

Gillispie, Charles Coulston, editor-in-chief, *The Dictionary of Scientific Biography*, Volume IX by A.T. Macrobius and K.F. Naumann, Charles Scribners Sons, New York, 1974.

Guberlet, Muriel L., *Explorers of the Sea: Famous Oceanographic Expeditions*, The Ronald Press, New York, 1964.

Hart, James D., *The Oxford Companion to American Literature* (fourth edition), Oxford University Press, New York, 1965.

Harvey, Paul and J.E. Heseltine, editors, *The Oxford Companion to French Literature*, Oxford University Press, 1959.

Herzberg, Max J. and the staff of Thomas Y. Crowell, *The Readers Encyclopedia of American Literature*, Thomas Y. Crowell Company, New York, 1962.

Heuvelmans, Bernard, *In the Wake of the Sea Serpents*, (translated from the French by Richard Garnett), Hill and Wang, New York, 1968.

Hope, Ronald, editor, *The Harrap Book of Sea Verse*, George Harrap & Company, London, 1960.

Hugo, Victor, *The Toilers of the Sea*, (translated from the French by Isabel F. Hapgood), Thomas Y. Crowell & Company, New York, 1888.

Idyll, C.P., editor, *Exploring the Ocean World: A History of Oceanography*, Thomas Y. Crowell & Company, New York, 1969.

Kastner, L.E. and Henry G. Atkins, *A Short History of French Literature*, Blackie & Son Limited, London and Glasgow, 1925.

Kemp, Peter, editor, *The Oxford Companion to Ships and the Sea*, Oxford University Press, 1976.

Kennaugh, W.E. & Company, *Salvage Proposal to Marine Insurance Companies*, Griffin & Hall, Washington, 1860.

Latil, Pierre de and Jean Rivoire, *Man and the Underwater World*, (translated from the French by Edward Fitzgerald), G.P. Putnam's Sons, New York, 1956.

_____, *Sunken Treasure*, Hill and Wang, New York, 1962.

Lewis, Charles Lee, *Books of the Sea: An Introduction to Nautical Literature*, United States Naval Institute, Annapolis, Md., 1943.

Marcucci, Edmondo, *Les Illustrations des Voyages Extraordinaires de Jules Verne*, Société Jules Verne et Feret & Fils, Paris, 1956. The Library of Congress retains a copy.

Mathias, Peter, *The First Industrial Nation: An Economic History of Britain*, Charles Scribner's Sons, New York, 1969.

McDonald, Philip B., *A Saga of the Seas*, Wilson-Erickson, New York, 1937.

Miller, Walter James, editor, *The Annotated Jules Verne: Twenty Thousand Leagues under the Sea*, Thomas Y. Crowell, New York, 1976.

Mowat, R.B., *The Victorian Age*, George G. Harrap & Company, Limited, London, 1939.

Patterson, J.E., editor, *The Sea's Anthology*, William Heinemann, London, 1913.

Pesce, G.L., *La Navigation Sous-Marine*, Vuibert & Nony, Paris, 1906.

The staff of G.P. Putnam's Sons, compilers and editors, *The Nineteenth Century*, G.P. Putnam's Sons, New York, 1901.

Quatrefages de Breau, Armand de, *Souvenirs d'un Naturaliste*, Masson, Paris, 1854.

Quinn, Patrick F., *The French Face of Edgar Poe*, Southern Illinois University Press, Carbondale, 1957.

Rowland, K.T., *Steam at Sea*, Praeger Publishing, Inc., New York, 1970.

Ryerson, V.B., *A Brief Account of Submarine Machines and Especially of Ryerson's Patent*, Edward O. Jenkins, New York, 1860. The Chicago Historical Society has a copy.

Schlee, Susan, *The Edge of an Unfamiliar World: A History of Oceanography*, E.P. Dutton & Company, New York, 1973.

Selincourt, Aubrey de, editor, *The Book of the Sea*, W.W. Norton & Company, New York, 1963.

Shepard, Birse, *Lore of the Wreckers*, Beacon Press, Boston, 1961.

Siebe, Henry, *Conquest of the Sea: A Book of Divers and Diving*, George Routledge & Sons, London, 1873.

Smith, Myron J. and Robert C. Weller, *Sea Fiction Guide*, The Scarecrow Press, Metuchen, N.J., 1976.

Stern, Philip Van Doren, *The Confederate Navy*, Bonanza Books, New York, 1961.

Stevens, William Oliver and Allan Westcott, *A History of Sea Power*, Doubleday, Doran & Company, New York, 1920.

Sweeny, James B., *A Pictorial History of Oceanographic Submersibles*, Crown Publishers, New York, 1970.

Taton, Rene, editor, *Science in the Nineteenth Century*, (translated from the French by A.J. Pomerans), Thames & Hudson, Ltd., London, 1965.

Temple, M.L., *Du Scaphandre et de son emploi a Bord des Navires*, Arthus Bertrand, Paris, 1855.

Verne, Jean Jules, *Jules Verne*, (translated and adapted by Roger Greaves), Taplinger Publishing Company, New York, 1976.

Walker, Warren S., *James Fenimore Cooper*, Barnes & Noble, New York, 1962.

Waltz, George H., Jr., *Jules Verne: The Biography of an Imagination*, Henry Holt & Company, New York, 1943.

Ward, Ritchie, *Into the Ocean World: The Biology of the Sea*, Alfred A. Knopf, New York, 1974.

Williamson, William M., editor, *The Eternal Sea: An Anthology of Sea Poetry*, Coward-McCann, New York, 1946.

The Man Who Painted Under the Sea

FOOTNOTES

1. Moulton, Robert H., "Painting Under the Ocean," *Technical World* (*Illustrated World*) Vol. 19:49+, March 1913.

2. _____, "An artist who operates at the bottom of the ocean . . ." *Sunset* 41:46, July, 1918.

3. _____, "A Modern Merman Who Paints the World Under the Sea," *Outlook* (superseded by *Outlook and Independent* and *New Outlook*) 2(74) 499-501, 21 November 1923.

4. Holder, Charles Frederick, "The Glass-Bottom Boat," *The National Geographic* XX(9):761-767, September 1909.

5. Pritchard, Zarh H., dedication to Robert Rogers as incorporated into 1926 Grace Nicholson Gallery Catalog.

6. *The Literary Digest* 44(25):1319, 22 June 1912, "An Undersea Painter."

7. Danielsson, Bengt, *Tahiti*, Les editions du Pacifique, Papeete, Tahiti, 1976.

8. Pritchard, Zarh H., "The Under-Sea World – Experiences of an Artist Who Paints at the Bottom of the Sea," *Asia* (*Asia and the Americas*), pages 217-220+, March 1924.

9. Nicholson, Grace, A compilation of notes to Zarh Pritchard as incorporated into her gallery catalog for 26 February to 26 March 1926: from Narii Salmon, 13 December 1905, 18 December 1905, page 31.

10. Andersen, Antony E., "Art Under the Sea," *Los Angeles Times*, section VI, page 2, 27 May, 1906.

11. Field, Perez, "Walter Pritchard gives reception at his new studio," *Graphic* (formerly *Los Angeles Graphic* and *Western Graphic*), page 25, 23 March 1907. [The History Department of the Los Angeles Public Library has copies.]

12. Nicholson: from Jack London, 12 January 1912, page 31.

13. *ibid:* from John Burroughs, 12 April 1909, 3 March 1913, page 27.

14. *ibid:* from David Starr Jordan, September 1916, page 25.

15. *ibid:* from Charles Livingston Bull, 14 June 1912, page 27.

16. Townsend, Charles Haskins, to Zarh Pritchard, 31 July 1916, in "Undersea Paintings by Zarh Pritchard," page 22, Grace Nicholson Galleries, Pasadena, 1926.

17. Ritter, W.E., to Zarh Pritchard, Scripps Institute, 1 December 1916, in "Undersea Paintings by Zarh Pritchard," page 24, Grace Nicholson Galleries, Pasadena, 1926.

18. Hudson, Charles B., to Zarh Pritchard, 24 December 1917. In "Undersea Paintings by Zarh Pritchard," page 25, Grace Nicholson Galleries, 26 February to 26 March, 1926.

19. Harada, Jiro, "Under-Water Paintings by Zarh Pritchard," *The Studio*, XIIV Leicester Square, London, Vol. 91:177-181, January–June 1926. The Metropolitan Museum of Art and New York Public Library have copies.

20. Lucas, F.H., to prospective patrons for the Hall of Ocean Life, American Museum of Natural History, 14 August 1923.

21. Beebe, William, to Zarh Pritchard, 2 August 1923.

22. _____, "Color Under the Sea," *House and Garden* 52:58-63, December 1927.

23. Vaughan, Malcolm, "Painting Beauty Under the Sea," *Los Angeles Times* Sunday Magazine, pages 16-17, 8 July 1928.

ADDITIONAL REFERENCES

Anonymous, *The Civilian's South India*, John Lane, The Bodley Head, Ltd., London.

Andersen, Antony E., Review of Pritchard Exhibit at Grace Nicholson's Galleries, section III, page 19, 14 March, 1926.

Anthony, H.E., "Glimpses into the Hall of Ocean Life," *Natural History Magazine* 33(4):364-380, 1933.

Art Digest, Art Index 3:1127, October 1935-September 1938.

_____, "Undersea Paintings" (exhibit at Arthur V. Newton Galleries, New York), *Art Digest* 10(6):20, 15 December 1935.

Baird, Joseph Armstrong and Ellen Schwartz, *Northern California Art; An Interpretive Bibliography*, Library Association – University Library, University of California, Davis, 1977.

Beebe, William, *Beneath Tropic Seas*, G.P. Putnam's Sons, 1928.

Brooklyn Museum – Institute of Arts and Sciences, Original Drawings and Paintings of Natural History Subjects, Exhibition Catalog, Department of Contemporary Art, 25 October–17 November, 1935.

University of California (Davis) Art Department, "Fifteen and Fifty – California Painters at the Pan-Pacific Exposition of 1915," The University Library, 10 May 1965.

Carroll, Charles M., "Painting the Wonders Under the Sea," *Scientific American* 108:179+, 22 February 1913.

Cary, Elizabeth Luther, "An Artist Who Paints Under Water," *The Scrip – Notes on Art*, II(2):373, August 1907. The New York Public Library has copies.

Greutzner, A. and J. Johnson, *Dictionary of British Artists 1880–1940*, Antique Collectors Club, Woodbridge, Suffolk, England 1976.

Harada, Jiro, to Zarh Pritchard, 17 July, 1915 in San Francisco.

Lewis, Oscar, *San Francisco: Mission to Metropolis*, Howell-North, Berkeley, 1966.

The Literary Digest 58(4):22-23, 27 July, 1918, "Painting the Sea-Floor."

Mallett's Index of Artists, (supplement) 10(8):7, 15 January 1936, Zarh Pritchard at Arthur V. Newton Galleries.

Metropolitan Museum of Art, Library Catalog – Volume 18, plate 016643 (3 reference cards).

Millier, Arthur, Review of Zarh Pritchard exhibit at Grace Nicholson Galleries, *Los Angeles Times*, Part III, page 11, 14 March 1937.

Moure, Nancy Dustin Wall, assistance by Lyn Wall Smith, *Dictionary of Art and Artists in Southern California Before 1930*, Privately Printed, Los Angeles, 1975.

New York Public Library, *Catalog of Art and Architecture*, Volume 24.

Nicholson, Grace, A compilation of notes to Zarh Pritchard as incorporated into her gallery catalog for 26 February to 26 March 1926: from Sarah Bernhardt, May 1906, page 30.

ibid: from Jean Guiffrey, 13 July 1915, page 27.

ibid: from Percival Lowell, 17 April 1913, page 25.

Page, Henry Markham, *Pasadena: Its Early Years*, Lorrin L. Morrison, Los Angeles, 1964.

Perret, Ferdinand – Research Library of the Arts, File cards from the Library. Copies held by the Baird Archive of California Art, University of California, Davis.

Petit, Georges – Galeries, Peintures Sous–Marines par Zarh Pritchard, Exhibition Catalog for June, 1925, Paris.

Richardson, E.P., *Painting in America*, Thomas Y. Crowell, New York, 1965.

Robillot, P., *Flora et Faune Marines – Etudes D'Applications Industrielles*, C. Marsin, Paris, 1914. Portfolio in the New York Public Library.

Rolle, Andrew F., *California – A History*, Thomas Y. Crowell, New York, 1963.

Roske, Ralph J., *Everyman's Eden – A History of California*, The Macmillan Company, 1968.

Shepard, Paul, *Man in the Landscape*, Alfred A. Knopf, 1967.

Skinner, Cornelia Otis, *Madam Sarah*, Houghton Mifflin, Boston, 1967.

Smith, Gordon W., *Edinburgh*, Lutterworth Press, London, 1967.

Townsend, Charles Haskins, "Pritchard Exhibit at New York Aquarium," New York Zoological Society *Bulletin*, November 1913.

United States Immigration and Naturalization Service, Petition for Naturalization (4079963) and Certificate of Naturalization (265877) for Walter Howlison Mackenzie Pritchard.

Verneuil, M.P., "La Mer (Artistic use of its plant and animal forms)," *Art and Decoration*, (Paris), January–June 1910, Volume 27, pages 1–20 and 141–152; Volume 28, pages 161-176. The New York Public Library has copies.

The Brothers Who Made Undersea Films

FOOTNOTES

1. *The Virginian Pilot* (Norfolk), "Submarine Movies to Reveal the Wonders of the Deep," Special Features, page 1, 22 June 1913.

2. *Variety*, "Big Picture Exposition Next Week in New York City," page 8, 5 July 1913.

3. *The Virginian Pilot* (Norfolk), "Off for West Indies and Under-Sea Photos," page 3, 20 February 1914.

4. Gregory, Carl L., to Charles Williamson. Written during Williamson Submarine Expedition, but undated.

5. Williamson, J.E., *Twenty Years Under the Sea*, Hale, Cushman, and Flint, Boston and New York, 1936.

6. *The Boston Independent* (80):171, 2 November 1914, Review of *Thirty Leagues Under the Sea*.

7. Brownlow, Kevin, *The Parade's Gone By*, Bonanza Books, New York, 1968.

8. *Motion Picture Magazine*, Review of *The White Heather*, page 68, June 1919.

9. *The Philadelphia Telegraph*, "Goes to Bottom of Sea for Film," 30 April 1917*.

10. *The New York Times*, "German U-Boat Reaches Newport," page 1, 8 October 1916.

11. *Photoplay*, *Twenty Thousand Leagues* (preview), page 100, January 1917.

12. Weitzel, Edward, Review of *Twenty Thousand Leagues*, *The Moving Picture World*, page 240, 13 January 1917.

13. Shorey, George N., Review for *Twenty Thousand Leagues*, *Motion Picture News*, page 112, 6 January 1917.

14. *Photoplay*, Review of *Girl of the Sea*, pages 91 and 125, October 1920.

15. *Motion Picture News*, "Trade review and marketing information for *Wet Gold*," page 867, 13 August 1921.

16. *The New York Times*, Review of *Wonders of the Sea*, page 20, 16 October 1922.

ADDITIONAL REFERENCES

Anonymous, "J.E. Williamson Conducting Undersea Expedition Here for Explorers Club," article in unidentified Bahamian publication, circa 1940. On file with the Explorers Club, New York.

Allemandy, Victor E., *Wonders of the Deep – The Story of the Williamson Submarine Expedition*, Jarrold and Sons, London.

American Film Institute Catalog 1911–1920, Patricia King Hanson, executive editor, and Alan Gevinson, assistant editor, University of California Press, 1988. *Thirty Leagues Under the Sea*, page 922; *Twenty Thousand Leagues Under the Sea*, page 956; *The Submarine Eye*, page 897; *Girl of the Sea*, page 328.

American Film Institute Catalog 1921–1930, Kenneth W. Munden, executive editor, R.R. Bowker Company, New York and London, 1971. *The Mysterious Island*, page 534; *The Uninvited Guest*, page 847; *Wet Gold*, page 878; *Wonders of the Sea*, page 925.

Barnouw, Eric and Iris Newsom, editors, *The Sintzenich Diaries*, from *Wonderful Inventions: Motion Pictures, Broadcasting, and Recorded Sound at the Library of Congress*, Library of Congress, Washington, D.C., 1985.

Bowser, E., *Twenty Thousand Leagues Under the Sea*, review for "Films from the Archive," Museum of Modern Art Department of Film, New York.

Brent, Loring, "A Motion Picture Drama from the Ocean Bottom," *Scientific American* CXV(4):78–79, 22 July 1916.

Croy, Homer, *How Motion Pictures are Made*, Harper, 1918, pages 328–350.

Davis, Robert H., *Deep Diving and Submarine Operations*, Saint Catherine Press, London, 1935.

De Koven, John, "Undersea Film Opens New World," review of *Twenty Thousand Leagues, Cleveland Leader*, 4 May 1917.*

Dugan, James, *Man Under the Sea*, Harper and Brothers, 1956.

Electric Boat Company, Outline specifications for a proposed Exploration Submarine, Design 174-A, Groton, Connecticut, 16 June 1932.

Estes, Oscar G., "First Undersea Cameraman," review for the *Classic Film Collector*, undated article on file with Museum of Modern Art, New York.

Falls, Cyril, *The Great War 1914–1918*, G.P. Putnam's Sons, 1959.

The Film Index – a Bibliography, Museum of Modern Art Library and H.W. Wilson Company, New York, 1941, Volume I – The Film as Art.

Franklin, Joe, *Classics of the Silent Screen*, Citadel Press, New York, 1959.

Gray, Edwin A., *The Killing Time – The U-Boat War 1914–1918*, Charles Scribner's Sons, 1972.

Gregory, Carl L. and J.E. Williamson, "Submarine Photography," *Journal of the Society of Motion Picture and Television Engineers*, December 1973 reprinted from: *Transactions of the SMPTE*, 12 May 1921.

Gresham, William Lindsay, *Houdini – The Man Who Walked Through Walls*, Holt, Rinehart, and Winston, 1959.

Hall, Mordaunt, "J.E. Williamson's Film of Undersea Life," review of *With Williamson Beneath the Sea, The New York Times*, page 35, 24 November 1932.

Harrison, Louis Reeves, review of *The White Heather, Moving Picture World*, page 1070, 17 May 1919.

Hart, James, editor, *The Man Who Invented Hollywood*, Touchstone Publishing, Louisville, Kentucky, 1972.

Jacobs, Lewis, *The Rise of the American Film*, Harcourt, Brace and Company, New York, 1939.

Josephy, Alvin M., editor, *The American Heritage History of World War I*, American Heritage Publishing, 1964.

Koenig, Paul, *Voyage of the Deutschland*, Hearst's International Library, New York, 1916.

Latil, Pierre de and Jean Rivoire, *Man and the Underwater World*, (translated from the French by Edward Fitzgerald), G.,P. Putnam's Sons, 1956.

The Lecture Agency Limited, Outer Temple, Strand, London, "Into the New World Under the Sea," Pamphlet for lecture series of Mr. J.E. Williamson, 1935.

The Ledger Star (Norfolk, Virginia), "Underwater Specialist Dies at Eighty-Four," page 28, 18 July 1966.

Leish, Kenneth W., *Cinema*, Newsweek Books, New York, 1974.

Moen, L.C., "Trade review and marketing information for *The Uninvited Guest*," *Motion Picture News*, page 992, 1 March 1924.

Motion Picture Magazine, Review of *Twenty Thousand Leagues*, page 13, March 1917.

Motion Picture News, "Another Williamson Undersea Film for Universal" (*Twenty Thousand Leagues*), 16 October 1915.

Moving Picture World, "Submarine Pictures on Exhibition. Unusual Subjects Photographed by Williamson Brothers being shown at Museum of Natural History," 21:1106, 22 August 1914.

_____, "Taking Pictures Underwater," 21:226, 11 July 1914.

Mullett, Mary B., "Ernest Williamson's Adventures in Making Motion Pictures Under the Sea," *American Magazine* 98:46-49, November 1924.

The Nassau Daily Tribune, "Post Office on Bahamas Ocean Floor," 9 August 1939.

The New York American, review of *Twenty Thousand Leagues*, 25 December 1916.*

The New York Dramatic Mirror, "Williamson Brothers Complete Their Organization," 16 December 1916.

_____, display advertisement for Williamson Corporation, 16 December 1916.

_____, review of *Twenty Thousand Leagues*, 6 January 1917.

_____, display advertisement for *Twenty Thousand Leagues* (with trade information) and accompanying trade article, 24 February 1917.

The New York Star, trade article on *The Submarine Eye*, 2 May 1917.*

The New York Times, "See First Pictures Taken Under Water," 12 August 1914.

_____, "German Submarines Sink 6 to 9 Ships Off Nantucket," page 1, 9 October 1916.

_____, "Inventions Make Film Possible," review of *Twenty Thousand Leagues*, page 7, 25 December 1916.

_____, review of *The White Heather*, page 11, 5 May 1919.

_____, obituary: "John Williamson, Sea Explorer, 84," 17 July 1966.

The New York Times Directory of the Film, Arno Press, New York, 1974.

Perelman, S.J., "Roll On, Thou Deep and Dark Scenario, Roll," *The New Yorker*, 24+, 16 August 1952.

Photoplay, *Twenty Thousand Leagues* (preview), page 133, October 1916.

_____, review of *Wonders of the Sea*, page 118, January 1923.

Pratt, George C., *Spellbound in Darkness; A History of the Silent Film*, University of Rochester Press, Rochester, New York, 1966, and New York Graphic Society, Greenwich, Connecticut, 1973.

Reid, Laurence, review of *Wonders of the Sea, Motion Picture News*, page 2289, 4 November 1922.

Ryan, Roderick T., "Carl Louis Gregory; an historical note," *Journal* of the Society of Motion Picture and Television Engineers, page 1008, December 1973.

Scientific American, "A New Apparatus for Submarine Operations," XCVIII(14):243, 4 April 1908.

_____, "Photographing Under Water," CIX(1):1 & 6, 5 July 1913.

_____, "Taking Motion Pictures at the Bottom of the Ocean," CXI(2):25, 11 July 1914.

Select Pictures Corporation, Buffalo, New York, invoices to Citizen's Theatre, Oxford, New York. Itemized costs for film rental and promotional material on *Twenty Thousand Leagues*, 20 November 1917.

Spear, G.Y., of Electric Boat Company, to George Williamson, 17 June 1932.

Talbot, Frederick A., *Moving Pictures*, Lippincott, Philadelphia, 1923.

Twist, Stanly H., foreword to *Twenty Thousand Leagues Under the Sea*, Grosset and Dunlap, 1917.

Time-Life Books, *This Fabulous Century*, Volume I: 1900–1910, Volume II: 1910–1920, Volume III: 1920–1930, Time-Life Publishing, 1969.

The Virginian Pilot (Norfolk), "Williamson Submarine Movies Make Big Hit," page 1, 17 July 1914.

_____, obituary: "John Ernest Williamson, 84, Undersea Camera Pioneer," 17 July 1966.

Williamson versus Universal Studios, November 12 to 23, 1917. Direct testimony from New York State trial records transcribed in segments by Richard Koszarski in 1975.

Williamson, J.E., Diary for the production of *Twenty Thousand Leagues* as entered into the trial testimony for Williamson versus Universal Studios and transcribed in segments by Richard Koszarski in 1975.

_____, Personal History originally compiled for the records of the Motion Picture Pioneers and Foundation, New York. Currently on file with the Explorers Club, New York.

Williamson, G.M., to Ruth Maccann, 19 March 1914.

_____, to Paul Koster, 6 October 1932.

Williamson, George, Jr., and Shirley, taped interview, 16 November 1978.

_____, additional tapes, 24 June 1979.

*Unpaginated articles contained in the Robinson-Locke Collection of Dramatic Scrapbooks – Lincoln Center Library for the Performing Arts, New York.